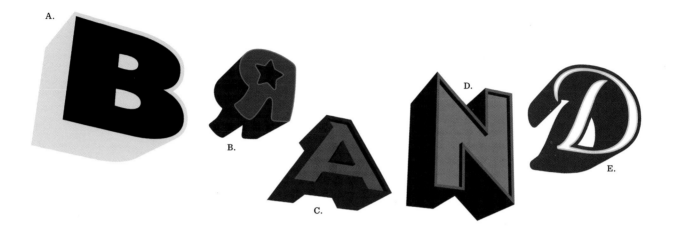

A. B. C. D. E. F. G. H. I. J.

First published in the United States of America by
Rockport Publishers, a member of
Quayside Publishing Group
100 Cummings Center
Suite 406-L
Beverly, Massachusetts 01915-6101
Telephone: (978) 282-9590
Fax: (978) 283-2742
www.rockpub.com
Visit RockPaperInk.com to share your opinions, creations, and passion for design.

Library of Congress Cataloging-in-Publication Data
Millman, Debbie.
 Brand Bible : the complete guide to building, designing, and sustaining brands / Debbie Millman.
   p. cm.
 Includes bibliographical references and index.
 ISBN-13: 978-1-59253-726-6
 ISBN-10: 1-59253-726-X
 ISBN-13: 978-1-61058-198-1 (digital ed.)
 1. Branding (Marketing) 2. Brand name products. I. Title. II. Title: Complete guide to building, designing, and sustaining brands.
 HF5415.1255M548 2012
 658.8'27--dc23

                                          2011040806
                                          CIP

ISBN: 978-1-59253-726-6

Digital edition published in 2012
eISBN: 978-1-61058-198-1

10 9 8 7 6 5 4 3 2 1

Editor: Jeremy Lehrer, unifyingtheorymedia.com
Producer: Taryn Espinosa
Principal Photographer: Brent Taylor

Printed in China

THE COMPLETE GUIDE *TO* BUILDING, DESIGNING, *AND* SUSTAINING BRANDS

EDITED BY DEBBIE MILLMAN

RODRIGO CORRAL DESIGN

BRAND BIBLE

THE COMPLETE GUIDE TO BUILDING, DESIGNING, AND SUSTAINING BRANDS

CONTENTS

FOREWORD

What do the words *brand* and *bible* have in common? Branding is storytelling elevated to narrative, often embellished with myth to enhance a product's identity. The branding story, conveyed through signs, symbols, and other elements, results in a manufactured legacy that appeals to consumers. *Bible* is storytelling elevated to narrative and mythically embellished to appeal to adherents' faith. Brand and bible are indeed linked by intention, if not function.

The Bible is a collection of origin stories. Some of it can be taken literally, while other parts can be considered symbolically. *Brand Bible* is also a collection of origin stories. Here, they can be taken literally, as they present part history, part commentary. Yet branding is not pure truth or even partial truth. The histories of most branded products should never be accepted at face value. To brand a product means to impose a personality, character, and heritage that will ultimately influence the way the branded product, institution, or object is perceived by the public. Devising, maintaining, and perpetuating the myth is job number one of branding experts.

So, what should the reader of the *Brand Bible* expect—fact or fiction?

The answer: This unique book gathers together many facts and fancies that inform the branding practice. It presents a narrative of the history of branding, of how branding emerged in its early forms and evolved into something much more pervasive. The goal is to provide a guide for professionals and an origin narrative for those engaged in aspects of contemporary branding, which include a broad range of projects: Branding books, restaurants, and media, as well as hotels, cities, and cultural institutions. Readers will receive a holistic understanding of brand procedures, brand languages, aesthetics, and ethics.

This book is a brand in its own right. It not only documents branding practices, it reinforces the "rightness" of branding. This "Bible" does not simply recount information; taken as a whole, it argues for the profession, its enormous influence, and its standards. It supports branding's validity and viability—and its myths. This book is "the word."

So, is branding religion, as the word *bible* implies? Not in the strict sense. But in branding, there is a deity—the product being branded—and a host of disciples—the secondary brands that both feed off and help nourish the main brand. And it certainly has devotees—those drawn to worship a particular deity.

Branding is not an organized religion, but branders must be devout. Read the interviews here with those involved with contemporary brands ranging from MTV to Lean Cuisine, and there is religiosity in their voices and fervency in their mission.

In branding there is a deity—the product being branded—and a host of disciples.

They are committed to spreading the word (which they've helped to develop) and then to recruiting converts. The best brand campaigns not only sustain but also attempt to grow their congregations—I mean their consumer base.

Brand and *bible.* This book will help the reader understand what it takes to build, design, "activate," and sustain brands. But if read carefully, it might actually cement the idea that during these hard times, when soaring debt is rampant and economic growth is stagnant, anything that motivates the economy is good, and that branding is indeed a calling—or at least a tool—in that mission.

—Steven Heller

For at least 4,000 years, man has marked cattle with red-hot branding irons to prove his ownership. Literally millions of designs have been originated—some romantic, some dignified, some even comical—to distinguish herds. There is a true story behind every brand, frequently a tragedy, a comedy, a tender romance, more often a proclamation of hope.

— *Irons in the Fire: Cattle Brand Lore,*
Oren Arnold

Hot iron branding
device for cattle

INTRODUCTION

My entire life has been punctuated by brands. I became aware of their transformative power, albeit subconsciously, when I was little girl and first discovered packages of Goody barrettes hanging on the dazzling display racks in my father's pharmacy. I'd ogle these colorful accessories and imagine that the act of donning them would remake me into a prettier girl, though I had no real reason to believe this. Nevertheless, I was bewitched by the abundant array of hair accoutrements until my teens, at which point my yearning transferred to what I considered "cool" brands: Levi's jeans, Puma sneakers, and Lacoste polo shirts. From there, I turned to decidedly more adult brands, including the Ford Escort, Tiffany ring, and Cuisinart mixer. Nearly thirty years later, I look back on my all-consuming need for branded goods with both nostalgia and pity. I bestowed such power on these inanimate totems. I believed that by the sheer virtue of acquiring these objects, they would magically convert me into a dramatically different person—the person I longed to be.

Contrary to the way we think of brands now, the brand has not always signified the imprimatur of a manufactured product. The word *brand* is derived from the Old Norse word *brandr*, which means "to burn by fire." Ancient Egyptians marked their livestock with hot irons, and the process was widespread in Europe during the Middle Ages, not to mention in the American West centuries later. Such branding helped ranchers, both ancient and contemporary, to separate cattle after they grazed in communal ranges; in addition, herders with high-quality livestock were able to distinguish themselves from those ranchers with inferior animals. The dynamics of brand reputation helped build better businesses even back then, and the role of the brand—as a barometer of value—has continued ever since.

In 1876, after the United Kingdom passed the Trade Marks Registration Act during the previous year, Bass Ale became the first trademarked brand in the world. Its quintessential red triangle, submitted to the government for trademark protection, became the icon for a new era of branding, one in which companies had legal protections for their brand identities. In addition to clinching "Trade Mark Number One," Bass's trailblazing history includes its appearances in Edouard Manet's 1882 masterpiece, *A Bar at the Folies-Bergère*, and Pablo Picasso's 1912 painting, *Bouteille de Bass et guitare*, ostensibly providing the brand with the cultural distinction of "first product placement."

A century later, we are living in a world with over one hundred brands of bottled water. The United States is home to over forty-five thousand shopping malls, and there are over nineteen million permutations of beverage selections you can order at your local Starbucks. Is this a good thing or a bad thing? The observations Naomi Klein made over a decade ago in her seminal critique, *No Logo*, still resonate today.

Openings of every sort—in schedules, in urban space, on clothes, in events, on objects, in sight-lines, in democracy, in philanthropy, in cultures, on bodies—are all inscribed with an impression of the market. Things once thought free from this—even opposed to it—the museum, public space—find it ever more difficult to retain autonomy in the face of corporate culture and its sponsorships, educational initiatives, and so-called civic gestures.

Those who do not share Klein's antipathy will inevitably counter her stance with the argument that free-market economies are just that—free—and a plethora of choice is what fuels freedom and innovation. Then they might point to brands such as Toms Shoes and Newman's Own, a design studio like Alex Bogusky's FearLess Cottage, or movements like John Bielenberg's Project M as evidence of designers and marketers advocating change via brands or branding. Perhaps then, the question of whether this behavior is good or bad is secondary to the imperative of understanding why we behave this way in the first place. Why do humans create tribes? Why do we have a drive to telegraph our affiliations and beliefs with symbols, signs, and codes?

Scientists and anthropologists tend to agree that humans are pack animals, which explains why we feel safer and more secure in groups. And psychologists such as Harry Harlow and John Bowlby have proven that humans feel happier and better about themselves when the individual brain resonates with those of other like-minded humans. Perhaps our motivation to brand, and to be branded, comes from our hardwired instinct to connect— perhaps not. In either case, what is indisputable is the breakneck speed with which brands have become more pervasive over the past

Early Bass Ale packaging

century, and the number of people who have literally and figuratively bought into these brands. Any knowledge of culture is impossible now without an understanding of the implications of "brand." We have entered a day and an age where brand is an extension of human facility, whether it is psychic or psychological.

This discussion was the centerpiece of the Inaugural Masters in Branding program at the School of Visual Arts in New York City. Twenty three students, along with faculty Richard Shear, Rodrigo Corral, Jeremy Lehrer, and myself spent nearly a year researching the history of brands and the impact they have had on our culture, our behavior and our evolution. As we investigated mankind's first markings on the cave walls of Lascaux to our most recent status updates on the walls of Facebook, we came to realize that the need to document our place in the world with symbols, statements, and brands seems to be inherent in our humanity. This book is the result of that investigation—and that realization..

—Debbie Millman

PART ONE /
BUILDING BRANDS

01

MEANINGFUL MARKINGS AND THE GREAT LEAP FORWARD

MYLES GAYTHWAITE

Perched high on the tallest hilltop overlooking a vast plain surrounding the modern-day Vezere River, the entrance to the Lascaux Cave would have had the same visual prominence to the local inhabitants as the cathedrals that would later come to dominate this landscape many thousands of years later. The cave itself was practically tailor-made for the purposes to which our ancestors used it. Its entrance was high on a hill facing north-west, and the opening passage led down a long, slow slope into the main chamber, such that, at most times of the year, the setting sun would have shone down gloriously into the cave. Within these chambers some 18,000 years ago, Upper Paleolithic man created a stunning collection of images that capture their symbolic and mundane world—one of the few remaining artifacts of the ancients.

The main chamber of the cave, the Hall of the Bulls, is massive; it measures 62 feet long by 22 feet wide (19 x 7 m), with gently sloping walls that arch upward into a domed ceiling some 22 feet (7 m) from the floor. The ceiling is not only stalac-tite free, but is coated in a thick layer of calcite, which gave it a smooth, translucent white surface upon which to paint.[1]

Although this first chamber contains more than thirty-four paintings, it is four massive bulls that dominate, the largest measuring 17 feet (5 m) across. Not only are the bulls exquisitely rendered, but they are drawn so that their propor-tions are correct only when viewed from the center of the space. The entire ceiling is a masterful

BELOW:
Vogelherd, horse; photograph by Hilde Jensen, copyright University of Tübingen

RIGHT:
Upper Paleolithic cave paintings from Lascaux, France, estimated to be 17,300 years old

composition that appears to have been planned out before its creation. These are not the paintings of individual shamans but are instead the result of a concerted tribal project, a stunning example of Upper Paleolithic technology and collaboration.

A community that poured so many resources into such a creation would clearly have valued it as a centerpiece of tribal life. The size of the hall and the compositional planning of its walls and ceiling suggest that it was used for large gatherings, a place where significant numbers of people gathered for social ritual.[2] Although it's impossible to say whether or not these paintings had a religious purpose—especially in our modern sense of what that entails—Lascaux, with its geographic prominence and the incredible art that it contained, would have occupied a significant place in the imaginations of the regional population at the time.[3] While not the oldest, or the largest site of its kind—the cave at Chauvet, also in France, dates to 32,000 years ago—it is certainly the most famous, impressing modern viewers as much for its technical as well as artistic achievements.[4,5] Unlike the adroitly composed Hall of the Bulls, a further chamber called "the Apse" was covered with thousands of engravings, rendered one atop another with complete disregard for composition or narrative. The chamber has been called one of the most vital areas of the cave, an exquisite palimpsest of personal psychic expression. The space, curving gently from floor to ceiling, would have enveloped the artisans' entire visual field in an immersive aesthetic experience. Awash in the cacophony of shared tribal history, the ancient artists' present moment would have been intimately connected to the tribe's past through the shared act of creation

in this space—giving participants an unbroken link from past to future, a moment free from the constraints of time and space.[6]

The exact meanings of the engravings may be lost—debate still rages about them—but the process of the paintings' creation conveys something of great importance: Recent discoveries seem to indicate that humans used these caves for thousands of years, continuously adding new imagery as well as repainting the existing drawings.[7] This act of creation, of communicating through drawn representations, clearly played a fundamental and long-lasting role in the evolution and identity of this ancient society. Even if we can't decipher the intended content of the message contained in these images, it seems clear that the caves at Lascaux and Chauvet served as an important locus for the society; they enabled a process of discovery and at the same time, an expression of social mores through ritual.[8,9] A similar act of expression and human evolution was evident in the tools made by our forebears. Initially, some 2.5 million years ago, our *Homo habilis* ancestors made simple stone tools such as a "chopper," a handheld tool made from flint, presumably used for activities like chopping wood and butchering animals. As our ancestors evolved, they began to improve their tools to the much more refined and varied forms that began appearing about 150,000 years ago, coinciding with the arrival of *Homo sapiens*—the modern human.

Over this span of evolution, the tools began to take on a meaning relating to social status and its owners function in society. The tools that individuals carried would reflect the role they had during the hunt or taming of the local environment.[10] And this burgeoning communication of social stature

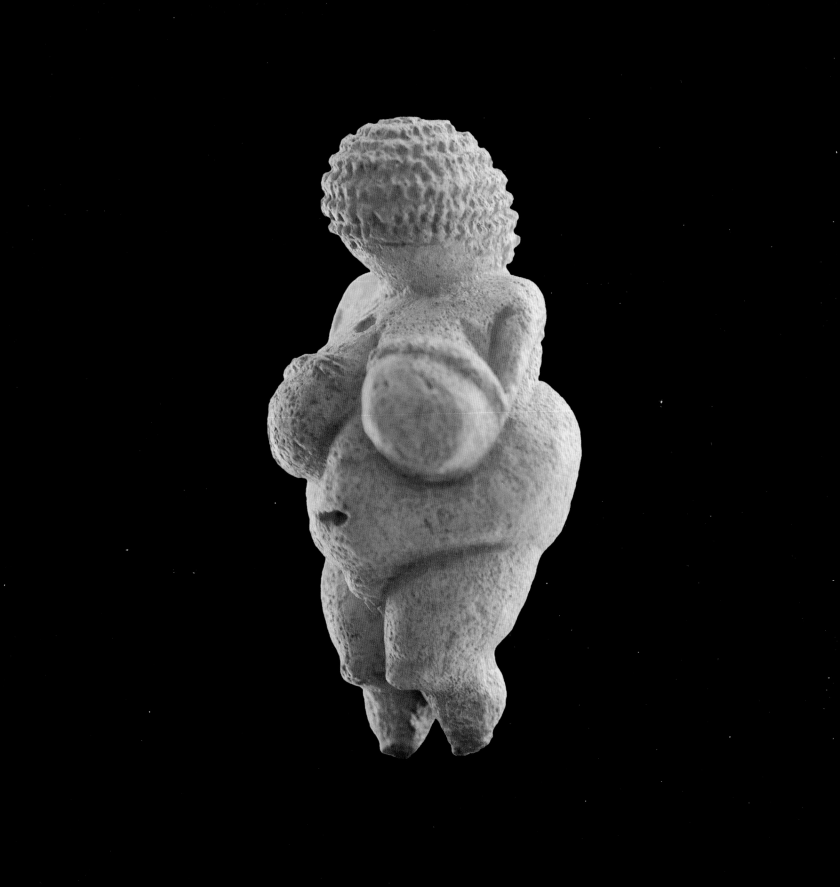

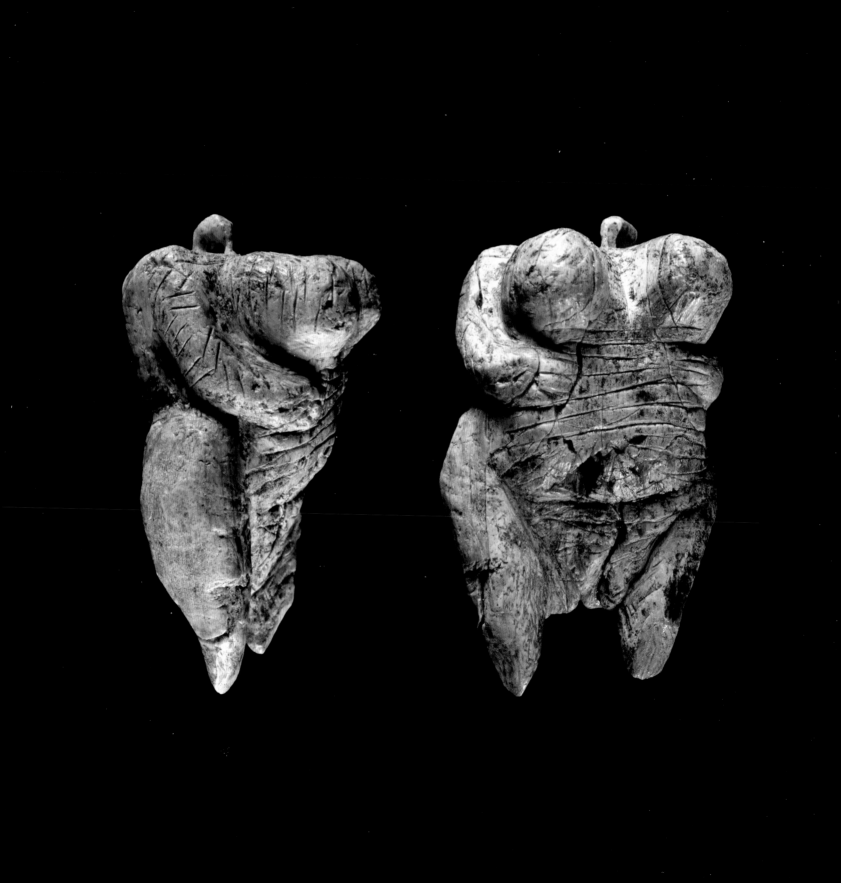

began to take expression in ever more varied forms. As early as 100,000 years ago, humans began fashioning necklaces and other adornments from petrified shells and the teeth of slain predators such as wolves and cave bears.[11] These items were highly prized and were traded from tribe to tribe across ancient Europe.[12] Elaborate burial rituals would sometimes involve hundreds of decorative pieces, far more than a single person could make—hinting that a communal system of creation had emerged at this time.[13, 14]

The most significant bellwether of change emerges about 45,000 years ago, conveying an important transformation of our interior life: Humans began creating objects that had no function other than to communicate ideas through designs, symbols, and archetypes. They carved small horse figurines and other decorative items from mammoth bone; they made the so-called Venus figurines, the carvings of women that had pronounced sexual features.[15] At the same time that they were starting to create these objects, humans began to make aesthetic modifications to their tools as well. They crafted spear throwers, used to extend the hunter's reach and leverage, in the shape of reindeer and other animals, an alteration that serves no "useful" function other than communicating an abstract idea.[16]

The meaning of these designs is still debated: They may have communicated social status, imbued the object with symbolic power, or been of purely aesthetic motivation. To modern eyes, the Venus figurines might seem to represent the archetype of fertility, but the exact significance is lost to time.

What cannot be disputed is that these objects mean something; they tell stories and communicate ideas far beyond their practical functions.

If cave paintings could be said to speak on behalf of the tribe to the individual, the tools and adornments conveyed social status and personal meaning to the society—a communication directed outward, from the individual to the larger group.[17]

Through these tools, objects, and adornments, ancient humans spoke to each other—and they are also speaking to us. These paintings, decorations, and other creations mark the beginning of our stories, our myths, and our ways of understanding the world. The caves are just as alive for us today with symbolic import and possibility as they were for humans thousands of years ago. We may not know the original intention of the creators, but the art speaks, has meaning, and communicates something, however ineffable, between two people across the gulf of time. When Pablo Picasso emerged from his visit to the Lascaux Cave, he is reported to have pronounced, "We have invented nothing." Picasso's pronouncement could easily mean that the subtle refinement of form and artistic mastery on display at Lascaux is equal to any contemporary art. However, one can also say that the will to communicate through artistic expression has been with us since the dawn of time—and perhaps it is not we who invented art, but art that invented us.

ABOVE:
Hohle Fels, bird
RIGHT:
Hohle Fels, venus

02

FRUITS OF THE ELIZABETHAN ERA

ZACHARY LYND

Historians often point to the Industrial Revolution as the genesis of the contemporary age of branding, arguing that the businesses of the era "manufactured" new consumer tastes right along with the mass-produced goods that signaled the onset of our modern world. In fact, the enormous increases in productivity that began in the late eighteenth century were possible only after the revolutionary transformation in consumer tastes, desires, and aspirations that occurred during the rule of Queen Elizabeth I, which lasted from 1558 to 1603. Once that shift had taken root, the societal transformation began in earnest.

Sixteenth-Century Elizabethan England

Queen Elizabeth I was a true renaissance woman, agile in political dealings, savvy in economic matters, and well versed in the arts. She spoke several languages, and she led her country through a time of peace that had been unparalleled until her reign. She had ascended to the throne after a tumultuous history: Her mother, Anne Boleyn, was executed after being convicted of infidelity to Elizabeth's father, King Henry VIII, leaving the child motherless from the age of two and a half. Her half-sister, Mary, had her imprisoned in the Tower of London.

Yet, from these unusual circumstances emerged a monarch whose wisdom and political acumen allowed her to preserve her power and expand the scope of her country's interests. The queen faced challenges to her rule both from inside the country—Mary, Queen of Scots (not her sister, who had died), was seen as a threat—and outside of it, so she developed a strategy that would keep the members of the nobility—and their capital—away from military intrigues. Elizabeth turned her court into a parade and theatrical spectacle.

Not only were the noble classes required to maintain temporary residences in London in order to attend the lavish rituals of the court, the dictates of sixteenth-century hospitality required them to host as extravagant parties at their country estates as well. A reputation for generosity was a sign of

Queen Elizabeth I

social distinction, an idea which Elizabeth masterfully exploited. In fact, the most lavish of all feasts at that time was in honor of Elizabeth herself: The annual Accession Day, celebrating the queen's ascension to the throne, was a feast of such epic scale that it was forever immortalized in Edmund Spenser's poem, "The Faerie Queene."

Her predecessors in the monarchy had controlled the elite by way of economics, and in that sense, Queen Elizabeth's system was neither new nor revolutionary. Yet, by transforming the framework for what and how the nobility would spend their wealth, she dramatically altered the system of consumption.

The East India Company

The East India Company was charted by Elizabeth in 1600, her forty-second year as queen. The company brought colorful fabrics, calicoes, spices, and other exotic items from the Indian subcontinent to English shores. These items quickly found a receptive audience in British noble society and began to transform not only the tastes and buying habits of the nobles but also courtly society as well. These treasures had an exotic appeal. Back at Her Majesty's court, the attending nobility impressed and wooed the queen with these delights.

Up to this time, matters of patina and family heirloom were the key indicators for conveying a family's social status. Patina referred to the wear on a family heirloom—the oxidation on a gold or copper piece, for example—showing how long a family had been in high standing by communicating how long they had been in possession of these particular

luxury items. Members of British society counted on these signifiers to interpret others' social standing and to communicate, and elevate, their own.

The East India Company introduced novelty into this generations-old system of social and class distinction. The cornucopia of goods from abroad had an appeal relating to the exotic and the new. Queen Elizabeth gave these new charms her full embrace and, in so doing, encouraged the nobles to curry her favor through the endless competition of acquiring and showing off the latest fashions from abroad. The shift to the celebration of the novel presented a serious challenge to the orthodoxy of inherited social status, and the cachet one could achieve by presenting gifts to the queen—as well as displaying one's own wealth with the new purchases—soon made spending as a form of social competition both necessary and desirable. Keeping up with the Joneses—or the Duke of Norfolk, as the case may be—had begun in earnest.

In his book *Culture and Consumption,* cultural critic Grant McCracken writes about the shift to novelty that took place in the Elizabethan era. "This development represents a triumph of style over utility, of aesthetics over function," he observes. "More important, it represents a radical redefinition of the idea of status and the use of goods to express status."

The ensuing social competition also changed the emphasis on how individuals thought of their family legacy. If patina no longer mattered, then members of the nobility—whether actual or aspiring—could simply focus their efforts on social climbing through conspicuous consumption rather than obtaining, or preserving, heirlooms that would be valued for the status they afforded. That shift

enslaved the nobility to fashion, luxury, and trends. The new, exciting objects of fashion and faraway lands hijacked social cachet from the Old World, becoming the dominant means of expressing one's identity, and generating a snowballing cascade of new desires. As spending led to further spending in a kind of economic arms race, the ritual of consumption began to gain enough traction that it would seriously challenge previous customs relating to social cachet.

More Than "Mere Consumption"

Before the Elizabethan era, it was a radical concept to celebrate the novel, particularly from outside one's own culture and social vocabulary. As consumer culture flourished in the aftermath of the Elizabethan shift, the enjoyment of novelty became less alien, and over the years, patina took on less significance. These new rituals of consumption and social peacocking instigated an entirely new set of behaviors, which had a significant implication for British society. The newly baptized consumers were simultaneously exploring and charting new territory, unwittingly inventing the rules and mores of the very dance they were participants in.

Writing in *The Origins of Modern English Society,* the British social historian Harold Perkin has observed, "If consumer demand, then, was the key to the Industrial Revolution, social emulation was the key to consumer demand." The rituals of consumerism gave the British an accessible, achievable way of emulating the grander life, and the appeal of that accelerated path to social success was irresistible.

The legacy of family lineage had long defined one's status in society; and while that system hadn't—and still hasn't—ended, the new paradigm of consumer spending allowed people to convey and lay claim to status in a wholly new way. The new patterns of consumption established at the end of Elizabeth's reign spread from the upper classes of British society to the wider populace, creating a more powerful economic impact on the country as a result of a surge in buying and trading. But while the British found the new goods aesthetically pleasing, the new economic behaviors still hadn't been embraced as the norm. Slowly, British society changed and, what initially seemed a novelty, began to gain more appeal.

The economist Nicholas Barbon, writing in the 1690 treatise *A Discourse of Trade,* considered this new culture of consumption. Barbon writes, "The wants of the Mind are infinite, Man naturally Aspires, and as his Mind is elevated, his Senses grow more refined, his Wishes, which is for everything that is rare, can gratifie his Senses, adorn his Body and promote the Ease, Pleasure and Pomp of Life." Barbon's analysis of society could be as easily applied to the modern-day mindset as it was to those of British society at the end of the seventeenth century.

The Fable of the Bees

By acting in their self-interest and indulging their desires for luxuries, the rich contributed to the expansion of commerce and to higher employment throughout England. Merchants and laborers found work in ports where the goods from abroad arrived; workers got jobs in factories where the fruits of English domestic production and foreign imports were processed and manufactured. Through their own selfish drives, then, the upper classes had led to an improved economic state for the lower classes—even if that meant sometimes horrifying conditions working in factories. The transformations and contradictions of the new economic reality led the philosopher Bernard Mandeville to craft a seminal satire, *The Fable of the Bees,* that would examine the shifts occurring in his time, and the human drives that instigated them.

The Fable of the Bees was a satiric and paradoxical comment on contemporary British society. It tells the story of a bustling hive where the bees hypocritically complain about their own vices, their own penchant for dishonesty and fraud. In a fury, the bees' god, Jove, eliminates vices from the society. When he does, the hive begins to decay.

FLAGS OF ALL NATIONS.

NEW ZEALAND	PERU	BRAZIL	CHILI	BOLIVIA	SANDWICH ISLANDS
LIBERIA	COCHIN CHINA	KINGDOM of SIAM	BIRMAH	EGYPT	TUNIS
ARABIA	GREEK NATIONAL	ITALIAN STANDARD	EMPEROR of AUSTRIA	HOLLAND	PERSIA
JAPAN	BRITISH STANDARD	IRELAND	MOROCCO	STANDARD of the GERMAN EMPIRE	CHINA
DANISH ROYAL STANDARD	Union Jack			Revenue Flag	NORWEGIAN STANDARD
SWITZERLAND	Admiral's Flag	UNITED STATES of AMERICA		Flag of the Secretary of the Navy	SWEDISH ROYAL STANDARD
PAPAL STANDARD	FRENCH STANDARD	VICE ADMIRAL	COMMODORE	RUSSIAN STANDARD	IONIAN ISLANDS
NICARAGUA and SAN SALVADOR	BELGIUM	ROYAL STANDARD of SPAIN	PORTUGUESE STANDARD	TURKEY	DOMINICA
COSTA RICA NATIONAL	U.S. of COLOMBIA	ARGENTINE REPUBLIC	ECUADOR	URUGUAY	PARAGUAY
SOCIETY ISLANDS	VENEZUELA	MEXICO	GUATEMALA	HONDURAS	HAYTI

Fruits of the Elizabethan Era

National Coats of Arms, 1902

Argentine Republic

Netherlands

Spain

Brazil

Argentina

United States of America

Mexico

Italy

Portugal

Peru

Russia

Chile

Austria Hungary

Great Britain

Norway

Sweden

Greece

Belgium

Denmark

Germany

Because the bees have become impeccably honest, they are no longer able to bargain productively in matters of money. In the completely virtuous hive, certain aspects of the society lose their relevance or luster—such as everything relating to law (no longer necessary) and to luxury (since partaking of luxuries is an indulgence that goes by the wayside). This leads to unemployment and stagnation. The weakened hive is eventually attacked by enemies, and the bees are driven out. Purged of vices, the once-thriving society falls apart.

The Fable of the Bees, published in 1714, provided fodder for the endorsement of the new economic order, and was widely read and debated. The story was immensely controversial because critics assailed the author, suggesting he advocated vices at the expense of virtue. His view wasn't that simplistic, yet he recognized the benefit that selfishness, consumption, and indulgence in luxuries provided for society. As he wrote:

> Thus Vice nursed Ingenuity,
> Which join'd with Time, and Industry
> Had carry'd Life's Conveniences,
> Its real Pleasure, Comforts, Ease,
> To such a Height, the very Poor
> Lived better than the Rich Before.

Setting the Stage

By the late 1700s, the increase in spending had raised standards of living for all levels of society. A great sum of people had enjoyed an increase in wages, a greater distribution of wealth, and a boom of aspirations and desires inspired by the dawning consumer marketplace. In London, where the social hierarchy was most concentrated, spending as a form of status climbing continued to push consumption to new heights.

The city of London itself played an important role in creating the new consumer society and influencing buying behavior. The city's merchants and entrepreneurs were quickly developing a new system of commercial techniques that would allow them to tap the market's potential. Because London was a world epicenter of economic activity, the city and the sensibility of her businessmen had a strong influence on the way that marketplace offerings would be produced, packaged, and sold. In the book *The Birth of a Consumer Society,* an analysis on the burgeoning culture of consumption in the eighteenth century, the authors write, "A mass consumer market awaited those products of the Industrial Revolution which skillful sales promotion could make fashionably desirable, heavy advertisement could make widely known, and whole batteries of salesmen could make easily accessible."

The Branding of the East India Company

In the modern era of companies deemed "too big to fail," it's interesting to reflect that there once existed a business so powerful that it had the ability to coin money, negotiate treaties, establish colonies, and even wage war. The East India Company, as it was called, was a multinational, joint stock corporation whose fleet of ships led England in a new age of state-sponsored expansion and global trade.

Historian Antony Wild, author of the book *The East India Company: Trade and Conquest from 1600,* writes that the company "was a supremely Elizabethan invention." Fiercely ambitious and powerful, the company had a fleet that was the largest merchant navy in the world. With Queen Elizabeth's blessing, the East India Company had unprecedented power in its dealings with other countries and commercial enterprises throughout the world. And as part of its "brand," the company's coat of arms gave a potent illustration to this purpose and attitude. In the image, the ships have full sails

and are facing east, signifying the beginning of an auspicious journey as well as the company's relationship with the Far East. The roses incorporated into the coat of arms represent England, and the blue globe on top signifies the world. The "sea lions" in the image convey the company's strength and royal imprimatur. The Latin motto below, "When God leads, nothing can harm," is part slogan, part war cry. The coat of arms was as grand as the company's mission.

Where the official coat of arms, formally called the Armorial Bearings of the Company, signified its naval excellence and capability, the corporate mark distinguished

The trademark, applied to cargo and money, among other things, evidences an understanding of branding—of laying claim to ownership and quality

its goods. The mark was initially a simple heart-shaped figure placed underneath the number four, which evokes a ship's sail. Later, a cross was added, to suggest the shape of an anchor, with the letters *E, I,* and *C* placed within the outline of the heart, standing for the company's official name. The trademark, applied to cargo and money, among other things, evidences an understanding of branding—of laying claim to ownership and quality—at a

time when such techniques were still in their nascent phases. The symbol also had other practical benefits—it gave a clear warning to would-be thieves who would be deterred by the company's naval power. The East India insignia is considered to be the first commercial trademark, and because of the company's travels in far-flung places of the world, it became the most widely known brand logo of its time.

Today, in a turnabout of its history, a businessman from Mumbai now owns the company and has transformed it into a purveyor of premium food products. To this day, the company maintains a clear language of branding and a strong embrace of its storied history.

03

POTTER'S GOLD

JESSIE McGUIRE

At the dawn of the eighteenth century, the stage had been set for a great economic transformation. Though people's buying habits had always been driven by personal preference and societal norms, most individuals in the years before the eighteenth century tended to buy and use only what was necessary. But the development of new technologies in the England of the Industrial Revolution led to innovations in manufacturing and production. The subsequent rise of factories and proliferation of mass-produced goods allowed consumers to choose among many options—a luxury they had never known before. Building on the transformations that had occurred in the Elizabethan era, the Industrial Revolution created a shift in the marketplace and ushered in a new culture of consumerism.[1]

ABOVE:
Josiah Wedgwood,
circa 1870

RIGHT:
Vintage Josiah
Wedgwood blue
pottery

The First Modern Entrepreneur

The eighteenth century marked the onset of many of the branding, marketing, and advertising techniques widely used today. Yet, before branding became the ascendant communicative and marketing tool, many goods were, to a significant degree, anonymous—an approach evidenced by the earthenware industry of the mid-1700s. Throughout England and Europe during the mid- to late 1700s, the earthenware industry—creating everything from dinnerware to vases and other decorative pieces—was growing exponentially; and abroad, the wares were selling particularly well in the New World. The industry was flourishing, yet there hadn't been much innovation in the field. The stage was set for someone with the passion and strategic insights to transform the industry.

Josiah Wedgwood was a potter who had learned his family business and then set up his own shop for producing pottery in its various guises, including earthenware. Wedgwood began learning the craft in 1739, at the age of nine. He later emerged as a very modern entrepreneur, becoming what *Forbes* describes as "the 18th century's most famous potter through innovation, artistic products and a lean production system."[2] Indeed, in 2005, *Forbes* readers and editors ranked him as the nineteenth most influential businessman of all time. Through a strategy of clever craftsmanship, sales, and invention, Wedgwood dramatically transformed his industry and the very nature of business itself. He spurred the evolution that led to today's rituals of consumption and branding, and his vast legacy continues to be relevant and very much influential today.

Design Thinking

Wedgwood was born in England in 1730 into a family and community of potters. After his father died, Josiah began an apprenticeship with his eldest brother, Thomas, which lasted for five years.[3] He entered into the family business at a time when pottery was gaining some ground in an earthenware market that had previously been dominated by porcelain, and particularly china. Though the young Wedgwood possessed no great skill as a potter, he took a strong interest in new materials and processes and was a tireless researcher, recording all his pottery-making and materials experiments in detail. In the early 1750s, Wedgwood began studying the process by which porcelain was finished, which included glazing techniques, so as to better understand the craft of pottery. Wedgwood's older brother was not enthusiastic about the experiments, however, and in 1754, the younger Wedgwood broke with his brother and entered into a partnership with potter Thomas Whieldon of the company Fenton Vivian; with Whieldon, he established a small factory in which to continue his investigations.[4]

Wedgwood's experiments can be seen as early signs of what we now call "design thinking"— the process through which a design is tested and refined. Using his unique methodology, Wedgwood would research a material or design, quickly create a prototype to test it, and then craft his findings into new wares. With this approach, Wedgwood spearheaded innovations that are now taken for granted but were evolutionary for the time. Among them: He created an assembly line approach to production, where individuals specialized in one aspect of the production process. He noticed that pottery was typically designed, produced, and

stored without any kind of consistency in sizing, which meant that pieces couldn't be stacked; to avoid this and to standardize sizes, he chose to use molds instead of relying on the vagaries of the potter's wheel. This allowed plates to be more easily stored in piles.[5]

The eighteenth century marked the onset of many of the branding, marketing, and advertising techniques widely used today.

Wedgwood also analyzed clay mixtures and finishes, which eventually led to important breakthroughs in glazing techniques and design. His first major achievement in this arena came in 1759 when he determined the formula for green glaze, which expanded his creative palette, since the new glaze allowed a piece to be an even color and could be placed in the kiln at the same time as other varieties of finishes.[6] This glaze would become the cornerstone of Wedgwood's early products and his entry into the consumer market.

Celebrity Endorsements

In 1759, equipped with these innovations in production and design, Wedgwood set up his own business. His observations of the buying public's habits informed the decisions that would shape what would become the early Wedgwood brand. He noticed, for one, that the possessions that younger generations had once inherited from their parents—things like plates, silverware, furniture, and other household goods—had become a

Wedgwood blue

Sky-color of a perfect day—

in a cotton cord that shows

the news from every angle.

Ours alone. Sizes 8 to 16, 39.95

Budget Town Shop, Second Floor

Lord & Taylor, New York. Also

Manhasset, Westchester,

Millburn, West Hartford

Lord & Taylor

class of consumable luxury goods that people now wanted to buy new.[7] Moreover, it had become more common for families and individuals to replace their belongings with newer versions of the same items—a behavior that had once been unthinkable. In the new economic order, one could elevate one's social status—to a degree—through conspicuous consumption, and the members of British society were increasingly falling under the sway of this ritual. Wedgwood, cognizant that this would lead customers to buy the latest products in order to demonstrate their wealth and their cultural accomplishment, took advantage of this by creating specialized lines and limited editions.

In the book *The Birth of a Consumer Society*, the authors note that one of Wedgwood's first commercial triumphs was "to turn that pursuit of ceramic luxury by the rich into the pursuit of useful pottery for many."[8] Ironically, the first step toward achieving this goal was when Wedgwood garnered the imprimatur of the royal family. In 1763, the potterymaker patented a technique that allowed him to create a new form of cream-colored pottery—the so-called "creamware." Queen Charlotte, the wife of King George III, admired it so much that Wedgwood christened it Queen's Ware in her honor.

The queen enlisted Wedgwood to create dinnerware for the royal court, and Wedgwood also made the line in a version that was available to the general public—and which became immensely successful. He sought out other members of the monarchy, the nobility, and art connoisseurs to create custom lines and limited editions for them; he would name each after the person he was designing for. Recognizing the value of these "celebrity endorsements," he began advertising

himself as Potter to His and Her Majesty. He believed that, as the authors of *The Birth of a Consumer Society* observe, "if he had the patronage of the great, he would have the custom of the world."[9] With this strategy, he acknowledged the power that a few had over the many—a cultural dynamic now known as "influencer theory." Wedgwood also understood the importance of being fashionable. He believed that if he could create a particular social cachet for his wares, he could appeal to all classes of society. Traditionally, pottery and porcelain had not been inscribed with the name of the artist or company; they were, in effect, anonymous wares. Wedgwood, however, wasn't satisfied with anonymity. After he went into partnership with Thomas Bentley in 1768, he began stamping each piece "WEDGWOOD & BENTLEY," creating, in essence, the beginnings of brand identity. Consumers came to know that

the Wedgwood & Bentley stamp was a guarantee of quality and a signifier of style. It conveyed a business that embodied both innovation and cachet. Thus a brand was begun.

Modern Marketing

Through his rigorous process of experimentation, Wedgwood had refined the earthenware he was making, but he came to a realization that his innovation had a limit. He realized that he was not likely to invent pottery superior to his creamware; his black basalt, a fine-grained stoneware; or his jasperware, an unglazed stoneware typically colored blue and decorated with bas reliefs. Having extensively refined his system of production, he resolved to do the same in sales and distribution.[10] Understanding that he had to fully comprehend his customers in order to be effective in selling to them, Wedgwood studied what people were buying, wearing, and reading. He sought out consumers and asked them direct questions about their lifestyles and purchases, trying to detect patterns of preferences in specific niches of society. His investigations are some of the earliest forays into ethnographic research.

During the process of information gathering, Wedgwood discovered that people who were interested in fashionable products had a particular predilection to see and touch the items they were buying. That observation led him to create what would be a milestone in the history of branding: a London showroom. As Robin Hildyard notes in the book *English Pottery,* "It was ... logical that, in a climate where manufacturers' names were being attached to traditionally anonymous pottery and porcelain, Josiah Wedgwood should consider capitalizing on his appointment as potter to the queen in 1766 by opening the first single-factory earthenware showroom in London."[11] The showroom's location in the city was selected with great care: Though not the most fashionable area of the metropolis, the shop was in the heart of a neighborhood inhabited by artists and cultured, well-read—and well-dressed—men of society. For good measure, Wedgwood adorned his shop with a sign showing the Queen's Arms, a symbol that conveyed the favor of the queen.[12]

Though his techniques in branding, sales, and distribution may now seem ordinary, the strategies were completely novel at the time.[13] Wedgwood passionately believed in his brand, and he came to an intuitive understanding of his consumer. This combination allowed him to continually imagine new objectives for his growing business, and he consistently sought out new markets. With elegant showrooms, he showcased his wares in new climes. Relying on a group of salespeople—another novel idea at the time—he broke into new markets in Russia, Germany, Spain, Sweden, France, and the United States. By 1785, at least five-sixths of the earthenware manufactured in the business's Staffordshire home base was for export.[14]

Imitation as Flattery

Through the great advancements Josiah Wedgwood made in marketing, manufacturing, and experimentation, he laid the foundation for the longevity of the Wedgwood brand; his children would take over the company after his death in 1795. As part of the legacy, the early 1800s saw the younger Wedgwoods contending with the emergence of copycat brands. Many companies began imitating not only the Wedgwood products themselves (and selling them at a considerably reduced price), but also Wedgwood's sales techniques and showrooms. In time, the sales, display, and manufacturing techniques that Wedgwood had innovated spread from the pottery industry to other arenas. With numerous companies relying on the same strategies—and contending with copycat brands—there needed to be another point of differentiation and brand assurance. Copyright and trademark protection would soon be introduced.

Vintage Josiah Wedgwood blue pottery

Understanding that he had to fully comprehend his customers, Wedgwood studied what people were buying, wearing, and reading.

> "Beautiful forms and compositions are not made by chance, nor can they ever, in any material, be made at small expense. A composition for cheapness and not excellence of workmanship is the most frequent and certain cause of the rapid decay and entire destruction of arts and manufactures."

—Josiah Wedgwood,
late 1700s

Josiah Wedgwood and Steve Jobs

In eighteenth-century England, owning creamware, a white-glazed piece of pottery, signified that one was a member of an elite—or at least had some aspiration to be so. This particular kind of earthenware meant that one understood quality and appreciated the best of culture. In the modern-day world, Apple's high-design products communicate a similar message. The computers and devices the company makes are not simply functional pieces that serve a practical purpose; they also convey an aesthetic, even existential, sensibility.

In that sense, Josiah Wedgwood and Steve Jobs would seem to share some common ground. They both recognized and capitalized on trends in design, branding, and technology. Wedgwood became the eighteenth century's most famous potterymaker, not only through his ability to shepherd such elegant creations, but because he knew how to sell. He understood the importance of making a product and, ultimately, a brand, a seemingly integral part of remaining relevant in society. He recognized the value of making people want to be a part of a cultural experience.

The showrooms that displayed Wedgwood's products were an integral part of the company's brand experience; Apple has used the same tack for its own branded stores, acknowledging the value of engaging customers through a space that is both showcase and destination. As Wedgwood himself wrote, "I need not tell you the many good effects this must produce, when business, and amusement can be made to go hand and hand."[15] Wedgwood, for his part, created his showrooms to make the elite feel elite—and to tap into the common folk's

—Apple CEO Steve Jobs, 1997

desire to feel so as well. The retail spaces were crafted to generate a feeling of aesthetic appreciation for all who walked in. Apple showrooms have the same aim: With the array of computers and other devices on display, customers are transported into a world of magic, vibrance, and possibility evoked by the latest must-have technology. The stores' boutique atmosphere of personalized attention only enhances the experience.

Jobs and Wedgwood have followed the muse of other similar strategies: For one, they both comprehended the value of building anticipation for new products. Apple product launches are first closely guarded secrets that are eventually announced with great fanfare and coverage. For each product announcement, Jobs was a masterful showman, creating theater from the marvels of Apple creativity and generating the buzz that went along with it. And the Apple ethos is potent: Eager customers have been known to camp outside stores for days in advance of new product launches.

During the eighteenth century, Wedgwood, too, offered his customers "spectacular productions," particularly as relating to new debuts. The description of these spectacles given by the authors of *The Birth of a Consumer Society* is as applicable to Jobs' performances as it is to Wedgwood's: "These were carefully stage-managed. Great care was taken in timing the openings, and new goods were held back to increase their effect."[16]

"Here's to the crazy ones, the misfits, the rebels, the troublemakers, the round pegs in the square holes . . . the ones who see things differently— they're not fond of rules. You can quote them, disagree with them, glorify or vilify them, but the only thing you can't do is ignore them, because they change things. They push the human race forward, and while some may see them as the crazy ones, we see genius, because the ones who are crazy enough to think that they can change the world are the ones who do."

04

TRADEMARKS AND THE GROWTH OF CONSUMER PACKAGED GOODS

**MANAL NASSAR,
MYLES GAYTHWAITE,
NOAH ARMSTRONG**

The Trademark Protections Act was substantially revised in 1905, affording trademark holders increased legal protection. The explosion of branded consumer packaged goods soon followed.

As far back as the first millennium B.C., artisans would stamp a unique symbol onto their wares to prove their provenance. This was useful since the trade in these goods, such as earthenware pots and other durables, could reach far and wide, extending across the entire Mediterranean world. These marks provided some assurance as to their origin. This practice continued with the growth of trade and commerce and became commonplace during the rise and prominence of the guilds of medieval Europe. However, as today, these marks were certainly no guarantee of authenticity.

One of the first formal, mark-related laws was implemented in England in 1266, during the reign of King Henry III. The Bakers Marking Law required bread makers to mark every loaf of bread with pinpricks or stamps. The law was passed to ensure that the bread met certain standards and that bakers would be accountable for the goods they produced.

WHEN IT RAINS

First Trademark Challenge

The first known case of fraud concerning a trademark was Southern v. How in 1618 England: A prominent clothier accused a rival of affixing his mark upon an inferior product. While the case was ultimately decided for the plaintiff, the government didn't institute many protections to assure the rights of the first users of a particular mark.

Indeed, long after this first legal challenge, most marks were seen as signatures, simply denoting authorship. They were not utilized to secure trade protections, nor were they seen as a means of protecting buyers from fraudulent goods. Beyond the sale of luxury goods that enjoyed a prosperous trade across regions, most goods that entered into commerce did so, and remained so, at the local level. Therefore, the purchaser and seller typically had an innate trust for each other. This trust, often with roots in a relationship developed over time, existed irrespective of the maker's mark. Yet all of this changed with the Industrial Revolution.

The onset of the Industrial Revolution in England brought with it an explosion of goods and services for sale as well as a proliferation of new consumers with the means to purchase these products. Most importantly, for the first time, goods were being mass produced at a central location and shipped to far-flung locales. It was during this time that brand names and trademarks became increasingly important. In order to protect their offerings—and profits—from fraud, manufacturers in England began clamoring for official legal protection.

The first step toward legal protection for trademarks was the 1862 Merchandise Marks Act, which made it illegal to knowingly copy another's mark for fraudulent purposes. However, enforcing this law proved difficult, as it was extremely hard to prove who had used the mark first. To solve this, in 1875, the United Kingdom passed the Trade Marks Registration Act, which allowed for the formal registration of unique trademarks with the United Kingdom Patent Office, formally creating the infrastructure for the modern consumer brand. When the law went into effect on January 1, 1876, the brewery, Bass Ale, registered the world's first officially recognized trademark, the company's famous red triangle logo; the symbol remains in use to this day.

In the United States, protection of trademarks was not as well defined at the time. Although the United States *Constitution* established the legal groundwork for a patent system, it wasn't until Congress enacted the Federal Trade Mark Act, in 1870, that that brands began to enjoy legal protection.

Early Bass Ale packaging

Registering Trademarks

The first mark registered under the auspices of the act was for the Averill Chemical Paint Company—the mark was a logo that showed an eagle holding a pot of paint in its beak; below, a pennant displayed the slogan, "Economical, Beautiful, Durable." This 1870 law was ruled to be unconstitutional by the Supreme Court in 1879. Recognizing the importance of trademark protection—and spurred on by business—Congress developed a new law, the Trademark Protection Act, which passed in 1881. This law was substantially revised in 1905, affording trademark holders increased legal protection. The explosion of branded consumer packaged goods soon followed.

Though the Industrial Revolution saw the creation of many branded durable goods, perishable and dry goods enjoyed the benefits of mass production yet remained unbranded. Instead, they were sold in bulk under the purview of the local merchant. As late as the mid-1800s, not only were ingredients such as flour and sugar sold in bulk from large bins, but prepared goods, such as crackers, were also sold in bulk. Interestingly, this is where we get the term "the bottom of the barrel"—as the remnants that one could purchase in bulk from the bottom of the barrel were often of excruciatingly poor quality. Additionally, the consumer didn't always have direct access to the goods. Purchases were made from behind a counter where a patron would ask the merchant for flour or some other sundry and would subsequently be sold what the merchant suggested and packed.

From this informal rite of turn-of-the-century commerce would emerge an idea that would forever change branded consumer goods.

Following the lead of certain key innovators—National Biscuit Company (later Nabisco) among them, with its Uneeda Biscuit—manufacturers started to put their offerings in small packages, and consumers started buying these prepackaged goods instead of buying from bulk containers. Product labels, complete with promotional text and imagery, began to appear, as did the iconic symbols that helped to identify and convey the brand sensibility. Companies that recognized the value of this—among them Procter & Gamble and the company that made Genuine Bull Durham Smoking Tobacco, which used a bull as its logo and became a business known around the world—were able to build brands and the consumer loyalty that went in hand with them.

Classic Brand Trademarks

Brands without packaging seem to be an unthinkable possibility in the modern-day world. Numerous companies have taken the platform of the package into realms of the cultural sublime. Some of these icons include the Coke contour bottle, the Brillo box (re-created by Andy Warhol in his artwork), the Band-Aid tin, the Crayola Crayon box, and numerous others. Three classic American brands helped to define the possibilities of the visual palette.

IVORY®
IVORY Soap
99 44/100% PURE · · IT FLOATS
IVORY®
IVORY
LARGE
© P & G Co.
HANDS UP!
Have hands with
"That IVORY Look"—*pretty!*
Wash dishes with gentle IVORY.
For skin care—more
doctors advise IVORY
than any other soap.
IVORY SOAP
PROCTER & GAMBLE · MADE IN U.S.A.

Ivory Soap

MYLES GAYTHWAITE

In the mid-1800s, soap was mainly a secondary product created from remnants of the candle-making process. Most Americans at that time bathed just once a week; few homes had indoor plumbing, and carting water indoors and heating it for a bath was a laborious affair. Because of this, most people didn't give soap much thought and usually used the same bar for washing themselves as they did for washing their clothes and other items.

Procter & Gamble started as a manufacturer of candles, but founder James Gamble, keen on creating an American soap that could compete with the more luxurious castile soaps from Europe, wanted to expand the business. Working with a chemist on new formulations, Gamble succeeded in creating a unique, silky, white soap that he embedded with air bubbles in order to make it float. In 1879, this was a novel invention, one that provided a unique benefit that would set it apart from its competitors in the marketplace.

As the sons of P&G's founders came of age, they began to assume control of the family business. Realizing that the future belonged to soap manufacturing rather than candle production, they changed the direction of the company and started to increase marketing efforts behind the "White Soap."

According to company lore, a close cousin, Harley Gamble, was sitting in church one Sunday morning and was inspired by Psalm 45: "All thy garments smell of myrrh, and aloes, and cassia, out of the ivory palaces, whereby they have made thee glad." A devout

OPPOSITE:
Ivory Soap packaging, flat, 1954

LEFT:
"Something new"—
Ivory Soap being sold in 1879

man, Harley said that the word "ivory" reminded him of purity and would be an excellent association for soap. A new brand was born, and Harley was put in charge of sales.

The trademark for Ivory Soap was granted in 1879, featuring decorative serif type set beside P&G's "man in the moon" logo, which had been in use since 1851. What's remarkable about the original trademark is how unremarkable it was. Unlike the Coca-Cola trademark, which quickly became an American icon, Ivory's eventual popularity within the cultural imagination stemmed from the brilliant marketing and sloganeering of Harley Procter.

Looking back, it may seem as if Harley was particularly obsessed with the idea of purity, but the product he was marketing certainly benefited from his perspective. Not only did "it float"—a benefit that he touted ceaselessly—but this attribute seemed to reinforce the idea of purity. To that end, he hired chemists from across the country to test the actual purity of the product. The researchers reported that the "non-soap" elements amounted to 0.56 percent of the creation. Harley turned this to his advantage and pronounced that Ivory Soap was "99 and 44/100% pure." The slogan struck such a chord with consumers that it remains in use to this day.

1898

1904

1921

1935

In the mid-1800s, most Americans bathed only once each week.

1940

1947

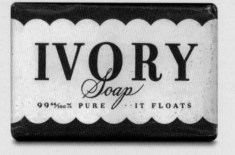

1947

1947

Purity and value was what made Ivory soap popular.

Like getting one free!

4 for the price of 3

NOW– TIED IN ONE BEAUTY BUNDLE

4 cakes of pure, mild Personal Size Ivory cost about
the same as 3 cakes of other leading toilet soaps!

Any way you look at it—Personal Size Ivory's new Beauty Bundle
is a beauty of a buy. Now—4 cakes all tied in one neat bundle—
so handy . . . so thrifty. And how those dainty cakes of mildness pamper
your skin! You see, the milder the beauty soap, the prettier your
skin, and Ivory Soap is mild enough for a baby's skin. So for that fresh,
radiant look, That Ivory Look, get your Beauty Bundle now.

99.44% PURE .IT FLOATS

THE BEAUTY BUNDLE IS YOUR BEST BEAUTY BUY

1921

1933

1941

Trademarks and the Growth of Consumer Packaged Goods

Coca-Cola

MYLES GAYTHWAITE

Coca-Cola, the world's most famous brand, sprang into existence one hot summer afternoon in Atlanta, Georgia, in 1886. Pharmacist J. S. Pemberton concocted a sweet, caramel-colored syrup to which he added soda water as a novel means of quenching his thirst. It was an immediate hit with soda fountain patrons and he began selling quantities on the order of nine glasses a day, according to legend. Pemberton's business partner, Frank Robinson, suggested the name Coca-Cola, remarking that he thought the two capital *C*s would look good together in advertisements. To prove his point, he drew up the logo in an elaborate Spencerian script, which was in vogue at that time, and the legendary logo was born.

Pemberton patented his concoction in 1887, but it wasn't until 1893, after he sold the company to Asa Chandler, that the words and logo were trademarked. Chandler was an astute businessman and marketed his product relentlessly, both through advertisements and an early form of promotional swag: He affixed his logo to all manner of items, from clocks to calendars and serving trays. Throughout the decade, Coca-Cola, though extremely popular, was sold only at soda fountains across the country. It wasn't until Chandler sold the bottling rights to two enterprising lawyers in 1899 that the product's sales flourished. Chandler's lack of business foresight on this point led him to sell the rights for the grand sum of $1.

Although the product was trademarked, the enormous popularity of the drink proved too irresistible not to copy. Hundreds of copycat colas surged the market, with names like King Cola and Pepsi-Cola, often with similar scripts and red coloration. Unable to stem

the tide through litigation, and with advertisements proving ineffective in convincing consumers to "buy the real thing," Coke sought a way to protect its unique product—to brand it more than it already was. The company patented the now ubiquitous bottle in 1915; the shape, designed by Alexander Samuelson and Earl Dean, was so distinctive that customers would be able to find it in the dark. Though it's now an icon of the Coca-Cola Company, the bottle was not granted trademark protection until 1977.

ABOVE:
Coca-Cola inventor, J. S. Pemberton (left)

Early Coca-Cola bottle rendering (right)

Drink Coca-Cola
Delicious and Refreshing

Refresh Yourself!

McClelland Barclay

THE COCA-COLA COMPANY
ATLANTA GA.

CHARM OF COCA-COLA IS PROCLAIMED AT ALL SODA FOUNTAINS

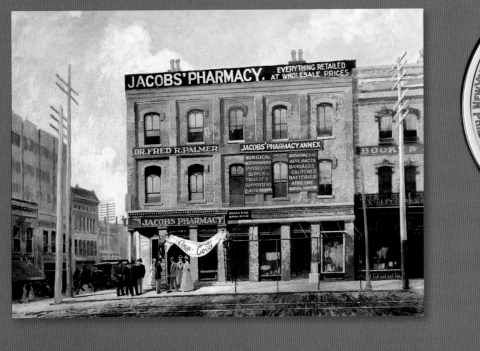

125 *Coca-Cola* years

In 1915 a bottle was designed based on the shape of Coca-Cola's two main ingredients: the cocoa leaf and the kola nut. This original curvy Coca-Cola bottle design had a diameter that was larger than its base making for a beautiful exaggerated shape but also making it unstable on conveyor belts, thus, unfit for production. A refined and slimmed-down bottle design followed later that year and the iconic Coke bottle was born.

1899   1900 through 1916   1915 (prototype)   1915

1957   1961   1991   1993   2007

Toasted Corn Flakes cereal was very similar to that made by the competitors W. K. Kellogg had inspired—forty-two of them to be exact—all based in Battle Creek.

Kellogg's
NOAH ARMSTRONG

In 1894, William Keith Kellogg took a batch of cooked wheat that had been left out overnight and ran it through a set of rollers. He had been using the method to create sheets of dough that were then ground to create a breakfast food. What he got from the process on that particular occasion was flakes of wheat; the accident would usher in a new era of breakfast foods. Kellogg continued experimenting with the new technique and eventually arrived at a new creation: corn flakes. William Keith (or W. K., as he was better known) had been working with his brother, Dr. John Harvey Kellogg, at the Battle Creek Sanitarium in Battle Creek, Michigan, where they advocated to patients the benefits of a healthy vegetarian diet. The brothers' ready-to-eat wheat- and corn-based cereals proved to be a healthy and tasty breakfast, becoming enormously popular with those convalescing—so much so that when these patients left the sanitarium, they told their family and friends about the cereals. The brothers soon found themselves filling orders and mailing boxes of their cereals to former patients, as well as their family and friends.

In 1906, W. K. changed the company's name from Sanitas Nut and Food Co. Ltd, a reference to the Sanitarium, to the Battle Creek Toasted Corn Flake Company, a reference to his most popular product—corn flakes. Unfortunately, the cereal was very similar to that made by the competitors he had inspired—forty-two of them to be exact—all based in Battle Creek. Kellogg added malt to distinguish the flavor of his corn flakes, but he needed customers to know that his was the original flaked breakfast cereal. He subsequently changed the company name to the Kellogg Toasted Corn Flake Company, and created a wordmark from his signature. With his name written in red stylized script and the phrases "None genuine without this signature" and "The Original" prominently displayed on each box, customers in Battle Creek, and beyond, knew they were getting an authentic batch of the original corn flakes—Kellogg's Corn Flakes—guaranteed by William Keith Kellogg himself. The wordmark, and the personal assurance it represented, is a tidy symbol of how businesses, and consumers, were bridging from one era to another.

LEFT:
Kellogg's Rice Krispies
advertisement, 1914

RIGHT:
Kellogg's PEP
advertisement, 1926

PEP

Takes *pep* to make that graceful flashing dive

POISED for the plunge! Muscles tensed. Back arched high. Picture of grace and health! Glowing pep in every movement! Radiant, riotous pep!

PEP is a wonder! A ready-to-eat cereal with a marvelous flavor! Fills you with glorious pep! Builds health, stamina, strength!

PEP is packed with nature's own health-bringing elements. Keeps you robust, alert, alive!

PEP is wonderfully fine for everybody. Contains bran

1.

2.

Character Icons Used in Advertising

MANAL NASSAR

As more legal protection was granted to trademarks, manufacturers began to utilize the trademarks more heavily as business tools. The marks, showcased on packaging and in advertisements, helped companies to build a valuable asset that would help them generate customer loyalty. These marks embodied something essential about the brand, and they built up strong cultural and emotional associations.

Part of the initial impetus for companies to develop trademarks was an interest in building that emotional connection: Packaged goods manufacturers needed to convince consumers that they could place just as much trust in a big brand as in the better-known local products.

Coca-Cola, Aunt Jemima, Quaker Oats, and Campbell's Soup are just some of the memorable brands that have emerged early on in the United States; these brand identities were a natural extension of a company's efforts to identify itself and ensure consumers' familiarity with its products. The ethos expanded as companies built a whole world of multimedia associations around the trademarks, with advertising taglines, product collectibles, as well as radio and television jingles; the elaborate culture of branding ensured that the brand would be deeply ingrained in consumers' psyche and, thus, unforgettably irresistible.

3.

4.

5.

6.

1914

7.

Popular Advertising Icons

1. Aunt Jemima was a character in minstrel shows during the late 1800s. She was adopted to represent a brand of prepared pancake mix, syrup, and other foods.
2. Breakfast cereals—many of them geared to children—have long had advertising mascots. Snap, Crackle, and Pop began advertising Kellogg's Rice Krispies in a 1933 radio advertisement. Other cereal-inspired characters include Cap'n Crunch, Count Chocula, and the Trix Rabbit.
3. The Quaker Man, one of the oldest icons of food culture in America, dates to 1877.
4. The cherubic Campbell's Kids have been gracing the soup company's advertising and various other obsessively collected paraphernalia since 1904.
5. Mr. Peanut, the dapper representative of Planter's Peanuts, has been showing off his top hat and cane on the American advertising scene since 1916.
6. The Morton Umbrella Girl first appeared on table salt packaging in 1914.
7. The Green Giant character first appeared on packaging in 1925, as the identifier for a variety of particularly large peas. He began appearing in ads three years later.

05

THE BEGINNING OF MANUFACTURER BRANDS

CHI WAI LIMA, JADA BRITTO,
and **MO SAAD**

At the turn of the twentieth century, technological innovations in printing and manufacturing proliferated, and businesses brought a great number of new products onto the market. As many Americans left agrarian life to seek their livelihoods in the city, they increasingly purchased these branded, packaged goods. This created a huge power shift: Consumers no longer needed to rely on storekeepers' opinions for what to buy, and manufacturers now spoke directly to their customers by designing packages and labels that promoted their brands' quality and consistency. Businesses realized that the potential to attract consumers lay not just in creating a product that would fulfill a need, but in creating the need itself. Enter the era of the brand.

Manufacturer Brands in Daily Life

From the 1880s onward, the emergence of factories that could produce seven times more iron and nine times more paper made mass production possible, decreasing prices of such essentials and the machinery associated with them. Where companies used to send out packaging to be made in factories, with new printing processes and high-production paper-folding or canning machines, they were able to purchase these massive machines and bring manufacturing of packaging and labels in-house. This, in turn, allowed them to brand large quantities of goods.[1]

By creating new products and packages, these pioneering businesses created a contemporary language for branding and marketing the items they produced. The most notable of these manufacturers—National Biscuit Company (which later became Nabisco), Colgate, Procter & Gamble

(P&G), and Johnson & Johnson—would advertise these products starring the package and label as "an integral part of the commodity itself," as early twentieth-century advertising expert Gerald B. Wadsworth put it in his 1913 book, *Principles and Practice of Advertising.*[2] If the package and label were integral to the product, then the brand had become similarly so. The biscuits were no longer just biscuits. They were Nabisco biscuits—and the packaging was as much a part of the product's identity as the product itself. As a result, the packaging—even the fact that the container was a particular size or made of a certain material—featured prominently in advertisements.

Transcending the "Art of the Artless"

Throughout history, packaging has been a tabula rasa for creative expression—for communicating a message, however straightforward (or not), about

LEFT:
Johnson & Johnson
Red Cross Bandages

ABOVE:
Crisco was introduced
in an airtight can,
which was opened
with a key. This paper
label was glued onto
the can.

Uneeda Biscuit was one of the first brands to take advantage of packaging innovation as a selling point in stores and in advertising.

the nature of the contents and the character of its creators. Before the nineteenth century, packaging might highlight the value and the nature of a product but would place little emphasis on its character. Paper, a common material for packaging even in ancient Egypt, was used to protect the wrapped contents but not to communicate with the purchaser.

The earliest known use of a printed label on a package is said to go back to 1550, when a German trading family used labels to mark goods such as silks and wool for shipment. But as a whole, commerce did not have a face of its own. The shops of traders, grocers, tailors, and shoemakers were strikingly similar in styling—all of them were adorned by simple signs, and there was no significant differentiation between competing purveyors. Nor were the packages that they gave to customers. In his book *Package and Print: The Development of the Label and Container,* Alec Davis describes packaging during this period as "the art of the artless."[3]

The first signs of major change in commercial enterprise came in the 1800s, when monochrome printing methods came into use. With the development of monochrome printing, more depth and variation could be added to the typical black-and-white printing methods. This allowed the reproduction of images, illustrations, and text to more visibly stand out. By the 1830s, it became possible to print color on paper as small as matchbox labels, and the era of "packaging innovation," as Davis describes it, began. In 1900, Artemas Ward, editor of various grocery and advertising trade magazines, would write, "It is wonderful to note the volume of package trading in food products, groceries, and patent medicines. Goods are no longer referenced as staples because they are no longer being sold in bulk but packaged."[4] Manufacturers had started to create a face for brands, taking packaging from artless to artful.

Uneeda Biscuit: A Fresh Approach

Uneeda Biscuit was one of the first brands to take advantage of packaging innovation as a selling point in stores and in advertising. In 1898, Adolphus Green and William Moore formed the National Biscuit Company (now called Nabisco and owned by Kraft Foods) and created Uneeda Biscuit, a cracker that would spur the revolution in how people thought about packaged foods. Crackers were once sold out of open barrels, where they were exposed to dirt and the elements; they would often become soggy. One anecdote goes that when a customer complained that mice were living in the cracker barrel, the merchant replied that this was impossible because "the cat sleeps there every night."[5] Obviously, the food industry was ripe for transformation. The evolution of packaging would be part of a progression that catalyzed a branding ethos.

For its part, National Biscuit Company set out to create sales—and thus brand appeal—through a more sanitary approach to selling foodstuffs. The first bit of branding was the name: Copywriter Henry McKinney of the N. W. Ayer & Son advertising agency suggested the name "Uneeda" to Green, who then combined it with "biscuit"—a term deemed more refined than "cracker." To keep the product fresh, National Biscuit invented the "In-er-Seal" package, a fully enclosed carton that was lined with waxed paper. Featured prominently in Uneeda's advertising, the In-er-Seal box was shown clutched by a five-year-old boy wearing a yellow raincoat, emphasizing the carton's effectiveness against moisture. Green added a trademark to the package when he discovered in a book an old printer's symbol that consisted of a cross with two bars and an oval; Green was moved by the meaning that Italian printers had given it of "the triumph of the spiritual over the worldly."[6]

Uneeda's campaign, from 1899, was one of the first in the United States advertising a ready-to-eat staple food sold in individual packages.[7] The In-er-Seal altered the public mindset about packaged foods—people used to be wary of such items because they couldn't see, smell, or taste the contents before buying them. But with the companies touting the benefits of packaging, consumers now realized its advantages in keeping food fresh longer.[8] Susan Strasser, a historian of American consumer culture, writes about the shift in *Satisfaction Guaranteed: The Making of the American Mass Market.* "In modern marketing terms, the emphasis on packaging in the National Biscuit advertising served as 'product education,'" she explains. "The company was promoting not simply its own products but the product category: packaged crackers and cookies."[9]

While it may seem an innocuous event in the history of branding, Uneeda's packaging was a milestone that led to other transformations. The transition from food sold in bulk to food sold in packages inevitably led companies to trumpet their advantages and differentiation. The innovation allowed customers to be able to get products without the assistance of a grocer, a radical shift from past years; it helped pave the way for the packaged food industry and ultimately, the supermarket.[10]

Growing Up with Colgate

Every morning and evening, most of us grab our toothbrushes and toothpaste for our daily regimen of dental care, but the concept of using a toothbrush and toothpaste is not much more than one hundred years old. Before the introduction of these products, people used to clean their teeth with concoctions such as crushed bones; eggshells; ground-up chalk mixed with lemon juice; ashes; and tobacco mixed with honey. The idea of cleaning teeth with a brush is generally attributed to William Addis, a prisoner who, while held in London's Newgate Jail in 1780, created the first toothbrush out of an animal bone and bristles. In the United States, the first patent for a toothbrush wasn't filed until 1857 (it received patent number 18,653). The design of the time still featured a bone handle.

Colgate, another manufacturer that used packaging and advertising to educate the consumer, introduced its first aromatic toothpaste—a powdery substance sold in glass jars—in 1873. In 1896, the company began selling the Colgate Ribbon Dental Cream, the first toothpaste in a collapsible tube (the container had originally been used for paints). In 1908, Colgate began selling toothbrushes and toothpaste with print ads that read, "Colgate's antiseptic dental cream: Comes out a ribbon / lies flat on the brush. Delicious antiseptic—more convenient, more efficient and less wasteful than powder. The Colgate quality in another original Colgate package." With these taglines, Colgate marketed the container as an integral part of the commodity.

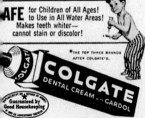

Colgate toothpaste was originally named Ribbon Dental Cream

In subsequent years, Colgate sought to build awareness of the brand—and of dental hygiene—through giveaways: In 1911, the company distributed 2 million tubes of toothpaste and toothbrushes to schools, with hygienists giving children demonstrations of how to properly brush their teeth. No longer would eggshells or tobacco mixed with honey be necessary. Colgate offered the effectiveness and convenience of its toothpaste and further complemented the pitch by the innovation of the package itself.

Crisco in the Kitchen

When Crisco was introduced in 1911 by Procter & Gamble, consumers didn't know what it was or that they would need it. The company described Crisco as "an absolutely new product, a scientific discovery which will affect every kitchen in America."[11] In the process of bringing Crisco to market, P&G also made some branding discoveries: Crisco is considered to have been the first brand to combine the branding techniques that would later become standard routine. But when—in its efforts to make Crisco successful—Procter & Gamble hired an advertising agency and enlisted scientific research and the accompanying sales pitches, the company was pioneering new territory.

P&G sought to ensure that Crisco was scientifically sound—and domestically appealing—before the company released it to the public. The shortening was created and tested in a laboratory, and before its debut, samples were given to cooks for further experimentation as part of P&G's culinary and branding due diligence.

As Crisco was manufactured—it wasn't a natural product, like butter, but rather was made through the industrial process of hydrogenating vegetable oil—P&G management recognized that they had to position the product correctly if it was to be successful. Before Crisco's introduction, the N. K. Fairbank Company had produced a similar shortening called Cottolene. The product had failed in the marketplace; many in the industry attributed the failure to the fact that consumers didn't trust a soap manufacturer to create a food product, since they thought the food would be created in the same factory as the soap, risking contamination. P&G realized, as the manufacturer of Ivory soap, that it could easily fall prey to the same pitfall. The company decided to focus on a strategy that would introduce Crisco with the assurance and information—that is, branding—necessary to ensure a market for the product.

To do this, P&G turned to advertising consultant Stanley Resor, who was running the Cincinnati office of ad agency J. Walter Thompson. It was the first time in the company's history that it had enlisted an outside agency to help advertise and market a product. Resor brought on JWT copywriter Helen Lansdowne, who became the first woman ever to attend a P&G board meeting. P&G management recognized the appeal to women would be a key part of the product's eventual success—or its failure. Lansdowne would bring in the woman's point of view and help the company reach female consumers.

Together, Resor and Lansdowne created an unprecedented marketing and advertising campaign for Crisco. They experimented with new methods of advertising, playfully seeing which method would work best in different cities,

The Story of Crisco contained 250 recipes and and cooking tips—P&G's attempt to make Crisco integral to popular culture.

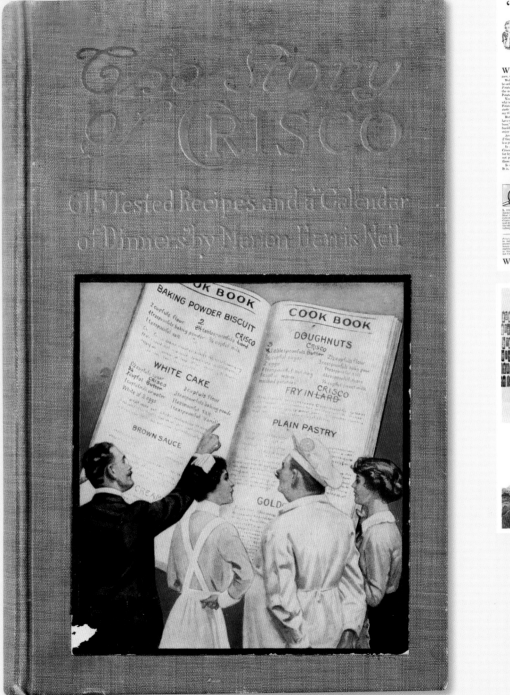

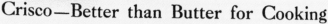

and used a plethora of advertising channels—streetcar ads, outdoor posters, and even house-to-house saleswomen. Lansdowne's copy touted Crisco's benefits, which included the fact that it would remain solid at room temperature and could be stored without refrigeration. Thrifty housewives could save money by using Crisco, since, in comparison to butter and lard, less of it could be used for cooking; the product could also allegedly be reused numerous times, since it wouldn't absorb the flavors of the food fried in it. Part of the product's branding itself included, of course, the packaging—a white paper overwrap emblazoned with the Crisco name—which enclosed the can inside.

In addition to the house calls, where salespeople would demonstrate the product to housewives, the company built the brand by making consumers feel like part of a community. The company arranged weeklong cooking workshops, during which women in cities around the United States learned what they could cook with Crisco. The sessions became so successful that they inspired a groundswell of enthusiasm, with home cooks eager to share their recipes with others. By 1912, housewives were sending in recipes to P&G to publish in a free paperback titled *Tested Crisco Recipes.* The publication of the book proved such a hit that P&G went a step further, publishing a second title called *The Story of Crisco,* which contained 250 recipes. With these strategies, P&G ensured that the shortening would become part of the popular culture at the time, and the company changed the habits of women and American cooking as a whole. The foray into branding, using the multipronged strategy—had reaped immense rewards for the company.

LEFT:
Early Crisco
advertisements

ABOVE:
Crisco taught people
how to use the product
by inserting recipes
into advertisements.

Changing Habits

While P&G was convincing consumers that they needed the new breed of manufactured products, other companies were endeavoring on similar brand-building efforts. Just as Colgate encouraged the new habit of caring for teeth and keeping mouths clean and thus created a new market for selling toothpaste and toothbrushes, Gillette in the early 1900s introduced a razor that men could use to shave at home—a significant switch in an era when they usually went to barbers. In the emerging arena of photography, Kodak pitched cameras as a necessary way of preserving memories; Johnson & Johnson debuted a range of products—including its famed Band-Aid—as an essential part of the home apothecary and modern hygiene. The Minnesota Manufacturing and Mining Company (today known as 3M) brought out Scotch Cellulose Tape, the first transparent adhesive tape.

With brand appeal conveyed through the very practicality, convenience, value—and ingenuity—of these new product offerings, companies swayed consumers of the necessity of such purchases. The brand was built through outreach to consumers and by investing in new techniques of marketing and advertising, helped along by advertising agencies that helped to forge brand identities. The innovations of the era are still resonating today—and, in some cases, the brand pitch is not all that different from what it was a hundred years ago.

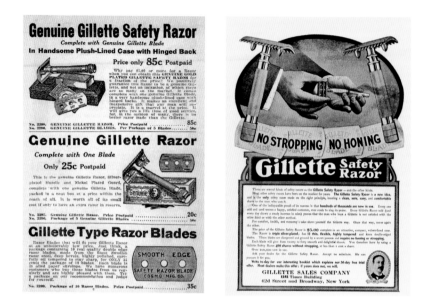

In the early 1900s, Gillette introduced a razor that men could use to shave at home—a significant switch in an era when they usually went to barbers.

3M Scotch Brand
Cellophane Tape

Reg. U. S. Pat. Off.

SCOTCH

BRAND

Cellophane Tape

NO. 600

2 Rolls - ½ x 2592 Inches

TRANSPARENT

7212T
7212T

KRAFT CHEESE

Adding Convenience to Quality

Our first thought in making Kraft Cheese is to make it good. Our second is to make it a convenience. We know that many prefer to buy Kraft Cheese in the original package, so to meet that preference we also pack Kraft Cheese in half pound and pound cartons, thus giving you the quality you like in the way you like to buy it. Your dealer will be glad to serve you the carton if you ask for it.

KRAFT CHEESE COMPANY
NEW YORK–CHICAGO–POCATELLO, IDAHO
KRAFT-MAC LAREN CHEESE CO., LIMITED
MONTREAL, CANADA
Made and Known in Canada as Kraft Canadian Cheese

Pasteurized

KRAFT CHEESE AMERICAN

KRAFT K CHEESE

To the man who wanted to marry Betty Crocker

Dear Sir:

Your letter with its charming proposal was very flattering, very nice . . . especially the part about applestrudel.

But we are afraid Betty Crocker cannot marry you.

For one thing (we must confess) yours is not the only proposal in the Betty Crocker files. Actually ten have been received, including one delightful one from South America.

But more important, the Betty Crocker home service staff is very busy right now helping test many new General Mills prod-

ucts. Some are foods, of course, but others are so different from the things we're making today you'll hardly believe it when they come out under the name General Mills.

And when you remember that the Betty Crocker staff already has a full-time job helping millions of American homemakers learn the secrets of fluffy fine-textured cakes, crisp flaky piecrust and golden-brown biscuits . . . well, you can see why Betty Crocker just *can't* marry anyone.

We hope you will understand.

Sympathetically yours,
General Mills

Band-Aid

We take many things in life for granted, and brands are no exception. We assume that they've always been the way they are in our present. Yet even classic brands have gone through evolutions over time.

In 1920, Johnson & Johnson introduced Band-Aid. Earle Dickson, an employee of J&J, created the bandages to help his wife, who continually cut and burned herself during household chores. The available remedy at the time—a piece of gauze that would be wrapped with a separate piece of adhesive—wouldn't remain on her boo-boos, so Dickson created an integrated bandage that would stick. After he told his boss about the invention, the bandage made its way into the Johnson & Johnson product family.

Since the introduction of the Band-Aid, the company has built the brand through a variety of strategies—innovative packaging, advanced technologies, and, more

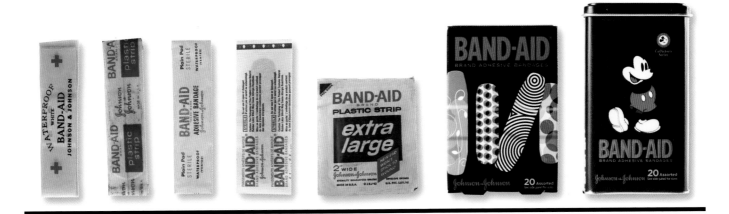

recently, collaborations with designers. The tin can—the timeless packaging reintroduced recently as a limited-edition release—became an integral part of the brand, and so did the red string, used to open the bandage wrapping, that made its first appearance in 1924. Band-Aid continued to innovate through the years by exploring new types of adhesives as well as integrating antibiotic ointment into the adhesive.

Creativity also became a part of the brand. Band-Aid introduced decorative bandages in the 1950s and instigated collaborations with artists. Most recently, in 2010, the brand teamed up with Disney to create bandages for adults featuring Mickey Mouse. Similarly, the company established a collaboration with renowned fashion designer Cynthia Rowley to position the bandages as fashionable accessories—an effort that generated donations to Design Ignites Change, a program that offers mentoring in design and architecture to high school and college students. The company's collaborations have been meaningful and sometimes, amusing,

elements of the evolving brand identity that nevertheless remains authentic to its original brand purpose.

Today, the company is emphasizing its brand values through innovative thinking and a commitment to sustainability. By creating Band-Aid packaging from responsibly managed forests in Brazil, the company is seeking to fulfill one aspect of the Johnson & Johnson credo: "We must maintain in good order the property we are privileged to use, protecting the environment and natural resources."

In a variety of ways, the company has reinforced the brand's heritage while still innovating in new directions. All throughout, Band-Aid has kept us engaged and built a loyal following—a companion through every scrape, graze, bruise, and blemish.

Band-Aid packaging through the years

The progression of the
Band-Aid box

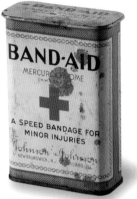
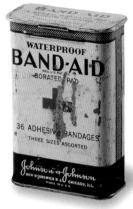

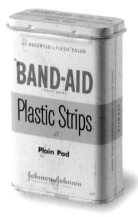

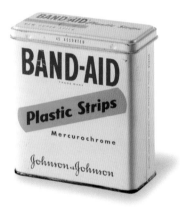

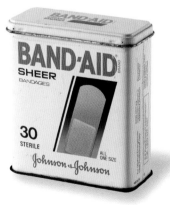
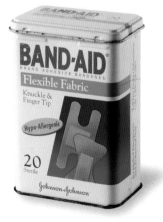

06

BREAKING THE MOLD: COCO CHANEL, KRUEGER BEER, AND LACOSTE

REBECCA ETTER *and* **MAXINE GUREVICH**

The early twentieth century was a time of great societal transformation, instigated and marked by the arrival of new products, technologies, and forms of visual communication. The emergence of continuous-process manufacturing, combined with the invention of offset printing, made the creation and marketing of mass-produced goods possible, and allowed manufacturers to use packaging and graphics to speak directly to consumers, who began asking for specific brands. In this way, the package itself became the hallmark of a product's quality and the point of differentiation. Then, as now, it was common for the various product offerings in a single category—beauty products, beverages, or food—to conform to a specific look. Traditionally, these product norms were defined by the company that was the leader or the first brand in a category. But in the early 1900s, a number of brands broke away from the "standard rule," establishing a new design aesthetic and altering consumer expectations. Three notable examples of such successful branding mavericks from this era are Chanel No. 5, Krueger Beer, and Lacoste.

Vintage Chanel No. 5 bottle

N° 5
CHANEL

PERFUME FROM 7.50

EAU
DE
COLOGNE
N° 5
CHANEL

EAU DE COLOGNE FROM 3.50

CHANEL

BATH POWDER 5.00

SPRAY COLOGNE WITH REFILL 8.50

every
woman
alive
wants
Chanel N° 5

N°5
CHANEL

CHANEL

PRESENTATION DE LUXE 17.50

SPRAY COLOGNE AND PERFUME SET 10.00

The perfume is surprisingly simple, yet deep at the same time, and that powerful simplicity carried over to the perfume's sleek package design.

Chanel Reinvents Scent

At the turn of the twentieth century, women's perfume had its own aesthetic of conformity: Bottles were highly decorative, often featuring embellished designs in an art nouveau style. The contents of these elaborate receptacles were also extravagant: Women's perfumes were lush and floral, based on essences of rose, lily of the valley, and lilac. The French fashion designer Coco Chanel, already famous by the early 1920s for her millinery and clothing design, thought these floral perfumes did not reflect women's true character. As she once said, "Women are not flowers. Why should they want to smell like flowers?"

With that as her guiding principle, Chanel sought to create a perfume manufactured specifically for women and made from synthetic ingredients. After enlisting the longtime perfumer Ernest Beaux to craft the scent, she achieved her goal with Chanel No. 5, one of the first aldehyde-based scents. The perfume is surprisingly simple, yet deep at the same time, and that powerful simplicity carried over to the perfume's sleek package design. Chanel No. 5's understated bottle, with its clean lines and pared-down label, embodied the sentiment often attributed to Chanel; that "elegance is refusal."

When it launched in 1921, Chanel No. 5 was sold exclusively in the Chanel store in Paris. Even without an initial marketing campaign or public relations efforts, the fragrance quickly became a brand synonymous with style and luxury. Its popularity was mainly driven by word of mouth, thanks to the connections Chanel had cultivated through her social milieu. This new style of marketing, or lack thereof, turned her social network into passionate brand advocates. And due to its prestige, women began to actively seek out the perfume and thus to dictate growth in the market. Just as Chanel's perfume redefined the fragrance category, it also redefined women's power as consumers.

Images from
Chanel No. 5
advertisement, 1961

Krueger Brewing Company and the "K-Man"

At midnight on April 7, 1933, a line formed outside a small, privately run brewery in Newark, New Jersey. After fourteen years of Prohibition, the government had declared that sales of beer and wine were no longer illegal. To celebrate, consumers gathered outside the G. Krueger Brewery, which had garnered a strong following. Beer drinkers had developed their enthusiasm for Krueger's during the dry years. Originally established in the late-nineteenth century, Krueger's managed to hold on to its Newark brewery throughout Prohibition by producing "near beer," a beverage that had the minimum allowable alcoholic content. This meant that when Prohibition was lifted, the company had a strong base of consumer loyalty as well as knowledge of the market as it existed at the time. Because of this, Krueger's was willing to take a risk and make a crucial jump into a new category: beer in a can.

In the beginning of the twentieth century, the increased mobility of Americans—traveling from place to place in cars and trains—gave rise to a greater desire for the convenience that would come from products that could be easily carried. Krueger's realized that beer in a can would satisfy that yen for convenience, while generating new profits for the company.

Even up to the 1920s, beer had been packaged primarily in bottles. Tin cans offered the advantages of being more lightweight, less likely to break during transit, and easier to cool in ice boxes. In 1927, the American Can Company had developed a patent for a beer can prototype that would replace bottles and was appropriate for holding beer: The can had to be specially lined in order to prevent the beer from spoiling because of contact with the metal, and the can had to be particularly strong, as it had to withstand pasteurization and the pressure of carbonation. The prototype was a success. While brewers around the country requested the can prototype during Prohibition, and were eager to experiment with the new packaging, no one wanted to be the first to introduce it into the market. It was not uncommon for consumers to be averse to new forms of packaging—whether tin cans or anything else; in particular, consumers didn't trust canned goods because they couldn't see what was inside the package. But this didn't deter Krueger's. The company enlisted American Can Company to create 2,000 cans of Krueger's Special Beer, a particular brew offered by the company, and the brewery sent 500 families four cans each, along with a mail-in questionnaire about the new container. The test run was a massive success, with 91 percent of the group approving the can. Since the new packaging had been embraced with such enthusiasm, Krueger's decided to extend the trial period. In September 1933, just two months before the amendment repealing Prohibition was ratified, the American Can Company installed the canning equipment for free. The arrangement was that Krueger's would pay for the machinery only if the venture was a success. The brewery conducted its second trial run in Richmond, Virginia, and soon enough, distributors and consumers were clamoring for Krueger's in a can. The company's market share grew significantly as a result. In 1935, other breweries such as Ansells Brewery, Pabst, and Northampton Brewing Company followed suit and started selling beer in cans. With the can, Krueger's had established itself as an innovative brand that was in tune with the needs of the common

ABOVE:
Krueger outdoor advertising

RIGHT:
Vintage Krueger Beer coaster

KRUEGER

Beer ☆ Ale

Since 1858

G. KRUEGER BREWING CO., NEWARK, N. J.

REG. U.S. PAT. OFF.

man. As other breweries started to invade the category and to chip away at the company's market share, Krueger's made some strategic adjustments of its own: It dropped the "'s" to become "Krueger Beer" and also sought to differentiate itself through graphic design. Integral to that was the company's logo, affectionately dubbed the "K-Man"—a silhouetted waiter in the shape of the letter K that had debuted on the trial run of the beer can. The illustration of the figure showed him carrying a tray that held a drinking glass and a bottle or can of Kreuger beer. The in-motion K-Man signaled an "at-your-service" attitude while simultaneously mirroring the emerging trend of mobility. The icon was a significant point of differentiation for the brand: Other brewers at the time were not known to use a character in their logo design, which set Krueger apart from competitors. While the K-Man's design brings a human aspect to a simple letterform, its geometric shape is key to its meaning: The most evocative aspect of the simplistic character design is that it leaves room for interpretation; its ambiguity allows consumers to project their own narrative onto it. By marrying this open-ended meaning with the underlying message of the company's values, Krueger created an iconic brand—one that was able to satisfy consumers' desire for products that could fit their newly "mobile" lifestyles. The brand mascot had longevity; throughout the span of the brewery's history, the design aesthetic remained consistent, with the K-Man appearing on several different beverage labels and in the company's advertising in the 1950s.

Krueger Revival

In its first incarnation, Kreuger's Brewing Company lasted from 1858 to 1961. Almost fifty years later, the brand is in the midst of a relaunch. Maxine Gurevich and Rebecca Etter spoke with a representative of the Krueger family about the prospects and strategies of reviving an historic brand.

Why have you decided to relaunch Krueger's now?

Heritage, mainly. The Krueger brand should be known for what it has always been known for throughout history: innovating beer. And of course, what better time than now to launch a family brewery, when beer is being equated with fine wine?

What design assets are you keeping? Will we be seeing a modern take on the "K-Man"?

The K-Man is a registered trademark of the Krueger Brewing Company. Though he is not the only concept, he is certainly the flagship icon of Krueger Brewing. Since the company is trying to maintain a retro feel, we will not be making many overt changes to the K-Man. However, since technology has moved forward, the K-Man will be seen in more modern contexts. Two of those platforms are, of course, Twitter and Facebook, which will help us bring him back to life.

Original Krueger
"beer-in-a-can"
announcement, 1936

Can you discuss the history of the K-Man?

K-Man was designed as a new concept for a trial run of the beer can, an eye-catching symbol that would bring more recognition to the brand he represents. He started out with a very simple, almost Pac-Man styled head, and though his body has not changed much, his face is now more elaborate than the original "baldie" character. The beer can itself changed almost every year since its inception, making a detailed history of it quite mundane if not impossible. People send us photographs of gimmicks used for promotions and nostalgic advertisements all of the time, and there are gimmicks that the company tried that confound even us. Some were used only one time and in one specific place.

Are there any stories or myths centered on this design? Do you know who created it?

A lot of history has been lost to time. The first beer cans were made in 1935, so most of the original plant workers—the ones who could share the authentic stories about the time—are no longer with us.

How has the market changed since Krueger Brewing Company last sold beer in the 1960s?

The market has changed immensely because people now have different tastes for beer than they did in the '60s. Micro-brews and "nanobrews" are becoming more the norm, and the companies that produce these products are not necessarily competing against the giant corporations, as they used to. People want choices, and they're also tired of the same old beer that tastes like water. This has given birth to the "craft brew," which is now very popular—that's the direction that we plan to take the company.

What pressures, if any, does today's Krueger Brewing Company feel in relaunching an iconic brand?

Ninety-eight percent of all localities that we pitch to have never seen or heard of our product; so for the most part, we're starting from scratch.

What do you envision for the brand in the next ten years?

Our intention is the keep the brand fairly small. Most businesses are not satisfied to just do that. They tend to outgrow themselves too quickly and then go bankrupt because they're not rooted in reality. In the next ten years, the brand should be recognizable by most people and hopefully, as time allows, we would like to do a lot of philanthropic work. Our main goal is to help people as much as possible, and in the process, they'll also get to enjoy our beer and ales.

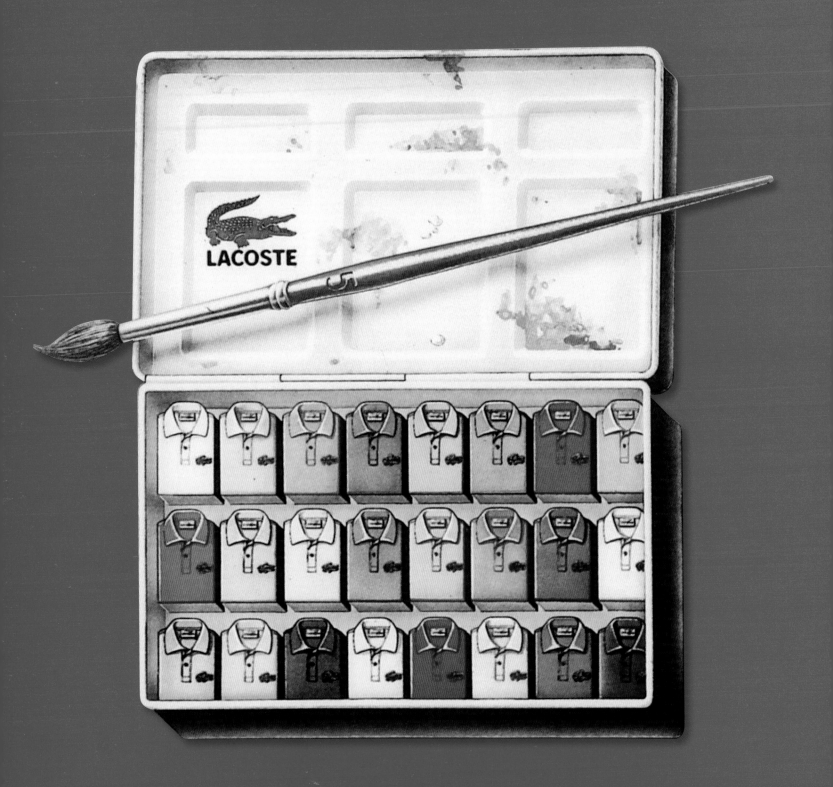

Lacoste and the Crocodile

Krueger, with its K-Man icon and innovative can packaging, wasn't the only early-twentieth-century brand whose appeal was rooted in design. Another design-driven brand from this era, also associated with an iconic symbol, was the sportswear company Lacoste, which launched in 1933 as a forum for the fashion sensibility of French tennis sensation René Lacoste. Lacoste, who was the brand's de facto ambassador even before the business started, coowned the clothier with André Gillier, the owner and president of the largest French knitwear manufacturing business. The company's iconic crocodile symbol has its origins in René Lacoste's personal history and character. Lacoste, himself, was known to affectionately recount how the "alligator" nickname—given to him by American reporters following a bet that involved an alligator skin suitcase—became his brand's icon (the main figures of these stories evidence some confusion about the difference between alligators and crocodiles). As Lacoste reminisced, the creature "conveyed the tenacity I displayed on the tennis courts, never letting go of my prey." In that spirit, Lacoste enlisted a fashion design friend to create a crocodile and embroider it onto the blazer he wore before matches. After Lacoste won a tournament at Wimbledon in 1925, an English journalist wrote an article titled "Fashion from France," focusing on the unique style of René Lacoste on the court and describing how his clothing and accessories embodied both elegance and functionality. This was to be the brand DNA for the fashion company that Lacoste launched. The tennis star had helped to innovate new designs for tennis clothing, and this creativity was matched by his grace and tenacity on the court. Lacoste exemplified the elegant style of the 1920s, and gave rich meaning to his company's alligator symbol. Unlike Kreuger's simply formed *K Design*, Lacoste's emblematic crocodile logo derived from a true story, one rich with values and history—one intrinsically connected with the man who gave the brand its name. And behind the man himself is myth—the myth of Lacoste's individuality and vitality; the legend of his affable character, of his agility and triumphs on the courts, and his sartorial acumen not only in creating new designs for sports but in placing a logo on the clothes—all these give the brand its resonance. It didn't take long for the Lacoste brand to gain popularity.

Lacoste exemplified the elegant style of the 1920s and gave rich meaning to the company's crocodile symbol.

Shortly after World War II, the Lacoste crocodile was appearing not only on men's shirts, but also on women's and children's clothing, leather goods, fragrances, and even footwear. It is important to note that Lacoste was not the first clothing brand to put a logo on an article of clothing—during the 1920s, the Jantzen company had done just that with its "red diving girl" icon, and she had subsequently become an object of cultural fascination. But Lacoste had gone on to become a much more widely adopted cultural icon; its widespread popularity marked the onset of the logo craze of the twentieth century.

07
THE GREATEST GENERATION OF BRANDS

SASCHA DONN
and **TIMOTHY HARMS**

During the holiday season of 1947, hundreds of households across America received the same special delivery: the Sears Christmas catalog. Weighing in at 300 pages, it offered everything from argyle socks to fishing tackle to radios. In subsequent years, the catalog's page count would only grow, reaching 436 pages by 1958.[1] The magnitude of the catalog is evidence of a society that had started to purchase out of want rather than need. Manufacturers and advertisers had attained a newfound proficiency in imbuing objects with values and attributes that gave them relevance emotionally and psychologically, but had little to do with the objects' functional characteristics. This skill—an essential aspect of branding—helped lead post–World War II society to levels of consumption previously unimaginable.

Branding the American Dream

With the end of World War II and the reestablishment of peacetime industry, the United States began a transformation into one of the world's largest economies, primarily driven by the collective purchasing power of the burgeoning middle class. The passage of the G.I. Bill in 1944 made higher education and home ownership attainable for millions of servicemen as they returned home to take on new jobs and start families. They purchased split-level homes, ranches, and Cape Cods in rapidly expanding suburbs like Naperville, Illinois, and Levittown, New York, equipping their residences with all the accoutrements of a newly affluent society: KitchenAid appliances, RCA televisions, and Corning cookware.

As consumers eagerly indulged in the enjoyments previously impossible during wartime austerity, they also began forging a new national identity— one that linked consumption with freedom and contrasted American society with life behind the Iron Curtain. In the book *A Consumer's Republic*, historian Lizabeth Cohen suggests that home ownership, automobiles, and mass consumption enabled Americans to effectively "beat the Soviets at their own game of creating a classless society"; this rendition of the American dream challenged the assertion that "capitalism created extremes of wealth and poverty."[2]

A Philip Morris advertisement from 1953 featured the actress Lucille Ball

Cold War contrasts turned into political demagoguery at the highly publicized "Kitchen Debate" of 1959, when then Vice President Richard Nixon and Soviet Premier Nikita Khrushchev sparred over the superiority of their respective countries' domestic technologies. As throngs of reporters followed the leaders through the American National Exhibition in Moscow, Nixon eagerly showed a cutaway model of a typical American suburban home, complete with the latest modern conveniences and stocked with popular consumer brands. The suburban home, Nixon boasted, would be affordable for the average U.S. worker and come complete with modern appliances that would "make easier the life of our housewives."[3]

Branding for Women

While gender norms of the postwar decade reaffirmed the male role as that of the breadwinner, women were still often in charge of household finances—a fact not lost on advertisers. As consumers spent more money on time-saving appliances for the home, products were positioned as making *her* life easier, more productive, and stylish. KitchenAid courted housewives by introducing a series of stand mixers in hues that promotional materials described as "petal pink" and "sunny yellow"; to further convince homemakers, the company dispatched an all-female sales force door to door to demonstrate the machines.[4] Like many brands at the time, KitchenAid's design and advertising centered on the flexibility that the product gave homemakers to enjoy life away from the drudgery of housework. The strategy epitomized the effort to reach particular audiences with the message that products could allow them to live a more complete, fully modern life.

As modern appliances shaped domestic life, new convenience foods also changed the way meals were prepared. Minute Rice delivered fluffy rice that didn't need to be washed, rinsed, or steamed. Maxwell House gave a "cup-and-a-half of flavor" in every cup of freeze-dried instant coffee. Betty Crocker guaranteed that its cake mix varieties would produce "perfect cake, every time you bake."

While some of these brand offerings readily appealed to the new breed of consumer, not all of the innovations were immediately embraced. Food production technology made it possible to create "just-add-water" cake mixes, but homemakers were skeptical of a product that significantly diminished their role in preparing and providing food for their families. Time spent in the kitchen, it seemed, had an emotional value relating to the way that housewives saw themselves as nurturers and caretakers. To help assuage such concerns, Betty Crocker ultimately added back in the step of cracking open an egg and adding it to the mix, so at-home bakers would feel as though they were playing a meaningful part in the preparations. Similarly, recipes began appearing that showed women how to be creative with convenience foods; when preparing cakes, for instance, they were advised to add their own touches like cherries, crushed pineapple, and shredded coconut on top of the completed creation.[5]

Throughout the late 1940s and into the 1950s, companies realized more and more that a product's basic qualities and attributes weren't enough to differentiate or position their offerings. In an increasingly crowded marketplace, where standardized manufacturing ensured the same consistency throughout the different brands in a product

Maxwell House
advertisement, 1933

To a Lady

[SOMEWHAT SKEPTICAL]

.. A Word About Coffee

You are asked to believe so many things, dear lady . . . Especially about coffee!

We know that you, of course, want coffee that is *fresh*. So, about our Maxwell House Coffee, we ask you to accept only this:

Any can of Maxwell House Coffee you buy is sure to be perfectly fresh—just as deliciously fresh as the very hour it was roasted . . . (about other coffees we have nothing to say).

We wish only to add: It is, therefore, quite impossible for any coffee to be fresher than Maxwell House.

It is air, you see, that causes coffee staleness. It is air, the very air you breathe, that robs coffee of its freshness . . . and turns delicate flavor oils rancid.

So in packing our Maxwell House Coffee we use a special method called the Vita-Fresh process (a process, incidentally, which we control). It eliminates air from inside the can . . . protects each pound of coffee against its flavor-destroying effects.

Thus our Vita-Fresh way of packing assures you roaster-fresh coffee—always. And certainly no coffee can be fresher than that!

We think you will enjoy this fine coffee that pleased the epicures of the Old South years a[...] It is exactly the same superb blend today . . [...] blend the years have never matched for r[...] mellow, full-bodied flavor.

Your grocer has it for you—*fresh* as the ho[...] was roasted. Why don't you try a can—today[...] is a product of General Foods.

And by the way—do you own a radio? If you[...] tune it in next Thursday evening on Captain Her[...] Maxwell House Show Boat. One full hou[...] music and fun with real Show Boat atmosph[...]

A-B-C's OF COFFEE FRESHNES[...]

[A] AIR is the destroyer[...] coffee freshness and flav[...]

[B] Unless coffee is p[...] tected against AIR[...] becomes stale — quick[...]

[C] Maxwell House Co[...] is *completely* protect[...] against AIR . . . you ge[...] perfectly fresh — alwa[...]

© G. F. Corp., 1933

MAXWELL HOUS[E]

GOOD TO THE LAST DROP

Trust
Swanson

Their Swiss steak is the kind you can cut with a fork

There's no comparison . . . and no mistaking a Swanson TV Brand Swiss Steak Dinner! The lean, juicy beef is so tender and flavorful. Served up with rich brown gravy, green beans, and buttered whipped potatoes. For good frozen dinners, trust Swanson!

ELEVEN DELICIOUS SWANSON TV BRAND DINNERS

Made only by *Campbell* Soup Company   "TV" and "TV Dinner" are registered trademarks

category, promoting tangible benefits like quality, convenience, or novelty failed to generate a significant advantage in sales. Rather, the emotional motivations behind consumers' purchases were a key driver of sales. With this in mind, companies began observing the psychological needs of their customers so they could create products that would resonate with their values and aspirations. Fictional characters like Betty Crocker, Charmin's Mr. Whipple, and Palmolive's Madge the manicurist, although fictional, represented friendly personas that consumers could relate to and trust.[6]

Television Changed Everything

The rise of both convenience foods and television in postwar society is perhaps best encapsulated in the iconic Swanson TV Dinner. While not the first to market such a concept, Swanson Company was arguably the most successful at promoting an all-in-one frozen meal—Salisbury steak, meatloaf, or fried chicken presented along with three or more side dishes in a neatly divided tray. Swanson established a connection between dinner time and leisure time, and became a hit with consumers who had recently become television owners. For better or worse, the idea that meals could bypass the dining room and be enjoyed while watching *The Ed Sullivan Show* changed the entire ritual of dinner and further established a captive audience for mass-media advertising.[7]

By 1959, television sets had arrived in more than 1 million homes across the United States.[8] The increasing amount of free time Americans spent watching just three or four major networks meant advertisers could gain access to a growing captive audience. They quickly seized on the potential of the medium, a shift reflected in advertising expenditures, which skyrocketed to $11 billion by the end of the decade.[21] As television programming mirrored and became an extension of consumers' lives, it provided a visually seductive way of showing how brands fit within the everyday lifestyle. Advertisers like Philip Morris negotiated pricey contracts to sponsor popular shows like *I Love Lucy*—generating exposure and awareness of their brands and products—and started using strategies like market segmentation, which divided the market into specific demographic groups. This allowed companies to target specific consumers who would be most interested in certain offerings; and it allowed companies to hone their advertising, so it would be most effective for those groups.[9] Adhering to a market segmentation strategy, Procter & Gamble promoted its cleaning products during daytime soap operas, targeting the women who were arguably the biggest users of their brands.[10] Branded programming such as *Texaco Star Theater, Camel News Caravan, The Colgate Comedy Hour,* and *Kraft Television Theatre* catered to children and adults alike.[11]

OPPOSITE:
Swanson advertisement, 1961, pitching its TV dinners as a ready-to-eat accompaniment for nightly tube viewing

BELOW:
Vintage patch with Zenith trademark

While the 1950s saw the establishment of a consumer society in which mass-produced goods were marketed to an audience eager to spend, this unprecedented appetite for new goods, advertisers feared, would eventually become sated. To prevent this from happening, manufacturers began encouraging product obsolescence by continually redesigning goods and introducing upgraded models.[12] Zenith, one of the most popular television brands of the '50s, is one of many companies that followed a strategy of planned obsolescence. Because most consumers already owned televisions, Zenith needed a marketing approach to highlight the unique benefits of new models so consumers would feel compelled to replace the sets they already owned.

The manufacturer began the decade by positioning itself as offering the highest-quality television on the market, but within four years, its message shifted to focus on the advantages of the latest models. By 1954, Zenith began advertising its Model X using the line "Zenith for '55 brings you the revolutionary new Model X with Top Tuning,"[13] and in 1955, the pitch was only slightly different: "You have to see it to believe it! Flash-matic Tuning by Zenith. Only Zenith has it!"[14] A year later, the company introduced the "space-command" remote, and although the brand had brought out its first remote in 1951, the company claimed the new version was "the one and only thing NEW in television!"[15] By 1959, the slogan was "Who Else But Zenith."[16] The company's tactics were emblematic of other businesses in different industries, which sought to convince consumers why they needed the most current model of each product.

A Nation in Transit

Two postwar developments did more to change the way the Americans lived, worked, and traveled in the latter half of the century than any other: the rise of automobile ownership and the construction of the interstate highway system. Since new homeowners had purchased residences that were located far away from public transit and urban centers, owning a car was a necessity, often for both heads of the household. Automobile sales skyrocketed in the postwar decade to more than 50 million by the end of the 1950s, with almost 75 percent of Americans owning at least one car. Automobile manufacturers relied on marketing tools like market segmentation and planned obsolescence to further increase sales.

Inspired by the German autobahn network, President Eisenhower expanded the Federal-Aid Highway Act of 1954 to an unprecedented budget of $25 billion to build what would eventually become the largest continuous construction project in U.S. history. The establishment of the interstate highway system helped to open up vast swaths of the country that previously had poorly maintained infrastructures. It also provided an increasingly mobile society a chance to visit monuments and parks, and helped spark a renewed interest in national travel.

As Americans increasingly relied on their cars to travel greater distances between work, home, and shopping, new malls and restaurants sprouted up around suburban centers. Drive-in movie theaters, drive-up teller windows, and quick-serve restaurants catered to the culture of the car. After salesman Ray Kroc visited a McDonald's hamburger stand in San Bernardino, California, in 1954,

A vintage glass milk mug for McDonald's featured their mascot Speedee and only a single golden arch.

By 1958, McDonald's had sold its 100 millionth hamburger and could proudly claim that each one had the same quality and taste, no matter the location.

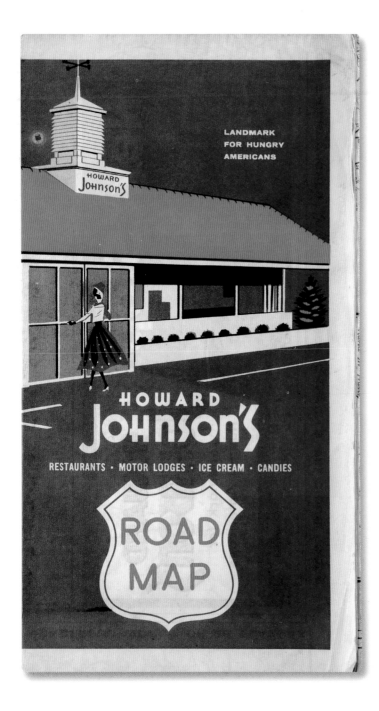

 LANDMARK FOR HUNGRY AMERICANS

HOWARD JOHNSON'S
RESTAURANTS · MOTOR LODGES · ICE CREAM · CANDIES

ROAD MAP

he took on the job of modifying and expanding McDonald's into a franchise that would become the template for the modern fast-food enterprise. Kroc realized if his restaurants offered a limited menu, they could focus on quality and uniformity across all locations. With this approach, he identified something most iconic brands still strive to deliver: a consistent experience.

By 1958, McDonald's had sold its 100 millionth hamburger and could proudly claim that each one had the same quality and taste, no matter the location.[17] Consumers could now go to a McDonald's anywhere around the country and know what to expect. Almost every decision Kroc made for McDonald's was influenced by the motoring culture of the decade. And car culture shaped the architecture of consumerism as well: As Americans spent more of their time in cars, franchises would have to do more to attract the attention of a culture traveling at 60 miles (96 km) an hour. Signs became bigger, taller, and more outlandish, incorporating rotating marquees and flashing neon elements. For McDonald's, the familiar golden arches became a (visible) symbol of consistency and reliability for those on the move.[18]

Another iconic roadside symbol of the '50s was the green, yellow, and red marquee for the rapidly expanding chain of Holiday Inn hotels and motor lodges. Known as the "Great Sign" by the chain's founder, Kemmons Wilson, it featured more than 500 flashing bulbs and a large neon boomerang arrow topped with a pulsating star. Its massive stature and frequent appearance on America's highways transformed it into a classic American icon—an emblem of clean, family-friendly lodging.[18] This particular brand was built from the passion born of personal experience: Wilson became interested in launching a hotel chain after a frustrating sojourn at a no-name roadside motel during a family vacation. Named after a Bing Crosby movie, his Holiday Inn franchises offered services now standard in the industry, such as air-conditioning, in-room telephones, and free ice. By the end of the decade, more than 200 Holiday Inns had been established, and other chains like Best Western, Howard Johnson's, and Ramada followed suit.[20]

The invention of both restaurant and hotel chains helped to give rise to the sensibility of branding, as travelers sought out the predictability and consistency of the branded experience—one that would be accommodating and comforting for families traveling in unfamiliar territory.

From the development of the suburbs to the widespread acceptance of the television and establishment of motor culture, the '50s saw marketers realize the importance of consumer insights, the benefits of market segmentation, and the necessity of meeting the actual and perceived needs of society. These realizations gave marketers the knowledge and skills to establish some of the most iconic brands of the century. With this new understanding and proficiency, companies sought to imbue products with meaning that would be culturally and psychologically relevant to the consumers of the time. Brands would now be defined by more than their functionality; it became essential for them to integrate layers of meaning that appealed to both minds and hearts of consumers.

Promotional materials from the past and the present for hotel chains Howard Johnson's and Holiday Inn, brands that sought to corner the hospitality market beginning in the 1950s

08

THE EVOLUTION OF REVOLUTION

CURTIS WINGATE
and **ABBY MCINERNEY**

In the 1960s and '70s, the civil rights movement, the sexual revolution, and an evolving youth culture transfigured the cultural landscape of the previous decades. These societal shifts provided a catalyst for political and social change; they also informed the evolution of brands. The new era brought with it an emphasis on authenticity and justice—and skepticism of government and big business. To be successful, businesses had to create brands that stressed honesty, projected a personality more than product features, and connected in a meaningful way with the cultural movements of the day.

Branding for Body Image

By the mid-'60s, nearly 50 percent of the American population was under the age of twenty-five,[1] the result of the post–World War II baby boom. In light of this dramatic demographic shift, some older brands repositioned themselves for young consumers. Only a few years earlier, in the '50s, Pepsi-Cola had appealed to body image to sell its signature drink, assuring consumers that it "refreshes without filling." Fast-forward to 1961, and the tagline had shifted from one of image to one of demographic: "Now it's Pepsi—for those who think young." The company would continue that tack throughout the '60s; in 1963, it informed young consumers, "You're in the Pepsi generation."[2] These ads marked a pivotal moment for the soft-drink maker. The company no longer sought to speak to everyone; rather it targeted one definable segment of the market, creating a dialogue—and a brand identity—that set Pepsi apart from the competing beverages of the time.

Pepsi advertisement,
1964

come alive!
You're in the Pepsi generation!

who is the Pepsi generation? Every[
with a young view of things! Livel[
people with a liking for Pepsi Co[
Famous regular Pepsi–with the bo[
clean taste and energy to liven yo[
pace. Or new Diet Pepsi–with that sa[
honest-to-Pepsi taste and less than[
calorie a bottle. The Pepsi generatio[
It's a whole lot of people like yo[

IF DIET PEPSI IS NOT AVAILABLE IN YOUR AREA, IT WILL BE SO[

"PEPSI-COLA" AND "PEPSI" ARE TRADEMARKS OF PEPSI-C[
COMPANY, REG. U.S. PAT. OFF. © 1964, PEPSI-COLA COMP[

Classic "Think Small"
advertisement for
Volkswagen, created
by Doyle Dane
Bernbach, 1960

Think small.

18 New York University students have gotten into a sun-roof VW; a tight fit. The Volkswagen is sensibly sized for a family. Mother, father, and three growing kids suit it nicely.

In economy runs, the VW averages close to 50 miles per gallon. You won't do near that; after all, professional drivers have canny trade secrets. (Want to know some? Write VW,

Box #65, Englewood, N. J.) Use regular gas and forget about oil between changes.

The VW is 4 feet shorter than a conventional car (yet has as much leg room up front). While other cars are doomed to roam the crowded streets, you park in tiny places.

VW spare parts are inexpensive. A new front fender (at an *authorized* VW dealer) is

$21.75.* A cylinder head, $19.95.* The nice thing is, they're seldom needed.

A new Volkswagen sedan is $1,565.* Other than a radio and side view mirror, that includes everything you'll really need.

 In 1959 about 120,000 Americans thought small and bought VWs. Think about it.

Defining "The Lemon"

In the early '60s, the advertising agency Doyle Dane Bernbach (DDB) was beginning to get a good deal of buzz for the firm's clever copy and uniquely positioned advertisements. Avis's "We Try Harder" campaign and a series for Levy's rye bread that featured the classic tagline, "You don't have to be Jewish," were just two examples of the agency's unorthodox yet highly effective work. One of the agency's partners, Bill Bernbach, was on a mission to elevate the advertising industry and establish the importance of the creative contribution to advertising. Bernbach created a structure in which art directors and copywriters worked in pairs—something that hadn't been done before—and his work helped shape the so-called "creative revolution" in advertising.[3] The agency's innovative work redefined the possibilities and techniques of the field, and DDB was instrumental in the success of many companies. But the agency's most groundbreaking campaign was for Volkswagen.

Business had been good for Volkswagen in the '50s, but in 1959, the president of Volkswagen of America, Carl Hahn, decided to turn to DDB for a preemptive strike against the encroachment of American compact cars.[4] At the time that Volkswagen hired DDB, the Beetle had its fans, but it also had some negative characteristics to address. Its homely design had none of the dash and grandeur of Detroit's streamlined vehicles. And its origins as a product of Nazi Germany were hardly in its favor. But the car had the appeal of practicality—for those marketing it as much as those buying it.

Helmut Krone, the DDB art director who worked on the Volkswagen account, was one of the earliest adopters of the Beetle, long before the agency landed Volkswagen as a client.[5] Arthur Railton, the editor of *Popular Mechanics* who first described the Beetle as "an honest car," ended up working for Volkswagen as a public relations manager in 1960.[6] People who valued the car's "honesty" aligned themselves as Volkswagen devotees. Fellow Bug drivers would wave to each other as a show of camaraderie. Clearly, there was something special about the car, and it became Doyle Dane Bernbach's task to express it.

After winning the business, Bill Bernbach and his team took a three-week trip to Germany to soak up every detail of Volkswagen's operations. During the trip, they met a production inspector by the name of Kurt Kroner who deemed one of the Beetles not up to par due to an imperfection in the glove compartment.[11] This was the inspiration behind the now legendary ad headlined "Lemon" and showing a photo of the rejected Beetle seemingly in perfect condition. The black-and-white ads described the rigorous inspection given to all Volkswagen cars (whereby flawed vehicles were kept off the market), and ended with the line "We pluck the lemons; you get the plums." The playful pairing of the photograph with a single word was bold in both its concept and its minimal design. While most automobile ads at the time used color drawings, DDB's use of black-and-white photography combined with an unexpected, droll headline broke the mold of typical advertising.[7] The ads embraced the Beetle's quirky characteristics and the German engineering, designed for longevity, which was a counterpoint to the newly prevalent trend for planned obsolescence.

The other ads in DDB's Volkswagen campaign built the car's brand with the same strategy of charming wit and honesty. The "Think Small" ads touted the car's cost-saving features, such as excellent gas mileage and an air-cooled engine.[8] This modest, self-deprecating tone continued in the "Ugly" ads, which poked fun at the car's bug shape.

The Volkswagen campaign was incredibly successful. Sales of the Beetle went from 100,000 in the late '50s to 600,000 at the peak of the car's sales in 1970.[9] The ads' combination of candidness and creative eccentricity was a cultural hit. The Volkswagen buyer was eager for something different, both in car design and in advertising; she understood the ads' wit—she could appreciate the joke.

Branding Youth Culture

If Volkswagen, as a brand, implied humor and insight, Levi's, in the '60s, meant understanding the concept of cool. Emerging from the '50s, when denim was associated with delinquency and bad-boy, James Dean types,[10] Levi Strauss & Co. was in the position to generate the perfect storm of teenage desire. As Dick Pountain and David Robins observe in the book *Cool Rules: An Anatomy of Attitude,* "Cool is an oppositional attitude adopted by individuals or small groups to express defiance to authority... "[11] Defining who you *weren't* was a way to define who you *were,* and brands that opposed the buttoned-up status quo of the '50s were ripe for adoption by the youth of the '60s. Like Pepsi, Levi's spoke directly to young people by creating new fashion styles and featuring teenagers and college students in ads. Though denim conjured up the

Vintage label for Levi's jeans, circa 1960s

rebellious magnetism of icons like Marlon Brando and James Dean, Levi's also appealed to those who were drawn to a more wholesome identity. At the beginning of the decade, the company portrayed its consumers as clean-cut in its advertising; later, the sensibility would shift to include visual nods to the growing counterculture.

By the early '60s, Levi's had become a staple of youth culture, as demonstrated in the band the Majorettes' 1963 surf-style song, "White Levi's." Upbeat and optimistic, the song reflects the more innocent early years of the decade:[12] "He takes me to the soda shop wearin' white Levi's / At the record hop he's wearin' white Levi's..."[13] Later in the decade, Levi's ads transitioned to the aesthetics of the hippie culture. For a new line of "Sta-Prest" pants called Bravo, Levi's co-opted the psychedelic poster art of rock 'n' roll, pairing it with taglines like "The American Way of Pants" and "Star Spangled Sta-Prest Styles."[14] This shift continued with the 1967 radio commercial featuring a cover of "White Levi's" performed by Jefferson Airplane.[15] A self-conscious homage to Levi's own evolution, the band's distorted sound was worlds away from that of the Majorettes. As Lynn Downey, Levi Strauss & Co. historian, notes, this "shows the dramatic cultural change that happened between the assassination of JFK and the Summer of Love."[16] Levi's had been a mirror to the cultural movements of the '60s; through a strategy of creating a resonance with several cultural niches, it was able to be the couturier for a full gamut of personalities and social cliques. Edgy enough for those moving against the grain, wholesome enough for those too timid for a walk on the wild side, Levi's could befriend nearly anyone.

Rock 'n' Roll History Is Made

Some brands in the '60s adapted themselves to suit the rebellious youth culture, while others were created by young people themselves. The decade was a time of speaking out, of communicating passion for a particular message. *Rolling Stone* magazine, launched in 1967 by twenty-one-year-old Jann Wenner and cofounder Ralph Gleason, reported on the musical manifestation of the counterculture; the magazine covered the movement while representing it at the same time. The editors of the magazine, which was based initially in San Francisco, the epicenter of the hippie revolution, believed that rock 'n' roll was, as Wenner has written, "more than just music."[17] The magazine created a passionate, youthful community, and explored music and politics alike in lengthy,

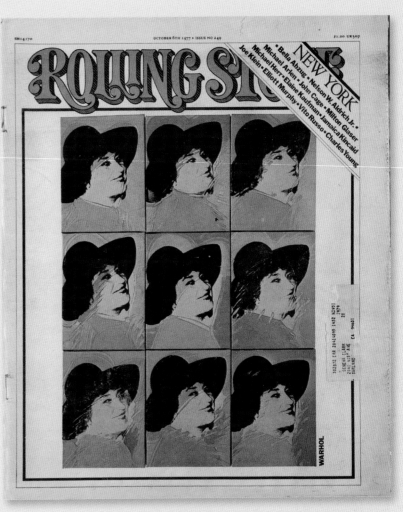

in-depth articles[18] by the likes of Hunter S. Thompson,[19] Ralph Gleason, and, later, Cameron Crowe.[20]

The brand was not only conveyed by the words of the magazine's writers, however. Just as the countercultural movement found expression in the proliferation of poster art and underground "comix," Wenner believed the cover was one of the most effectual means of expressing the magazine's identity—the cover would always

A cover of *Rolling Stone* in 1977 featured a painting by Andy Warhol

LEFT:
Vintage label for Levi's
jeans, circa 1960s

RIGHT:
Promotional 8-ounce
(235 ml) bar glass
for Levi's, featuring
vintage label design

The Evolution of Revolution

change yet would convey a sense of credibility and personality. Wenner had an eye for design and typography and, above all, photography. *Rolling Stone* became the first periodical to define rock imagery, fostering new and established talents such as photographers Annie Leibovitz and Richard Avedon, as well as designers including Roger Black and Milton Glaser. The covers carried controversial images such as a naked John Lennon and Yoko Ono (in 1968) and intricately eerie illustrations by Ralph Steadman for the famous "Fear and Loathing in Las Vegas" cover story, for the magazine's fourth-anniversary issue in 1971. Over time, the cover of *Rolling Stone* grew to signify more than just the magazine's identity—it became the big break that every band or musician coveted.

Celebrating Celebrity

In 1974, another magazine emerged, this one catering to the masses instead of the counterculture. *People* magazine redefined celebrity journalism and established itself as one of the highest-grossing magazines in history.[21] The magazine's brand conveyed a sensibility that was informal and safe. This was conveyed in part through purposeful typography. Instead of opting for a serif typeface, which was the predominant publication typeface at the time, the magazine's leadership chose a sans-serif typeface; with the ragged right margins, the magazine had a casual, friendly feel. Richard Stolley, who was *People's* first managing editor, has described the magazine as containing "stories about extraordinary people doing ordinary things and ordinary people doing extraordinary things."[22]

IN THIS ISSUE

William Peter Blatty
'The Exorcist':
"A sermon nobody
sleeps through"

Marina Oswald
Finally at peace
with herself

Gloria Vanderbilt
A fourth marriage
that really works

Solzhenitsyn
From his own writing:
A chilling account of
a good man's arrest

Stephen Burrows
Fashion king
of the sexy cling

The Loud Family
Broken up, but
closer than ever

Palm Beach Whirl
The parties, pets
and personalities

Vietnam MIA Wives
Demanding answers
that nobody has

Jim Croce
Million-dollar
music legacy

Richard Petty
Daredevil
at Daytona

The Hearsts
During the nightmare

People Puzzle

People weekly
March 4, 1974   35 Cents

Mia Farrow
In 'Gatsby,'
the year's next
big movie

The first issue of *People* debuted on March 4, 1974, and featured actress Mia Farrow.

May 19, 1975 ▪ 40¢

People

weekly

14227

A Lindbergh
son lives
with monkeys

David Burpee:
a man for
all seeds

**LIZ
TAYLOR**

In Russia with
her man and
comeback hopes

Jockey
Mary Bacon
thinks the Klan
is a winner

Quiet creator
of the two-fisted
Travis McGee

Replaced by Mia
Farrow for the debut
issue of *People* maga-
zine, Elizabeth Taylor
finally made the cover
on May 19, 1975.

The initial consumer response to the magazine
was similarly extraordinary, which made the
magazine more attractive to Hollywood execs and
advertisers, who were skeptical of the magazine's
unconventional approach. *People's* test issue was
released August 20, 1973, and featured Elizabeth
Taylor on the cover. Andrew Heiskell, chairman
of the parent publishing company Time Inc., sent
a copy to the writer and politician Clare Boothe
Luce. She brought it with her to the beauty salon,
and as she read it people started peeking over
her shoulder. It sparked a conversation between
the hairdresser and the manicurist that was so
intriguing that Clare wrote a letter to Andrew
quoting the dialogue and giving her two cents on
the viability of the brand: "It was a great success
with those two women. And my guess is that for
whatever this may be worth, it is bound to be the
best read magazine in any hairdressing salon in
America…. Furthermore, if the reader has time, it
will probably be read from cover to cover, because
reading it is like eating peanuts—you can't stop
once you begin."[23]

The magazine officially launched March 4, 1974,
with Mia Farrow on the cover, and by July of
that year, *People* had its first million-sale issue
with a somewhat risqué cover showing a shirt-
less Telly "Kojak" Savalas. This cover generated
hundreds of letters from readers, asking *People*
"when they would show the other half."[24] *Rolling
Stone* was creating personalities through journalism; *People* created journalism out of personalities. Both brands found resonance through
giving readers access, in their own unique ways,
to cultural superstars.

The Pan Am trademark,
from a 1970s uniform
patch

Branding the Skies

Just as *People* appealed to everyday readers with glimpses into the lifestyles of the rich and famous, Pan American World Airways (Pan Am) sought to create a world traveler out of the everyday citizen. Into the early '60s,[25] the jet-set lifestyle had primarily been the province of the well to do and glamorous, and Pan Am set its sights on making flight accessible to the masses through travel innovation. The airline created the first worldwide airline reservation management system, PANAMAC, which debuted in 1964.[26] With its hub in New York City, PANAMAC linked hundreds of agents across the world, allowing for lightning-speed flight reservations and a reassuring, easy experience for travelers.

The next step in making travel more widely accessible was to enlist a plane that could hold more passengers and fly longer distances while using less fuel. In 1966, Pan Am invested in twenty-five new Boeing 747s—a wide-bodied aircraft capable of doing just that.[27]

Even with these advancements, the coming decade posed challenges for Pan Am. The '70s began with a recession, and a 1973 oil embargo created fuel shortages and higher prices for airfares.[28] These two factors made consumers unwilling to spend on travel,[29] with the result that Pan Am saw a succession of annual losses until 1976.[30]

Throughout its history, the company's brand consistently stood for one thing: opening up the world to its customers, in style. PANAMAC made travel arrangements easier, but the real

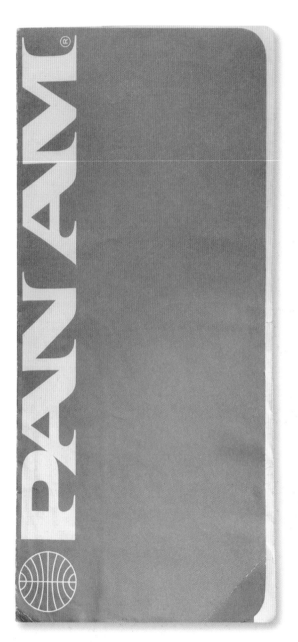

The Pan Am design sensibility was conveyed through the airline's printed materials.

magic occurred on board. Prior to the introduction of 747s, Pan Am planes represented the height of luxury. Travelers were welcomed into spacious interiors and were given gourmet multicourse meals from such esteemed restaurants as Maxim's of Paris. As travelers flew from departure to arrival, they were doted upon by young, beautiful flight attendants dressed in designer uniforms. The stewardesses—multilingual, educated, youthful, and slim—became one of the more glamorous attractions of flying Pan Am. Even as the company moved from expensive flights that only the wealthy could afford to flights for the masses, it maintained this aspect of the Pan Am experience.[31]

Heading into 1970s, Pan Am's communication materials lacked a modern tack. Ads often portrayed exotic locations and people, but graphic styles were inconsistent, with approaches ranging from photography and quirky illustrations to typographic treatments.[32] In 1970, Pan Am hired the creative studio Chermayeff & Geismar to reinvigorate the brand with a new identity program.[33] The epitome of sleek Swiss Modern style, Chermayeff & Geismar's Pan Am identity would, sadly, only be in use for two short years. By 1973, under new leadership who didn't see the value of the design revision, the company reverted to a slightly modified version of the original logo, and the new Helvetica-infused system would be relegated to the annals of design history.[34]

In the '60s and '70s, numerous brands were given an opportunity to ride the wave of cultural transformation and rebellion or to resist it. Regardless of the specific tactic, brands during these the two decades crafted new media platforms and new

ways of communicating with customers to convey compelling experiences beyond the product. The droll wit and restrained design of DDB's Volkswagen advertising provides a counterpoint to the lively palette of *Rolling Stone* or the brand mission of *People*. Yet, each of these innovators tapped into a cultural vein; and the businesses set precedents that would shape American culture and the legacy of branding.

First to fly the 747

PAN AM® makes the going great.

Printed in U.S.A.   C-173   3/70

ABOVE:
Print material for Pan Am touted the airline's use of Boeing 747 planes.

RIGHT:
Pan Am advertisement, 1961

You can still save $136 on your round trip to Europe by Pan Am Jet...but hurry!

Time is running out on the greatest travel bargain in history. Complete your trip before March 31st and you can see Europe for the cost of some "close-to-home" tours! Choose any European city, or *many*. Leave from any of 11 U.S. gateway cities. On Pan Am's 17-day Jet Economy Excursion fares, you save $136. For instance, round-trip New York-London by Jet Clipper* is only $350! You'll be there in hours, enjoying Pan Am's wonderful food and service on the way. Europe is waiting, a bargain hunter's paradise, with hotel rates, gifts, almost everything priced lower now. Make your reservations now. Call your Travel Agent today or one of Pan Am's 66 offices in the United States and Canada.

09

BRAND IDENTITY, CONSUMER EXPERIENCE, AND THE INTER-CONNECTED PACKAGE

KATHRYN SPITZBERG, NOAH ARMSTRONG, BRIAN GAFFNEY, CHANGZHI LEE, *and* **JEREMY DIPAOLO**

The first video that the channel aired, "Video Killed the Radio Star," by the band the Buggles, made a similarly prophetic statement. MTV was changing the way we heard music—and who would be its superstars.

Once upon a time, there were three major television networks in the United States: CBS, ABC, and NBC. The networks offered vibrant and compelling shows but they were rather staid; the programming—whether entertainment, news, or educational—was drawn from a limited palette. Enter cable television, and then MTV. When the channel debuted in 1981, it created an entirely new paradigm for television, garnering millions of viewers eager for the channel's music-themed programming and its bold posture of irreverence.

MTV was a game changer. It and the seven brands profiled in this chapter transformed brand categories or completely invented new ones. With its search algorithm, Google became the Internet search destination without peer, sending sites like HotBot and Excite into obscurity. It has since built on its cachet, aiming to become the Internet application portal without parallel. Amazon, too, recognized a niche and swooped into it, becoming the top online shopping site.

Starbucks coffee branding and store design conveys the purveyor's identity as a "third place," a comfortable refuge away from work and home.

Game-changing brands are iconic. They act as catalysts, leading culture; they rely on breakthrough performances; and they had a certain cultural logic to them, emerging as the result of an intrinsic social need.

These eight groundbreaking brands—MTV, Nike, American Express, Starbucks, AOL, Amazon, TED, and Google—transformed specific brand categories or invented them completely. They went far beyond simply improving the way we live, work, buy, play, and learn; they revolutionized culture.

The brands profiled here reflect the seminal transformations taking place from 1980 to 2010. While a selection of companies that created paradigm-shifting innovations could never be complete, these companies showcase the dynamics of brand innovation and the necessity for it. These are the game changers.

MTV

KATHRYN SPITZBERG

As cable television expanded into more homes across the United States during the late 1970s, deregulation of the television industry increased the number of available channels. As media companies sought to target the interests of specific demographics—and the advertising dollars that went along with them—programming became more "narrowcast." In order to provide programming for Warner Amex's struggling cable system, Warner Amex Satellite Entertainment Company was created and given free reign to seek out new markets with cheaply produced media properties.[1] A channel that showed music videos seemed to fit that criteria, and on August 1, 1981, corporate America ushered a milestone premiere that both reflected the zeitgeist and defined it: Warner Amex Satellite Entertainment Company broadcast the debut of MTV, a.k.a. "Music Television," at 12:01 a.m.[2] The network's opening sequence, a minute-long montage of images relating to space travel, gave viewers a powerful branded experience, alluding to MTV's promise that, as station VJ JJ Jackson put it, the world would "never look at music the same way again."[3] The opener's most iconic section features the image of an astronaut juxtaposed with the American flag on the moon. In MTV's rendition, the flag is replaced with the brightly colored, undulating, electric-neon flag of MTV, which morphs from one design to another. By appropriating and then altering historical imagery, the channel made clear that it was speaking to a new generation.

The first video that the channel aired, "Video Killed the Radio Star," by the band the Buggles, made a similarly prophetic statement. MTV was changing the way we heard music—and who would be its superstars. Through the network's influence, music became a multisensory experience too big for radio; the brand itself became a portal into the fashion, the flaws, the glamour, and the rebellion of our favorite entertainers. The channel's nonstop flow of continuous video fed the cravings of a new generation eager to experience their rock icons through the visual medium, and gave rock stars a new way of expressing their artistry. MTV gave record labels a new means to promote artists, and satisfied a youth culture constantly on the hunt for the latest thing. The MTV brand was unlike anything television viewers had seen up until that point. The channel had attitude, which was conveyed through its regularly changing promos, the channel's punk-influenced on-air graphics, and the "countercultural" programming. Walter Cronkite was not welcome here. The Pretenders, Iron Maiden, Elvis Costello, and Fleetwood Mac were.

The nonstop flow of programming made MTV groundbreaking in an even more significant way. It established MTV as the first network that viewers watched for the holistically branded experience—it essentially was a streaming brand promotion. As Naomi Klein observed in her book *No Logo*, "Viewers didn't watch individual shows, they simply watched MTV."[4] The brand became a stream of constant self-promotion with a point of view that transcended the platform of television and went on to influence and permeate pop culture. This media-brand-as-experience format stretched branding into a new realm that would eventually become the preferred form of major media brands. Adding to this new and unique brand positioning was the ever-changing MTV logo. The logo broke out of the framework of the conservative corporate identities of the time to reflect the uniquely expressive and ever-changing nature of the brand. A modern-day shape shifter, MTV adopted the attitude and appearance of its target audience—the fashionable, savvy, moody youth generation. And the logo itself became a phenomenon whose "animated mutability," as design critic Steven Heller observes, "made it as much an anticipated feature of daily programming as the music videos themselves."[5]

Though MTV had all the makings of the world-changing brand it would become, it wasn't an instant hit, due to its initially limited distribution. Cable television disrupted the monopoly of broadcast networks like NBC, CBS, and ABC, and after its debut, cable was still considered "alternative." Being a new concept in a new medium made finding like-minded cable operators a big challenge for MTV. The channel's leadership decided to make a bold move and launched a promotional campaign targeting cable operators. MTV enlisted the help of major music celebrities like Mick Jagger, Sting, Pat Benatar, and Stevie Nicks to encourage viewers to call their local cable operators and demand that they carry the network. The challenge was to be conveyed through the now-famous line, "I want my MTV." The call to action resonated deeply with the rebellious streak of MTV viewers. The brand was asking them to stand up for their generation—to stand up for rock 'n' roll. The campaign was a huge success; thousands of viewers called their local cable operators just minutes after the promotion debuted. Within months, MTV had significantly expanded its reach into households across America.

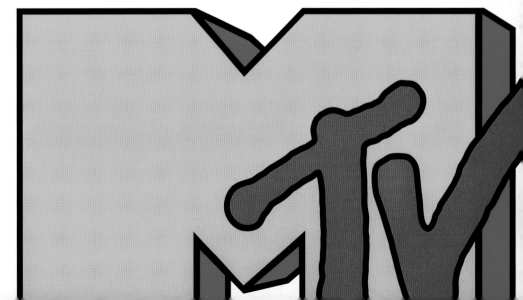

Nike and Michael Jordan

NOAH ARMSTRONG

In the early years of Nike, the company's owners, Bill Bowerman and Phil Knight, sold shoes at track meets out of the trunk of a car. Twenty years later, the company originally named Blue Ribbon Sports had become the top-selling brand in all of sports. As Nike expanded, the company's leadership continually returned to one essential question: How could they cement Nike's status as the undisputed leader of the sports apparel and accessories category? In the early '80s, athletes were commonly paid up to $10,000 to wear a certain brand of shoes. But the company's leadership recognized the limitations of the average endorsement deal, and they wanted Nike to achieve superstar status—to be the singular player dominating the sporting goods industry. If Nike wanted to achieve that elite standing, it needed to rethink its endorsement strategy.

Thus, brand innovation: Instead of signing numerous athletes for modest sums of money, Nike settled on the strategy that it would offer only multimillion-dollar deals to the most elite athletes. Nike wanted the brand to be synonymous with the superstars.

The brand's first potential recruit was Michael Jordan, who was then a twenty-one-year-old point guard from the University of North Carolina. Jordan had become famous for his ability to leap from the basketball court and soar through the air with such an upward trajectory that he appeared to have taken flight. He helped his team win games while under enormous pressure. He worked harder than anyone else. He was the epitome of commitment, passion, and pure athleticism. Nike management felt that Jordan was destined for a meteoric rise to stardom—if Nike could attach the brand to Jordan, Nike would be in an elite class unto itself.

Jordan was the perfect icon for Nike's new strategy, but he happened to be happily devoted to a different brand—Nike's longtime rival, Adidas. He wasn't interested in the Nike ethos. In order to convince Jordan to leave his brand of choice, Nike needed to come up with a special enticement. And so it created a new contract that forever changed the rules of the game for sports endorsements. In addition to paying Jordan $2.5 million over a five-year period, Nike would also design for him his own signature basketball shoe. The shoe would synthesize the technical expertise of Nike with Jordan's one-of-a-kind talent. It would be as representative of innovation as it was of raw talent and individualism. The Nike Air Jordan would be an icon that would showcase the heroism and accomplishment of both brand and player.

The Air Jordan's debut in 1985 marked not only a new era in professional basketball, but also the beginning of a shift in brands—certain brands would derive their relevance not simply from their own advantages but from a cult of personality that made their products irresistible. And like most game changers, the shoes would stir controversy. The NBA had mandated that shoes for all the

league's teams would be white—yet Air Jordans
were black and red. Since Jordan violated the rule,
the NBA fined him and attempted to ban the shoes.
Nike used the controversy to its advantage, happily
paying the fine and turning the hullabaloo into
an ad campaign highlighting its latest cutting-
edge product. Of course, Air Jordans stuck out
on the basketball court; there was no other shoe
like them, just as there was no other player like
Michael Jordan. The man and the shoes he wore
attained a mythic status. When Jordan's NBA
debut came to a conclusion, he would be named
Rookie of the Year—and $130 million worth of Air
Jordans would be sold.

American Express

KATHRYN SPITZBERG

In 1988, Michael Douglas won an Oscar for his portrayal of Gordon Gekko, a young, impatiently ambitious stockbroker in the movie *Wall Street*. The character pithily summarizes the sentiment of the 1980s with the now-classic line, "Greed is good." Though scholar Dinesh D'Souza and others have argued the era was nowhere near as gluttonous as its billing, the period that has been called "the age of greed" began with the 1980 election of President Ronald Reagan, whose administration slashed taxes for the wealthy and deregulated the markets, allowing big corporations unmitigated financial freedom. The enormous baby-boomer generation was in prime position to spend its newly accumulated earnings, the oldest among them nearing forty and the youngest just out of college. The emerging yuppie culture derived meaning from making money. A new breed of self-important billionaire was born in Donald Trump and Leona Helmsley. Television personality Robin Leach brought the gluttonous lives of the über wealthy straight into Americans' living rooms with the popular television series *Lifestyles of the Rich and Famous*, just as the Forbes list of richest people became more popular than the magazine's list of richest companies.[6] Pop-culture icons like "material girl" Madonna, as well as J.R. Ewing on the hit series *Dallas*, gave further impetus to the trend, placing enormous emphasis on wealth, status, and privilege, even if it was conveyed with irony.

Noting this paradigm shift, American Express led the charge in personal finances with products and services that catered to the desire for exclusivity and all things elite. AmEx had first tapped into this powerful motivator decades earlier when, in 1966, it introduced its Gold Card. The invitation-only Gold Card carried an annual fee but came with a bundle of services. Recognizing how this concept of being "invited" or "selected" could appeal to the "me, me, me" generation of the 1980s, the company launched the even more exclusive Platinum Card in 1984. With a $450 annual fee and no set spending limit, the Platinum Card kept right in tune with the shop-'til-you-drop, mall-madness mentality of what writer Tom Wolfe described as the "splurge generation."[7] Flashing a Platinum card meant the holder was paying a fee for it, but it also meant this particular consumer had the financial means to foot the bill, turning the Platinum into a signifier of the cardholder's wealth and status.

To further embed the idea of elitism into the brand's DNA, American Express developed a language branded around the idea of exclusivity, referring to its customers as "cardmembers" and offering them "membership rewards." Though the concept of loyalty marketing was nothing new, AmEx charted new brand territory with its membership rewards program by linking loyalty with luxurious branded experiences. AmEx rewarded its loyal cardmembers with access to luxury services like premium tickets to exclusive concerts, entrance into airport lounges when traveling, and access to a global, twenty-four-hour personal concierge service. AmEx created experiences that went well beyond what one would expect from a financial institution, making the brand a gateway to lifestyle. By handpicking its cardmembers and focusing intently on customer service, AmEx generated a unique symbiotic relationship between cardmember and card provider, with each profiting from the interaction. It was a groundbreaking arrangement in the financial services category: Cardmembers used their cards as status symbols and badges of elitism, while American Express used its cardmembers' potential purchasing power as a way to entice merchants into paying higher fees. If they would accept only American Express, they could take advantage of the big-spending, AmEx-carrying patrons. These strict agreements with merchants created yet another level of social exclusivity, relegating those patrons without AmEx cards to the shameful act of paying with cash.

By understanding the key cultural drivers of the decade, American Express successfully harnessed the power of exclusivity and privilege, and defined the AmEx brand as the card with the greatest cachet. The company nearly tripled the number of its cardholders by the end of the decade.

Have you got what it takes to spend The New Money?

Being one of the most famous cartoonists in the world didn't hurt Al Capp when he applied for the American Express Card —The New Money.™

*American Express Card Member
040 072 493 6 400AX
Creator of "Li'l Abner"*

Doing well won't do *you* any harm either. To qualify for The New Money, you must earn a minimum of $7500 a year, although your chances will improve immeasurably if you make more.

But even if you *do* make enough of the old money, ask yourself if you can use The New Money before you apply. Not every man can.

Do you travel on business? 97% of American Express Card members do. The average member spends $2500 a year on travel. Do you fly? A third of our members make 25 air trips a year.

If you're our kind of man, pick up an application wherever the Money Card is honored. Or write: American Express Card, Box 671, N.Y., N.Y. 10003.

© 1970 American Express Company.

Advantages of The New Money:
1 The New Money is accepted worldwide wherever you see the American Express Card shield. ☑ **2** The New Money is welcome on the best airlines, at hotels, motels, restaurants, rent-a-cars, gasoline stations, specialty stores worldwide. **3** The New Money is not a revolving charge card—there is no automatic *finance charge* of 1½% per month on your outstanding balance. **4** The New Money lets you extend payments for airline tickets. There is a *finance charge* for these extended pay plans, but the *annual percentage* rate is only 12%—one third less than many conventional revolving charge cards. **5** The New Money's exclusive "Be My Guest"® service lets you host someone to dinner halfway around the world—even when you can't be there. **6** The New Money can get you a guaranteed hotel or motel reservation through a free new telephone service, "The Space Bank."℠ Pick up an application wherever the American Express Card is welcome. Or write: Box 671, New York, N.Y. 10003.

THE NEW MONEY

AMERICAN EXPRESS
040 072 493 6 400AX
AL CAPP

AMERICAN EXPRESS
FOR PEOPLE WHO TRAVEL

A 1971 American Express ad sought to build cachet by appealing to the well to do. (At the time, $7,500 was a significant annual income.)

Starbucks

CHANGZHI LEE *and* **JEREMY DIPAOLO**

In 1983, Howard Schultz went to Italy. What he saw there would change his career, his company, and the way we think about consumption.

On March 30, 1971, three partners (two teachers and a writer) opened Starbucks Coffee and Tea in Seattle's Pike Place Market. Inspired by entrepreneur Alfred Peet—whose Peet's Coffee & Tea had introduced artisanal coffee to the United States in the late '60s—the first Starbucks sold high-quality coffee beans and high-end coffee-making equipment. Other than the occasional sampler, the early store didn't feature the beverages for which the company is now so renowned. By 1980, the company had four stores in Seattle, still focused on selling gourmet coffee beans and their supporting accessories. The shift that would transform the company came from Howard Schultz, who joined as director of marketing in 1982.

While in Milan for a housewares convention, Schultz was struck by the extraordinary environment of the espresso bars that dotted the city. Not only did these bars serve excellent, robust coffee, but they were also gathering places. People called each other by name.[8] These spaces formed a big part of Italy's societal glue. Instantly recognizing an opportunity for Starbucks to capitalize on this model, Schultz sought to extract the essence of Italian coffee culture—high-quality hand-crafted drinks in a convivial setting—and import it to the United States. However, it would take a falling out with the partners, the formation of his own company, and the eventual acquisition of Starbucks, in 1987, to see his vision come to light. When Schultz finally became CEO of Starbucks, he immediately set to work on implementing his entrepreneurial vision for the company's expansion and eventual dominance of the specialty coffee market. And selling great coffee was only part of the equation.

Starbucks' relevance as an iconic brand is evidenced by its ability to capture the spirit of Schultz's beloved Italian espresso bars and not simply offer a great product, but build a culture around the way people consume it. The brand, in short, was establishing a platform for personalized experience.

Before Starbucks, aficionados had to rely on their relationship with a coffee vendor to ensure they would receive their beverage "their way." And still, enter any neighborhood coffeehouse, and the consumer's cup is at the relative mercy of the barista's skill and interest level. Starbucks, through its rigid, systematized process of drink making and its accompanying language—which has been parodied since its inception—allows consumers to receive the same "iced triple grande two-pump vanilla nonfat latte" at any location, any time.

During the 1990s, the very moment Starbucks began its massive expansion into multiple U.S. markets, Generation X, with its emphasis on individual values, found a particular resonance with the ability to personalize (and identify with) a coffee concoction. The brand's Seattle roots gave it a special kind of authenticity, as the city would become a cultural beacon of music, fashion, and film during this time.

Offering customers a place to gather and share in the Starbucks experience was a key factor of the brand's significance and popularity in the marketplace. Schultz set out to create an environment that was a midpoint between the workplace and home, a goal again informed by his experience in Milan. This "third place," as he would later articulate it, was to be that convivial gathering spot for people to use as they wished: reading, chatting, or simply enjoying a moment over a frothy cappuccino. In those moments, consumers were taking in the entire multisensory experience: the flavors of "their" beverage, the call and echo of drink names, the punctuated hissing of the espresso machine and the rich aromas that followed, the mellow tunes, and the variety of customers waiting their turn for the same experience. Starbucks was building a community all its own, and the company did it on both sides of the counter.

Every employee of Starbucks is called a "partner," even Howard Schultz. This corporate meta-tag very simply illustrates the company's commitment to an internal culture that fosters the wealth of the company through collective achievement. Intensive training for all "partners" is met with competitive compensation packages that include stock options and health benefits for part-time staff. This attitude toward employees was almost unheard of at the time. But it allowed Starbucks

to build a passionate culture of people who took stake in the company's success, whether they were company leaders or part-time baristas.

Schultz captured the essence of that first trip to Milan and built a place where people could share in it. That first experience, which is now eloquently pruned and articulated as legend in Starbucks history, has gone through many iterations as the company has evolved. That the essence of it is unmistakably brewed into every cup, felt in every store, and understood through the appearance of the green-and-white Siren is testament to the deep equity the brand carries across the countries where it has arrived. The Starbucks phenomenon also speaks to the enormous potential for personal experience to shape our world.

AOL (America Online)

BRIAN GAFFNEY

America Online had a bold mission, and its founders had a savvy anticipation of the future. Founder Steve Case has observed that, during its early history, the company's leaders understood that, "Someday, everybody is going to be online. Someday, we are going to be living in a more interactive world. Someday, people will feel like they are part of an electronic community." [9]

America Online, now known as AOL, was founded in 1983 by William von Meisteras. The company was then known as Control Video Corporation and it was the provider of GameLine, an online access provider for the Atari 2600. GameLine permitted users to download games and keep track of high scores. The company didn't fare well, and when it was on the verge of bankruptcy, its mission, leadership, and name changed—to Quantum Computer Services. The company had initially followed a strategy of providing online access through video game devices; as part of the new identity, it shifted to focusing on personal computers as conduits to the Internet.

In 1985, Quantum launched a dedicated online service for Commodore 64 and 128 computers, called Quantum Link; three years later, the company partnered with Apple to launch Apple Link Personal Edition, which provided Internet access for Apple II and Macintosh computers, followed later that year by the introduction of PC Link for IBM-compatible computers made by the Tandy Corporation. The company changed its name again in 1989, to America Online, after

the company's relationship with Apple ended. The same year witnessed the debut of a sound clip that was to become a cultural phenomenon: "Welcome! You've got mail." That signature sonic-brand statement achieved such widespread recognition that it permeated pop culture; it later became the name of a hit film starring Tom Hanks and Meg Ryan.

Initially, AOL built its infrastructure for online access by working with computer makers that already had a strong user base. From that platform, it shepherded an online revolution. The company helped usher in the online era by convincing IBM, to incorporate modems into its machines. With modems a standard feature and not an add-on, home users were able to connect to the Internet much more easily. And AOL, with the technological experience and infrastructure in place, was positioned to be the access point for home users as the mass market for online consumer services was burgeoning.

AOL helped to build that bridge by creating a simple, easy-to-use (and catchy) user interface that made online access less intimidating— "online" no longer would be a foreign land that required obscure lingo and commands. User-friendly email, chat rooms, and the company's curated content made the largely unregulated World Wide Web appear much safer, more stable, and more approachable. And the advantages of its services were an irresistible part of the brand appeal: Email made it possible to communicate with friends, family, and colleagues anywhere in the world, in a way that was faster and cheaper than postal mail or telephone. And the attraction of the Web itself was part of AOL's draw, as the Internet was gradually being built into a forum for an extraordinary range of content, shopping, entertainment, and interactive experiences. Instant messaging was engaging and allowed for a new form of conversational rapport. AOL built the wealth of online possibilities into its own brand.

The success of the AOL experience is evident in the company's numbers: It reached 1 million subscribers in 1995 and grew to 5 million members one year later. In the early 2000s, AOL was the world's largest Internet service provider, with 35 million subscribers, surpassing all its competitors. It merged with Time Warner in 2000, a move that was hailed as marking the ascension of new media and the beginning of an age of media companies and content.

But the merger didn't go smoothly, and as is often the case with category innovators (does anyone remember Netscape?), AOL started a revolution but wasn't able to continue it. The company grew until 2002, when it began to falter. In the fourth quarter of that year, AOL began losing subscribers and advertising revenue as a result of a two-front war: One set of competitors was offering cheaper prices for dial-up while another group was promoting high-speed Internet access over cable and telephone-based digital subscriber lines (DSL). Even if AOL today is no longer heralded as the groundbreaker it once was, much of what we take for granted in the online realm was made possible by the company's early forays into Internet access and user interface; the company established a familiarity with the Web, and an acceptance of it, that is second nature to us now.

Amazon.com

BRIAN GAFFNEY

In 1994, Jeff Bezos was a senior vice president at D. E. Shaw & Co, an investment firm. While there, Bezos became aware of a startling statistic: Internet usage was growing at 2,300 percent a year. Bezos recognized there was great potential in creating a business that would tap into that online audience. The main question: What would the enterprise do?

That Bezos settled on selling books is a historical given. In July 1995, he started Amazon.com, naming the company after the river that is the largest in the world—a reflection of the young founder's ambitions. In the first thirty days of operation, the company filled orders from all fifty states and forty-five countries. Just over a year later, in December 1996, Time declared Amazon.com the "best place to do holiday shopping without leaving your house."[10]

Books were but a logical point of entry for what would become the world's largest Internet retailer. Bezos believed that he could build an online store with a complete and competitive selection, surpassing the 150,000 titles that book superstores normally stocked. When Amazon launched, it offered site visitors a selection of 1 million books.

The company gradually built out its slate of offerings. In 1997, CDs and movies were added to the company's stock, followed the next year by software, electronics, video games, toys, and home improvement products. Amazon shifted from its billing as "Earth's largest bookstore" to "Earth's biggest selection," not simply by expanding its retail offering, but by including intangibles like computing, warehousing, and delivery services.

The company's brand is built on a relentless commitment to, as Bezos has described it, a "culture that obsesses over the customer." That brand value is reflected in the company's history of making the site both functional and vibrant. The company made the online shopping experience enjoyable through a user experience that was easy to navigate and also enabled the company to market its wares; simultaneously, the site allowed customers to become a part of the Amazon community, to establish their expertise. Users would contribute reviews of books; the site would give users recommendations and allow them to see what other buyers had purchased. Visitors could buy items with one click. The goal of customer satisfaction—in both product selection and experience with the company—is reflected in the brand mark, with the yellow arrow/smile pointing from the letter *A* to the letter *Z*.

Convenience is a part of the brand, as is innovation. The very notion of selling books by the Internet is one aspect of that history, but the company made other leaps forward. It was ideally positioned to capitalize on the ebook phenomenon, and its Kindle reader catalyzed the transition from print to digital books and has gone on to shift the dynamics of the book industry. In May 2011, Amazon had sold more ebooks than print books. With that accomplishment, it was clear that the company had entered new territory. With numerous successes under his belt, the question left for Jeff Bezos is, "What's next?"

Google

CHANGZHI LEE

Do you remember the search engines AltaVista and Excite? Chances are you don't. But if you want to find out more about them, you can do a Google search.

"Google it." Those two words have become essential in the modern-day lexicon, evoking the incontrovertible value of the Google search—and brand. Instead of libraries, card catalogs, the local wise man, or other means of research, we turn to Google to investigate every subject and question, whether that is Lady Gaga's latest antics, homeopathic remedies for the common cold, or directions from home to the local swimming hole.

Simply stated, Google's brand advantage was that it made Internet searching reliable, simple, and fun. You got the sense that if you couldn't find the information on Google, then it probably wasn't out there. The company's top-secret search algorithms are the best in the biz, and are being continually refined. The user interface, offering the option for the "I'm feeling lucky" result, gave the search process a level of entertainment.

The Google brand is built on simplicity and the value of the utilitarian approach to information design. The brand aesthetic features simplicity almost to the point of ugliness. The logo is not going to win any design awards, and neither is the look of its search pages—or Gmail, for that matter. But if they're not especially pleasing to the eye, Google's services are dependable; the company has built a reputation for the reliability of its online services and applications. If you want to get good search results, you use Google. No other brand has the same cachet. And while Gmail may take some getting used to, once you understand its aesthetic, you will find it eminently useful.

The Google brand ethos is built on its commitment to making the company's online offerings usable and practical, whether that's News, Voice, Maps, Finance, or any other rollout the company has made. The Google brand is built too on its effort to synchronize each of its programs into a seamless online experience that allows users to take care of modern-day tasks, responsibilities, and pastimes. Though the company has had some missteps— Google Buzz among them—it's continued to roll out new applications and features that have garnered enthusiasm and users. We now rely on the suite of Google apps for organizing our lives, for learning, for communication, for research. Google remains the online portal without peer—a search engine that has become a destination in its own right.

TED
BRIAN GAFFNEY

The TED Conference began in 1984 as the brainchild of architect, author, and graphic designer Richard Saul Wurman. Wurman had noticed that common themes had emerged in the fields of technology, entertainment, and design (thus TED), and he wanted to create a forum that would allow business and cultural leaders to share their thoughts and generate meaningful discussion on contemporary trends and innovations. The discussion, he hoped, would lead to further cultural evolution.

After years when the conference content was available only to attendees, the TED organizers made a conscious decision to share the discussion more widely, fulfilling TED's mission to share "ideas worth spreading," as the organization's tagline goes. In 2007, the TEDTalks debuted for free, on the Internet.

Today, nearly 1,000 TEDTalks3 are posted at TED.com; each one is fewer than eighteen minutes in length, and in total, they've been watched more than 300 million times.[3] Robert Hammond talks about creating New York City's High Line; Oliver Sacks speaks about the variety of hallucinations he's seen in patients; Amy Tan talks about creativity and her own metaphysical evolution.

The TED brand is expressed in the very nature of the TED presentations themselves. A speaker talks on a stage, using a screen as an aid and visual accompaniment to the narrative. The very act of watching is itself an adventure in curiosity, as each speaker brings his or her particular creativity and sensibility to the presentation, providing a source of dramatic intrigue. The typical classroom lecture is infinitely dull by comparison.

TED, it seems, has become a de facto educational institution, the go-to site for learning from leaders in culture, business, media, and art. In an article from *Fast Company* in September 2010, writer Anya Kamenetz suggested that TED is "the first new top prestige education brand in more than 100 years"[4] and "the global education brand of the 21st century."[4] Yet unlike traditional educational institutions, TED grants no diplomas, has no faculty, and has no official students; there is equality between the speakers and attendees alike, with conference organizers referring to them both as "TEDsters."

Certainly, the TEDTalks provide an education in contemporary culture for people all around the world, giving audiences the intellectual repast of a Charlie Rose interview combined with the ever-present online accessibility of Google. TED's brand sensibility is one of openness and inclusiveness—of encouraging and inspiring intellectual curiosity. Not everyone may be invited to the event itself, but millions of people all around the world are encouraged to explore and learn from TED. The organization has made intellectual curiosity contagious and developed a cachet for cultural innovation and reflection.

TED has sparked an online revolution, leading the world's online community to be exposed to artists, writers, inventers, diplomats, designers, and business leaders that might otherwise remain behind a media veil. The TED forum allows these innovators to share their thoughts from their own point of view and without the filtering of traditional news media. With the site's videos easy to integrate on other sites, viewers can easily share their favorite Talks with both personal and professional networks. Which of us hasn't watched—or forwarded—a TedTalk?

Under the leadership of media entrepreneur Chris Anderson, who bought TED in 2001, the TED brand has begun expanding. Anderson's curatorial goal has been to challenge members to "apply their collective brainpower to intractable social issues."[6] In addition to the TEDTalks, there is the TED Prize, awarded to spark positive social change, the Open Translation Project, an effort to translate the TEDTalks into numerous languages, and the TED Fellows program, which brings cutting-edge thinkers into the TED fold. The goal of all these projects is to inspire evolution, innovation, and social change. TED has introduced branded offshoots like TEDGlobal, TEDIndia, and TED@Cannes that take place in different locales yet offer the same sensibility.

In this same spirit, the conference allows organizers from around the world to apply for a free TEDx license that allows them to locally organize and curate a branded event—a kind of TED franchise operation. These offshoots, which have included TEDxEkaterinburg, TEDxFortGreene, TEDxCaltech, and TEDxJakarta, among hundreds of others, encourages the brand's meme to spread faster than it could if it was controlled by TED Central Office, yet they still fit with the TED ethos. The brand shines through.

When creating the website that would serve as TED's "global ideas platform,"[5] the design firm Method created a simple, easy-to-navigate design that presented the relevant information with elegance yet without design frills. Since the vast majority of TEDTalks watchers will never attend a conference themselves, the design of the site must handle the task of expressing the brand, conveying its transparency and the extensive content. The firm developed an unconventional rating system that allows visitors to use words such as jaw-dropping, inspiring, longwinded, obnoxious, courageous, and funny to rate the talks. TED has made cultural exploration and discussion compelling, transformative, and revelatory. It is a platform for cultural innovation and discovery.

10

BRANDAPTATION IN THE TWENTY-FIRST CENTURY

MARGAUX GENIN *and* **JEREMY DIPAOLO**

Times Square,
New York City

The innovation of technology has progressed at blinding speeds in recent years—the cellular phone has become the smart phone, and the desktop became the laptop became the tablet capable of connecting us anywhere, anytime—and it's only getting faster. In an era where the instant and open sharing of information is commonplace for almost everyone in the world—on platforms ranging from cell phones to Facebook, Posterous, Tumblr, and Twitter—brands are contending with new challenges. The modern brand is not simply a logo, a product, or a promise, but the collective whole of the perceptions, emotions, and projections that people place upon these elements, and the organization from which they originate.

Until recently, the major outlets of communication have been controlled and operated by brands. This means that brands were able to (mostly) control the messaging relating to their offerings, as the available media channels typically provided a one-sided monologue: Brands had the leading roles, with consumers in the audience. The mass adoption of the Internet in the late 1990s and of mobile technology in the early twenty-first century, however, has enabled consumers to not only co-opt, but also masterfully subvert the very channels at the heart of brands' successes for more than 100 years.

A Warhol-like rendering
of Lady Gaga

The emergence of powerful peer-to-peer networks allowed individuals to share their brand experiences in real time and broadcast them to the world without being filtered or censored. These networks allowed consumers to pull back the curtain from the "great and powerful Oz"[1] to reveal that brands did not always have consumers' best interests in mind.

There is a long history of skepticism about businesses' ultimate goals—just consider the criticism volleyed at companies involved in the "military-industrial complex," or the books *The Jungle* by Upton Sinclair and *Silent Spring* by Rachel Carson. But the accessible, democratic forum of the Internet is unlike any other medium, and it plays into the resistance we have to large, faceless institutions. We seem inextricably drawn to trust our fellow consumer; we have more faith in each other and less in brands.

This trust factor, and the fact that technology levels the media playing field, has resulted in a situation where brand and consumer are engaged in a global shouting match. The contemporary day and age is a period of disruption: A brand can no longer rely on its longstanding heritage to guarantee business success—the rabble has much to say about particular products and company policies alike. Brands have adapted to this landscape by either fighting the noise or by employing a strategy of embracing and even joining in with the new dialogue. But simply participating in the conversation doesn't mean consumers will talk to you. In order to truly engage existing and potential audiences, many businesses have realized that much more is necessary.

In the shift from mass-marketing to consumer segmentation in the 1960s, brands sought to divide the marketplace into manageable niches in the hopes that they could reach specific demographic segments with powerfully targeted messaging.[2] Yet in the new paradigm of the twenty-first century, the collective entity of the buying public is not so easily divided. It is a living, breathing organism populated by humans, which means it is messy, unpredictable, and in a constant state of evolution. In order to prevail in their missions, in order to truly relate to modern consumers, brands must embrace the messiness. They must leave space for the consumer to not only be a part of the conversation, but also be an active participant in the very messaging that brands have tried to control throughout the history of consumption. By adapting to this new model, successful brands are empowering their community of loyalists not only to amplify the brand message, but to do so on their own terms.

Obama '08 Political Campaign

Few events crystallize the notion of building loyalist communities like an election. The 2008 U.S. presidential election saw new tactics employed—centered on the use of social media—to reach and motivate the majority of the nation to vote the first African-American president into the White House. In some ways, Barack Obama's personal engagement with his constituents can best be described as a populist technique right out of the Reagan or Roosevelt playbook, but with one important distinction: Whereas radio and television allowed former presidents to deliver only a monologue to the masses, modern technology allowed Obama

Shepard Fairey's classic (and controversial) Obama poster incorporated the campaign's *O* logo.

to be an active participant in the conversation among them. By focusing on crystal clear, differentiated messaging and deploying a design system with a level of consistency that flabbergasted even the most experienced of design practitioners[3] the Obama '08 campaign established itself as one of the most iconic brands of the early twenty-first century.

At the heart of the brand was a universal icon, a simple logo in the shape of an *O*: open, shining, patriotic. Obama's vision of America for all Americans. Crafted by the designer Sol Sender to be a symbol of unity, the logo avoided the traditional red state/blue state rhetoric inherent in most election graphics, instead expressing all the colors of the American flag. Also doing away with primarily typographic-centered designs of campaigns past, the Obama '08 identity placed the graphic icon at center stage. It reinforced the notion of Obama as the human icon that people could believe in, no matter their age, race, or gender. The logo projected the values of Obama's politics, and allowed people to see their values mirrored through the broad range of interpretations utilized throughout the campaign. The gay community adopted the symbol to create web banners that read "Obama Pride" and featured the full-spectrum rainbow in place of the symbol's red-and-white stripes. "Women for Obama" transformed the outer *O* into the Venus symbol.

While the *O* mark served as the visual anchor for the campaign, the identity system's true engaging power can be attributed to its "ownability." Using a sophisticated combination of metaphor and recognizable iconography to modify the mark, the campaign was able to establish direct associations with many groups within the population. This allowed the identity system to simultaneously

project and absorb different narratives, all involving candidate Obama. These were inserted into various campaign signs, web banners, and other materials that correlated to different subsets of Obama's constituents among the fifty states and U.S. territories.

The campaign was an innovation in community engagement that still serves as a model to brands. By utilizing social media platforms such as Facebook, MySpace, YouTube, LinkedIn, and Twitter as well as text messaging, websites, email blasts, and other means, the campaign effectively disseminated information directly to supporters and promoters online—and allowed them to make the message, and the cause, their own. As brand strategist Marc Gobé observed, "The technology put in place by the Obama campaign and the programs made available to the volunteers helped create a movement because the actors had the freedom to act and [they had] the tools to operate and subsequently impact community."[5]

While one memorable bit of evidence of this strategy is Shepard Fairey's "Hope" poster, the campaign saw the *O* logo appropriated in almost every conceivable way, from stickers and signs to the icing atop cupcakes at fund-raising bake sales. By allowing supporters to organize in essentially any way they saw fit, the Obama campaign was not only granting power to the people, but was, in fact, powered by the people.

Martha Stewart

A human icon need not be the leader of the free world to be the centerpiece of a successful brand. Sometimes, this figure can also teach you how to decorate cupcakes. That is, at face value, one of the many utilitarian resonances of the Martha Stewart brand, but its perpetual popularity can be attributed to something considerably more powerful: the bond of trust between each consumer and Stewart herself. Loved and loathed by the masses, her character is famously enigmatic and her story, undeniably American. Emerging from humble New Jersey roots, the tale of Stewart's ascent to become the country's first self-made female billionaire is one riddled with drama and triumph, trial, and redemption. It speaks to both the monumental potential of the human as iconic brand and to the possible pitfalls along the way.

The duality of Stewart the homemaker and Stewart the media mogul informs the appeal of the Martha Stewart brand, as cultural critic Grant McCracken points out in *Transformations: Identity Construction in Contemporary Culture*. "Stewart is a cultural artifact shot through with complexity, conflict, and paradox. It is precisely this that allows her to speak powerfully to so many different groups." Her placid nature and matronly approachability on camera belie her shrewdness as a businesswoman, and it is her deft handling of the roles as perfectionist taste-maker, motherly enabler, and many identities in between that underpin her successes.

The visual experience throughout the Martha Stewart brand universe is one of careful curation, an approach that has increasing value in today's frenetic digital world, when we simply don't have time to sort through the morass ourselves. The brand relies on basic design principles to form powerful combinations of images across all of its touchpoints, creating a consistent narrative that seems to emerge directly from the icon herself: Every recipe, product, and editorial spread coalesces to form the cosmos of good taste of which Stewart is the creator. The vivid turquoise color scheme, not used much elsewhere in design, makes the brand highly distinct and instantly recognizable. The logo, hand-carved from a disc of plaster by graphic designer Stephen Doyle, reinforces the brand's willingness to embrace the imperfection inherent in the process of human creativity.[6]

ABOVE:
Graphic designer Stephen Doyle handcrafted the Martha Stewart logo from a disc of plaster.

LEFT:
Packaging for Martha Stewart melds the logo and the distinctive turquoise color scheme.

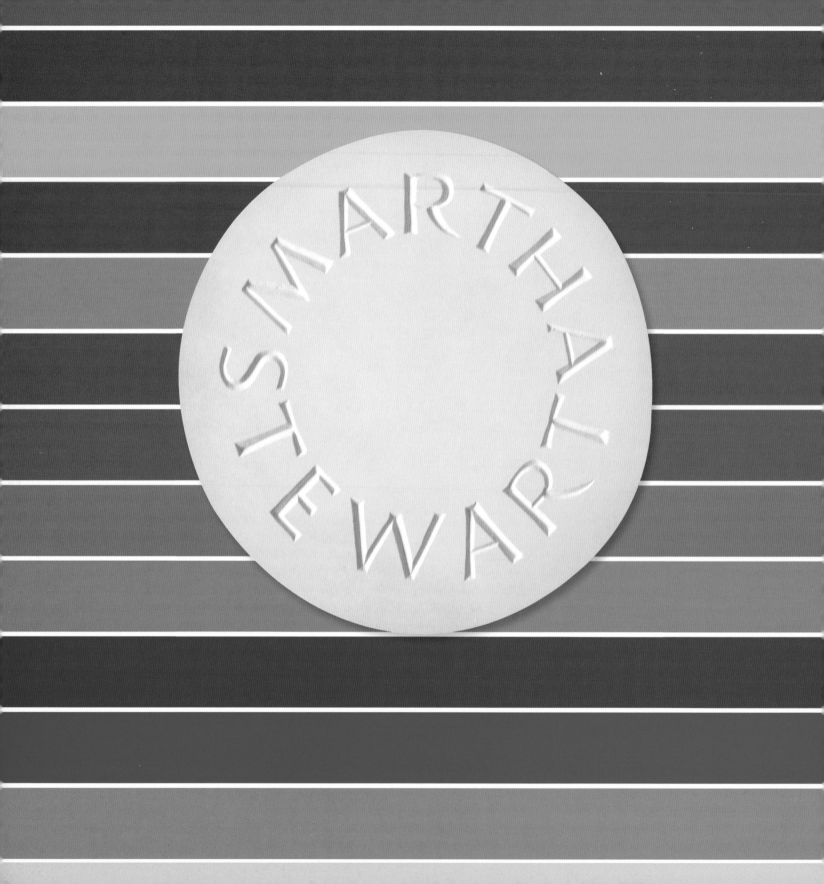

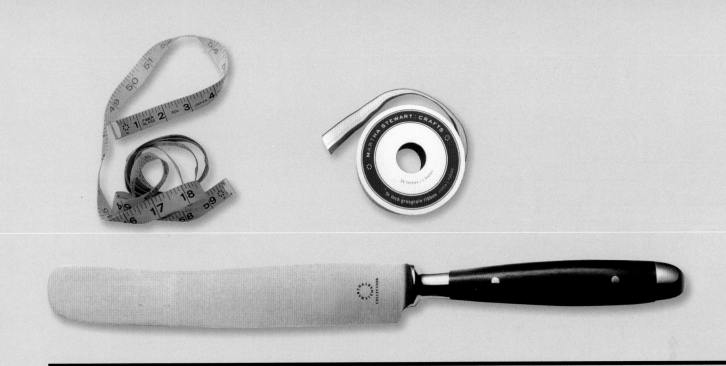

It's difficult to examine the Martha Stewart brand without drawing a correlation to religion. The full name of the brand is Martha Stewart Living Omnimedia. Much like organized faith, the goal of the brand is to be an omnipresent power able to reach and guide adherents through every major moment of their lives, from the ordinary and everyday to major occasions and rites of passage. The brand has developed Stewart's presence among myriad channels: Her magazines, her multiple television and radio programs, her websites, apps, community, ecommerce projects, and other venues, solidify the icon's brand into a bona fide empire.

One of Stewart's main distinctions as a leading brand, however, comes not only from the sheer scale of her empire, but from the way she empowers her community to express themselves creatively. Her constant presence within the brand system gives aspirants a role model to emulate, though it doesn't pass judgment on how they choose to do so. The brand's Facebook page states that "Martha Stewart Living Omnimedia is not just about lifestyle, but about tools for modern living—not just about the how-to but about the why-to."[7] In this way, Stewart has sought to instill an enriched sense of meaning in her consumers' lives by offering them the resources to beautify and elevate their surroundings, allowing them to follow their guru's guidance through the filter of their own muse. This willingness to let go and allow people creative autonomy is a testament to the brand's confidence in the strength and clarity of its messaging and the recognition of its iconic design elements—and the total uniqueness of the experience these represent.

ABOVE:
Martha Stewart branding is ever-present, elegant, and unobtrusive.

FAR LEFT:
The completed Martha Stewart logo, as crafted by designer Stephen Doyle

Apple Inc.

In the pantheon of companies that have created a bracingly unique and compelling brand experience, only a few companies have mastered the lexicon as adeptly as Apple. By placing human-centered, seductively minimalist design at the forefront of its strategic approach, Apple has developed a line of products that are immediately recognizable, a joy to use, and completely memorable; so much so that consumers are willing to pay a significant premium for them.

The Apple brand started as a small, disruptive tech start-up in the 1970s, and has grown into a powerhouse with a global tribe of loyal followers. And much of the success starts with the "i." IPod, iPad, iPhone, iMac: The naming of Apple products is key to understanding how the brand chooses to engage its consumers. The "i" nomenclature serves several purposes. It gives us, as consumers, permission to project our personality onto the product, invites us to define the devices with a curated collection of personal content, and allows us to signal affiliation and differentiation simultaneously (our iPods make us part of a collective culture; yet each iPod is unique according to how each of us have defined it). The manifestations of the "i" become platforms to enable creativity and expression, and signal lifestyle and status. The Apple brand, in a sense, seduces the user into a magical realm. Yet the company doesn't have a set narrative for the consumer to follow. The company's products are the blanks to be filled in, the platforms and software to be utilized, giving people the permission to literally craft their own story. The Apple offerings evoke an approachability that

OPPOSITE:
Apple iconography becomes totemic in its retail locations.

BELOW:
The original Apple Computer Co. logo graces the cover of the Apple-1 operation manual.

Before the MacBook and iMac, there was the Apple II, as seen in these advertisements from the 1980s.

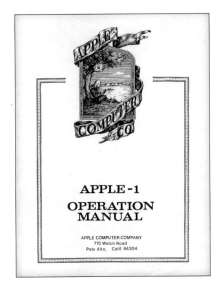

simultaneously signals design taste as well as an enticing "emptiness"; they want you to know that they are incomplete without you.

As Jonathan Ive, senior vice president of Industrial Design at Apple, puts it, "I don't have to change myself to fit the product, it fits me." It even seems at times that Apple's own tech stewards can only guess at the potential of their products; they rely instead on the massive community of users and developers to define and elevate the Apple experience by creating apps. In this way, Apple's vision supplies the overarching architecture, and the users decorate the interiors to their tastes.[8] Even the iconic iPod advertising campaign reinforces the notion that Apple's strengths as a brand lie in its ability to leave space for the consumer; its dominance arises, too, from its understanding of tribal affiliations as conveyed in the classic ad campaign

with the white wires; the dark figures dancing—all became a very literal representation of "standing out" and signaled affiliation with the iPod and, by extension, the Apple brand itself. Then came the "I'm a Mac. I'm a PC." campaign, which drew a line in the sand between old and young, corporate and creative, dodgy and functional, all with the intent to communicate once and for all that Apple is the tribe to be a part of.

All tribes need stomping grounds, and the Apple tribe is no exception. As Josiah Wedgwood demonstrated, the technique of marketing products in a showroom environment is not a novel concept. The Apple Store, on the surface, is little more than Steve Jobs channeling Wedgwood, but the result is no less magical. Apple's retail model is illustrative of the potential for success when a brand embraces the brick-and-mortar location as

In 1984, Apple introduced the graphical user interface and forever changed the way humans interact with computers.

Facebook

If a brand is a set of perceptions and emotions that must be carefully managed through consistent messaging and the continuous accumulation of positive associations, then Facebook allows each of its hundreds of millions of members to act as their own brand manager. Like Apple's products, the Facebook platform is an open framework, providing users with a tabula rasa on which to write their own brand stories. While this comes with the benefits of having a very visible and potentially wide-reaching platform that can be used to broadcast messages—a platform that, until recently, was available only to brands—it comes with a similar degree of responsibility that each member must take on as a member of the greater social network. One misstep within this environment can damage a person's reputation in very much the same way a brand's can be harmed. So, the rules of engagement on Facebook hinge upon the simple concept: Be real or be marginalized. Authenticity breeds trust, and without trust, the platform serves little purpose.[10] It's about the exchange of personality, thoughts, likes, and values among friends. In many regards, Facebook is the ultimate exercise in building and managing a tribe. Whereas Apple consumers rely on the brand icon and technological ephemera to signal group affiliation, Facebook members create their own personal tribes directly on the platform.

These are tricky waters for brands to navigate. While it can be argued that a brand's presence on Facebook is to build a dialogue with its consumers, many brands are still focusing on promotion over real conversation—to their detriment. Facebook has become a conundrum for brands and consumers alike because it creates a never-ending cycle of transactional interaction. In very

the greatest of brand-building experiences—as consummate fruition of the aesthetic and sensibility embodied in the product. As ecommerce has developed its foothold as a preferred method for purchase, retail stores must fulfill some other need. The Apple Store environment invites experimentation and play as a means to build a deeper connection with the company's products and with other tribal initiates. For the novice, classes are offered to enrich the experience. By making the retail location the epicenter for activities beyond "try and buy," the store becomes a staging ground for community building.[9]

ABOVE:
Apple's minimal design aesthetic conveys the brand message in its stores, as do the genius staffers.

Facebook's iconic
"Like" mark

much the same way that consumers use brands to signal status, brands have begun to achieve status on Facebook by displaying the number of consumers that are affiliated with them through "likes." This practice has extended far beyond the walls of Facebook and has spilled out across the Internet, where brands are relying on incentives such as product giveaways, access to limited-time discounts, and exclusive event invites to lure people to "like" them. This, in turn, creates another cycle. Brands offer people incentives for interaction, and in turn, people demand more and more incentives from brands.

Even though brands have been on Facebook for only a relatively short time, the evolution of this trend can be followed clearly. In the beginning, brands offered fans exclusive content such as sneak peeks, behind-the-scenes videos, and the like

which bestowed followers with the status of being in the "in crowd." However, as brands become more competitive on the platform and the shouting match between competitors grows louder, larger and more concrete incentives, such as travel givea-ways, are required to entice interest.

As a social platform, Facebook is "flat," an arena where all are equal: Other than your number of friends, very little distinction is made between the "brand called you" and the traditional brands that want you to "friend" them. In contrast to the open arena of the Web, the main Facebook feed allows little visual or interactive pizzazz; all comers must work within the confines of the limited palette and newsfeed. In the democratized world of social media, where every consumer becomes a producer,[11] the monumental challenge for brands becomes clear. To gain permission from consumers to be a part of their "conversation," a brand must emulate human behavior—to become another friend, and to achieve the authenticity that will garner the real-world "like," not merely the Facebook thumbs-up.

With a population of members that would rank it as the third largest country on Earth, behind China and India,[12] Facebook as a brand becomes a bit of a challenge to classify—yet it seems to have taken on the status of a nation. Much like a nation, Facebook is a federation of groups of people, rules, and codes of conduct; it has a large economy as well as the borders defined by the Facebook site architecture. There is a ruling elite that continually introduces new edicts—of interactive vocabulary and structure—to the delight and sometimes chagrin of the populace, whose outrage has yielded concessions on the part of the ruling monarchy. Facebook exerts a certain amount of power over its citizens, and if there is no formal constitution here, it's clear that are implicit rules: To be a member of this nation, each person is obligated to part with information about himself in a collective dance of compulsory show and tell.

The Facebook phenomenon presents implications for the way we will consider brands in the future. When brands start to surpass the scale of real-world nations, and in turn, begin to emulate them, how will we measure their influence? Certainly, there are brands in history that have achieved such scale, such as Procter & Gamble, which has spent almost two centuries shaping what and how consumers choose to buy. The difference with social platforms like Facebook, however, lies in our ability to witness and impact the narrative of the influence for ourselves. When over a half-billion consumers are responsible for actively shaping the messaging that builds and surrounds brands, the stakes of grassroots participation and brand cocreation become almost unfathomable. Only time will tell whether Facebook will continue to dominate the way we communicate with each other and with brands. But its adoption by so many people throughout the world, so quickly, speaks to two essential issues that brands must contend with for years to come: the ever-accelerating increase in the sophistication and scale of technology, and the exponential growth rate that defines how these digital civilizations rise and crumble. For now, it seems, brands' best hopes of surviving this constantly evolving ecosystem is to adopt and seek to truly engage the humanity that they've spent the past century attempting to manipulate.

Facebook, and platforms like it, are expressions of the evolution of our culture—they further our very human quest for the eternal life we gain through personal expression. The contemporary mediascape is the Lascaux of the twenty-first century; Facebook's "wall" the cave upon which we are carving our collective social history. On it, we make the same marks that we have made for millennia, whether scratched into stone, burned into a crate, embroidered upon a tapestry, painted onto a canvas, printed on a package, or flashed on a screen. They are the marks with which we let the future know not only how we lived, but that we existed.

Facebook has more
than 750 million
active users.

About 70% of Facebook
users are outside the
United States.

The average
user has
130 friends.

Facebook is translated into more than 70 languages.

50% of active users log on to Facebook in any given day.

People spend over 700 billion minutes per month on Facebook.

11

EMERGING MARKETS: BRIC* AND BEYOND

DANIEL LIN *and* **NATASHA SAIPRADIST**

For both multinational companies seeking to grow an existing business as well as entrepreneurs seeking to start a new enterprise, emerging markets have become a focus for expansion efforts during the past twenty years. Not only are these markets sources of cheap labor and inexpensive consumer goods, and destinations of choice for outsourced technical support, but they also drive many companies' economic growth. For brands that are struggling to increase profits in developed economies, emerging markets—with vast numbers of prospective consumers in all areas of trade, including food, clothing, and technology—can be a lifesaver, providing a source of new revenues and growth. But the effort must be handled adroitly. If managed badly, investment in emerging markets can prove to be devastating; damaging the brand equity a company has developed elsewhere. Achieving growth and success in these markets requires companies to be keenly attuned to the differences between cultures and to the complex nature of the markets they are entering. If successful, the relationship can be a boon for local populations, as the businesses provide employment for workers in managerial, production, and distribution roles. This additional financial ballast is especially critical during times of economic crisis.

LEFT:
A promotional button for Coca-Cola featuring the name in Chinese characters

RIGHT:
Vintage ad for Coca-Cola in China

* BRIC is the acronym for Brazil, Russia, India, China

Taking Western Brands to China

One might wonder how today's emerging-markets trade scene is different from that of 200 years ago, when "exotic" Western goods were first imported into China. Consumers in today's emerging economies desire cross-cultural goods now as much as in the past, but their decision-making process and purchasing behaviors are complex and not easy to predict. In many emerging markets, there is a huge difference between brand equity, the asset that has long been held in high value by Western companies, and brand preference, the actual purchasing choices that consumers make in local markets. Consumers might highly admire a certain brand— whether it is Nike or Adidas—but hesitate to buy the company's products. The failure of numerous companies to see and bridge this gap has caused foreign brands to stumble. To avoid that, several savvy Western brands have set aside the mindset of corporate imperialism when entering new markets. Creating their strategy from scratch, these companies have utilized basic concepts such as consumer research, cultural insight, and product development to navigate over the emerging-markets barrier.

Proctor & Gamble, the most successful fast-moving consumer goods (FMCG) brand in the world, entered China as early as 1984. The company's first product in China, the dandruff shampoo Head & Shoulders, was launched in 1988 in Guangzhou, capital city of the province Guangdong. Twelve months later, the company had captured a 15 percent market share in the province.[1] This was a dramatic coup, and it seemed to be effortless. P&G's triumph is all the more intriguing in light of the fact that consumers

P&G's triumph is all the more intriguing in light of the fact that consumers in that area of China only earned an average of 128 yuan each month.

in that area of China earned an average of only 128 yuan each month, yet were willing to buy a 28-yuan shampoo that was priced three times higher than the local brands. P&G's confidence in launching the product came from its reliance upon consumer research the company had been conducting since 1985, which revealed that dandruff was a common problem among Chinese consumers. P&G also entered the market at a time when China's emerging middle class began to care more about the issue of beauty, making the launch of this "luxury" shampoo a daring but reasonable move. In addition, the company, observing how the beauty trend was influencing the lower classes as well, decided to sell small shampoo sachets at the affordable price of 0.5 yuan.[2] The strategy made Head & Shoulders affordable to the masses of rural farmers and widely expanded its product saturation.

P&G's strategy is telling: The company did not simply pour its existing products into the Chinese market, labeling them at a high price in return for a high profit margin; it worked to understand consumers' buying behavior and how those consumers used the products in a unique cultural context.

Coca-Cola has sought to appeal to different markets by rendering its logo in characters from local languages.

Branding for India

Nokia used a similar strategy to succeed in India. Its current 30 percent market share,[3] as well as its reputation as the most trusted brand in India,[4] is due not solely to its early entrance into the Indian market in 1995, but also to the extensive market research the company conducted, especially in rural areas—which allowed for the development of a unique product tailored specifically to Indian consumers. As Nokia was doing research to improve its cell phone for the market, it turned its focus to truck drivers, who constitute a large segment of the country's working class. The company discovered that during long night drives, the truck drivers would get out of their trucks quite often to work or to load up the truck. There are seldom street lamps in many areas of India, so the drivers would carry a flashlight so they could see at nighttime.

This small observation turned out to be a significant insight into the needs of potential consumers. The company designed the Nokia 1100, its first cell phone specifically developed for India, with a built-in flashlight, a nonslippery grip, and a casing that was dust-proof (so phone circuitry would be protected from rough outdoor conditions). These innovations helped make the phone a huge success in the market. Interestingly, this move didn't cast Nokia as a working-class brand. With clever foresight, the brand had cast its net wide, tailoring its retail strategy to four different segments of users: "Live," first-time users; "Connect," entailing products with more advanced functions like GPS and camera; "Achieve," geared to business executives; and "Explore," targeting high-end users who prefer

phones with advanced capabilities. Nokia created diverse products that would fit the user behavior, income level, and lifestyle of different groups.

Success in emerging markets is not as easy as the preceding two examples might make it seem. The eagerness with which companies jump into these markets often comes from their belief that they can take the market by storm, which is almost never the case. Different consumer mindsets, a country's diverse demographic composition, great geographic distances, and government regulations are only a few of the imposing barriers to market entry.

In the 1990s, increased competition led the breakfast and snack foods company Kellogg's to seek opportunities in the developed world. The other markets where the company sold its products were already saturated, so the company entered the Indian market, seeing untapped potential in the country's 1990 population of 950 million citizens, 250 million of which were middle class. Launching the iconic cereal Corn Flakes without much understanding of Indian culture and eating habits, Kellogg's leadership thought they could convert Indian locals to eating breakfast the same way Americans do.[5] Indians, however, traditionally eat something hot—parathas in northern India, or dokla pohe (made of rice and milk) and sambar in south India—as their first meal of the day. In India, the concept of eating cereal for breakfast was nonexistent, as was the idea of starting the day with something cold—and Kellogg's cereals quickly get soggy when complemented with hot milk.

ABOVE:
Bottle caps from drinks available in India

RIGHT:
Coca-Cola bottles with the logo in different languages

in Mandarin, Coca-Cola means "delicious happiness"

Some consumers initially bought Corn Flakes as a novelty, but the product was considered expensive, and ultimately, locals still preferred the traditional options for breakfast. Kellogg's failed to lower the price of its cereals or to conduct market research. Instead, it kept launching a wide range of new products in India, even veering from its core of breakfast cereals to launch a biscuit brand. The company's strategy was to simply be as visible as possible on store shelves as it attempted—vainly—to establish brand awareness. Though Kellogg's is the dominant global brand when it comes to breakfast cereals,[6] the company lacked an understanding of the relationship between culture and cuisine, and it failed to acknowledge the psychology of Indian mothers, who make most of the food purchasing decisions for the country's households; it also underestimated the importance of tradition and culture in India. The company, as a result, failed miserably in the breakfast cereal category in the country.

Coca-Cola has sought to appeal to different markets by rendering its logo in characters from local languages.

Adapting to the Chinese Language

Another challenge to brands from the developed world is competition from homegrown brands that know their audience and are much savvier about local tastes and habits. Google, dominating almost 90 percent of the global search market, still fails in China to surpass Baidu, the country's domestically owned search engine. Like Kellogg's, Google tried to force China to adapt to Western ways—in this case, without thinking about how and why the Chinese conduct online searches; in addition, the company neglected to consider the unique nature of the Chinese language.

Because there are thousands of different characters in the Chinese language, Chinese Internet users prefer not to type when exploring online. Rather, they like to navigate through a portal site, browse around, and then link to something that interests them.[7] A search engine driven by a typed-in query or keyword simply does not function well, nor does it have the quick-linking appeal of portal sites. Chinese users also tend to search the Internet as a means of seeking entertainment, rather than as a way to find information for research or work-related purposes.

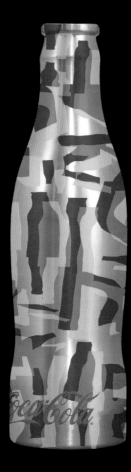

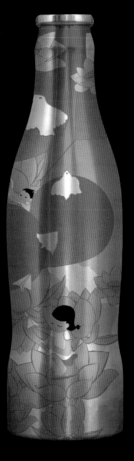

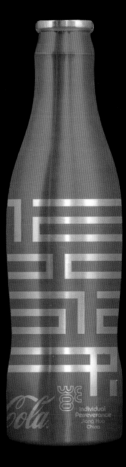

Limited-edition
bottles designed for
the 2008 Summer
Olympics in Beijing,
China

The context is made additionally complicated because the consumption-related behaviors of the Chinese are vastly different from those of people in the West. Traditional advertising does not persuade them as easily, as they rely more on blogs, user-generated sites, and word of mouth to make buying decisions.[8] When searching for products, Chinese web surfers are much less likely to do a search by typing in the name of a brand. Though Google has invested heavily in the Chinese market since 2006, the company still hasn't tried to understand the market's different needs. It has not changed its strategy, and in fact, the Chinese Google home page looks almost exactly the same as the one for the English language searches. In its overconfidence—and strategic immaturity—Google has failed to honor the most basic tenet of business: to know your customers.

As Western brands expand their presence in emerging markets, they are also indirectly creating a cadre of global competitors. More and more companies originating from emerging markets are becoming global brands that have great impact and meaning to consumers in the developed world. This is especially true in the technology sector, where the international labor division of the 1970s, in which different aspects of production were outsourced to facilities in different countries, had long-term benefits for then-emerging countries. In particular, these emerging markets gained both economic capital and industry know-how from the interaction.

HTC, a smartphone company, is a representative case. Founded in 1997, this Taiwanese company initially served as a design-and-manufacture house producing "white label" handheld devices for Western brands—meaning that HTC would create the devices and other companies would package and market them as their own. During the handheld operating system battle between Palm and Microsoft, HTC boldly bet on Windows CE, which lagged far behind Palm OS's 70 percent market share at the time. The decision not only allowed HTC to take advantage of the later market boom of Windows CE, but it also led the company to the position of innovator in the high-end smart-phone market; it entered the sector even earlier than Apple.

HTC foresaw how telecom carriers would dominate cell phone distribution and it collaborated with leading European carriers like BT and O2, providing white-label smart phones for these companies. For almost a decade, HTC settled on a strategy of choosing not to show its logo on such products and thereby gained a huge, if unacknowledged, market share. What the company envisioned, though, was the goal targeted by other companies from emerging markets: ownership of its own brand. In 2009, HTC unveiled "You," its first global campaign, in twenty countries, and announced "Quietly Brilliant" as the slogan representing the company's new positioning.[9] With every smart phone now sold, featuring HTC's logo juxtaposed with that of the cell-phone carrier, HTC's brand awareness is further increased.

Innovating in a technology sector is one way to succeed globally; capitalizing on a unique aspect of local culture to create an international sensation is another. Though this strategy is extremely difficult to bring to fruition, it can yield astonishing results. To wit: Havaianas, the world-famous sandal brand from Brazil, was initially a cheap rubber flip-flop brand manufactured mainly for local farmers. Before the 1990s, it was simply a commodity item that came in one style and one color and had no emotional appeal.

In 1994, Havaianas made a significant shift, rebranding itself as a young, free-spirited, zest-seeking Brazilian brand.[10] The company strategically expanded its product line, injecting more color and style into the sandal designs and creating an appealing advertising campaign promoting the brand's spirit. As the brand became a hit with celebrities and models in Brazil, Havaianas began expanding globally in 2000, marketing its products as high-end items. Evoking the pleasures of the exotic, Brazilian-style beach culture, Havaianas became one of the most successful lifestyle brands to come from an emerging market.

Havaianas's strategy could be termed "culture export," a tack widely used by most Western brands. The business impact of such a strategy—the return on investment—can be quite significant. Yet in the context of cultural impact, there is greater potential in targeting a more universal, generational lifestyle and creating a global community around it.

Innovating in a technology sector is one way to succeed globally; capitalizing on a unique aspect of local culture to create an international sensation is another.

Energy drink from Thailand

Bringing Red Bull to the Masses

Founded in Thailand in 1975,[11] Red Bull has managed to emerge from a small country in Southeast Asia to become a pioneer in the energy-drink category worldwide—it is now sold in more than 150 countries. In Thailand, the brand was named Krating Daeng, which literally translates to "Red Bull."[12] The energy-drink brand initially targeted Thai construction workers and truck drivers, two groups of people whose jobs frequently required them to work night shifts. In 1987, Dietrich Mateschitz, an Austrian entrepreneur, drank a Krating Daeng while in Thailand to cure his jetlag and he fell in love with the product.[13] Masteschitz and Chaleo Yoovidhya, the Thai owner of Krating Daeng, formed an equal partnership to launch the product in the West. The two partners decided to directly translate the name into English and to keep the logo drawn by Yoovidhya, which depicts two opposing bulls charging at each other, against the backdrop of the Sun—an image meant to convey power.

The partners also modified some ingredients and changed the appearance of the package to suit the new market's tastes—the original Krating Daeng is packaged in brown rectangular glass bottles. Relaunched in a carbonated format in 1987 for the Austrian market, Red Bull positioned itself not as a beverage for night-shift workers and truck drivers, but as the energy drink of choice for male teenagers and college students seeking stamina and energy—so they can experience life to its fullest. With the sleeker packaging, Red Bull generates a sexier image, in keeping with the sensibility of young

☑ IMPROVES PERFORMANCE

☑ INCREASES ENDURANCE

☑ INCREASES CONCENTRATION

☑ IMPROVES REACTION SPEED

☐ RESOLVES GENDER ISSUES

Red Bull does everything it says on the can. And nothing it doesn't.

RED BULL GIVES YOU WIIINGS.

17

men. Maintaining this same brand positioning, Red Bull entered Hungary and Slovenia in 1989; it entered the United States in 1997 and the Middle East in 2000.

Red Bull's wide success can be attributed to the company's ability to sharply assess the emotional needs of its new consumers and to the impact of its unique, nontraditional marketing strategy.[14] The Red Bull brand was initially built without much use of traditional mass-marketing techniques. Instead, the company employed buzz marketing tactics and established a close association and sponsorship relationships with extreme alternative sports such as whitewater kayaking, snowboarding, and Formula One racing; the company even made up its own extreme sports, such as Human Powered Flight, in which participants try to take off from the runway of a pier with homemade, human-powered flying machines.[15] By associating itself with these activities, Red Bull aligned itself with the elements of speed, power, and risk, all of which tie in with what the drink provides functionally: mental alertness. With these associations, along with the "Red Bull Gives You Wiiings" slogan,[16] the brand tapped into the archetype of an adventurer/explorer, suggesting that with Red Bull's help, consumers could accomplish more than what they previously thought possible. This message is on point for Western male teenagers and twentysomethings, who like to feel active and energized; these audiences tend to explore the world and learn about it through their own experiences, rather than relying on what their parents or other elders tell them. Whether they're charged with adrenaline and craving more, or in need of energy to pull all-nighters in college, Western teenagers have found a kindred spirit—spirits?—in Red Bull.

Red Bull's success outside of its original local market would not have been possible had it not changed its positioning and image to suit Western consumers. This same positioning would likely flop in Thailand, as young Thai men's behaviors and values are not at all similar to those of American teenagers. Thai children are brought up to be polite; in Thai society, respect for elders is considered highly important. The Red Bull image of danger and pushing the limits would not sell well in Thailand, where, additionally, the extreme-sports community is very small compared with that in the West.

Red Bull's global success may also stem in part from the fact that its makers concealed its real country of origin. The brand's shepherds understood that Westerners may not think highly of Thailand, a country known mostly as a travel destination, a fact that might lead consumers to have negative preconceptions about the drink. Adding to the obscuration, Red Bull states that the drink is "made in Austria." One would have to dig further or know of the original Thai roots to discover its true origin.

It's intriguing to see how important culture is both for Western brands that wish to succeed in emerging markets and for emerging brands that are trying to grow globally. Perhaps this is a mutual lesson that companies from both worlds learned by watching each other's experiences. In some cases, a company's original cultural context can be a significant aid in selling to other countries; in other cases, it can be a burden and an obstacle. To cross the cultural divide and be successful in the emerging market, it is vital that companies fully understand the psychological, sociological, and historical backgrounds of

Red Bull's success outside of its original local market would not have been possible had it not changed its positioning and image to suit Western consumers.

the local population and attempt to uncover and understand the different consumer mindsets, behaviors, and needs. Overly confident Western companies that fail to do market research and are blinded by potential sales figures will end up foundering. Only brands that are in sync with the norms and needs of the local people in these complex and new markets stand a chance.

When comparing the trajectory of brands from the two worlds, it's surprising to see how, in thirty years, emerging brands have sometimes achieved the infrastructure, revenues, and distribution that Western brands took almost 100 years to evolve. This compressed gestational stage may be due to the fact that emerging brands often harbor multiple capabilities under one roof: from R&D and design-and-manufacture to marketing, selling, and servicing. This is rarely seen in Western businesses nowadays, where a certain amount of outsourcing is common practice, particularly in technology. How these new types of conglomerates compete, both domestically and globally, with the legacy Western brands could be the next trend worth watching.

Red Bull bottle cap

PART TWO /
SUSTAINING BRANDS

12

RIDE ME

THE EVOLUTION OF BRANDING FOR TRANSPORTATION

ROCHELLE FAINSTEIN

In the modern era, numerous transportation brands offer to ferry us from location A to location B. If we want to travel by air on a low-cost carrier, we can choose from JetBlue, Southwest, or Frontier Airlines. Car brands range from Mercedes-Benz to Hyundai, Honda, Toyota, and Tesla. Motorcycles run the gamut, too: Harley-Davidson, BMW, and Ducati promise us exhilaration through a particular lens of pop culture and mechanical engineering. If we want to take a weekend jaunt from New York to Boston, let's say, we can opt for BoltBus, Peter Pan, or Fung Wah. Each brand, of course, offers its own particular experience and a unique strategy of appealing to our individual sensibilities. JetBlue has all those televisions, a reputation for efficiency, unique snacks, and a warm and fuzzy hospitality. Harley-Davidson offers entrée into an outsider culture. BoltBus has WiFi and brand-spanking new buses, while Fung Wah is unbelievably cheap. Toyota developed a reputation for environmental innovation until its production debacle of 2010 tarnished the company. Ford has gone from brink-of-bankruptcy irrelevance to hip, contemporary, and eco-advocate with its Fusion.[1]

Traveling by Rail

In the early history of the United States, the options for transportation were nowhere near as multifarious. Visitors and emigrants made the transatlantic journey to the country on ships. In 1818, the Black Ball Line established its "brand differentiation" from other transatlantic service when it introduced regular times for departure from the ports of Liverpool and New York. The line even had a brand mark—a "black ball" painted on one of its front sails. The company's success led to the ascension of the port of New York above other ports like Boston and Philadelphia, and it also inspired the competition and imitators. In later years—before trademark protection had been introduced—another shipping line copied the brand mark.

Once in the United States, travelers relied on wagon, carriage, canal, riverboat, and horses for journeys of varying lengths. The Baltimore and Ohio Railroad, which debuted in 1830, offered the first passenger train service with a train that was initially pulled along tracks by horses. Steam locomotion debuted later that same year, and the spread of railroads improved transportation for goods as well as passengers alike. As the railways evolved and enterprising inventers saw opportunities for innovation, more distinctions emerged. George Pullman established the first recognizable brand of train car; his Pullman car offered travelers comfortable sleeping berths for long journeys,

Photo: ChipPix / Shutterstock.com

and Pullman built on that brand in subsequent years, introducing innovations and refinements such as a dining car in 1868.

Auto Brands Step Up

Railroads ruled the American landscape until the 1920s, but their dominance ended as the automobile and the various forms of "internal combustion transport" became more widely adopted. Cars offered an autonomy that was unparalleled by previous modes of transportation, giving city dwellers a direct route to workplaces, a means of escape, and a new form of "touring" vacation. The emerging car brands—among them, Ford, Oldsmobile, Cadillac, Studebaker, and Fiat—sought to emphasize how their cars offered comfort, convenience, and quality. Henry Ford built his brand on the concept of "a motor car for the great multitude." Chevrolet appealed with "Quality at Low Cost," while the carmaker Willys-Overland made a more luxurious pitch with "A motorcar beautifully *engineered*, beautifully *built*—and stylish as the *Rue de la Paix.*"

Some companies advertised in women's magazines and tried to appeal to women's tastes by making cars available in smaller sizes and different colors. As the proliferation of brands bred competition, each company sought to emphasize its unique appeal and brand. In the arena of high-end cars, Cadillac has consistently positioned itself as a brand representing the luxury car of choice. It now has one of the longest histories in the automobile category—a testament to the efficacy of its positioning.

As car companies developed their capacity to produce cars—and to customize them according to aesthetic tastes, amenities, and performance—they increasingly sought to tap into niche audiences. Through this increasing specialization, different brands, and then subbrands, defined themselves more distinctly. Studebaker hired famed industrial designer Raymond Loewy to create cars for the company. The Chevrolet Corvette, introduced in 1953, and the Ford Mustang, which debuted in 1964, offered an unparalleled sports car experience and a design fetish alike, and the differentiation offered by driving experience and car design has continued to be a persistent theme in car brands. Recognizing the potential of these new subbrands, automobile company executives, beginning in the 1950s, decided on the name and positioning for the cars with a much greater degree of self-conscious deliberation than they had in past decades.

This paralleled a shift in which consumers similarly invested their decisions with greater significance. A car became a means of self-expression and self-actualization. The choice between a Cadillac and a Volkswagen was a statement about one's view of oneself and the world.

ABOVE:
Vintage photo of mechanics and employees in an auto repair shop

RIGHT:
Industrial design at its finest: A Ford V8 (top) and a Mercedes-Benz with Thai license plates (bottom).

Photo: Richard Thornton / Shutterstock.com

Photo: magicinfoto / Shutterstock.com

A car became a means of self-expression and self-actualization. The choice between a Cadillac and a Volkswagen was a statement about one's view of oneself and the world.

The Beetle defined the Volkswagen brand as an iconoclast.

Photo: Margo Harrison / Shutterstock.com

Classic automobile
print advertising from
the 1950s and 1960s

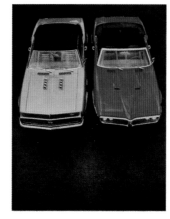

Airlines Emerge

In the same era that automobiles were becoming more widespread, the aviation industry was ascending. By 1928, with the first flight of Boeing's twelve-passenger transport plane, the age of air travel had begun in earnest, allowing passengers to quickly travel distances great and small.[2] The first national and international airlines began to crop up as early as the 1920s, differentiating themselves even then by experience and design. Airline advertising, from brands such as Martin and American Airways, showed how planes offered the sturdiness of war bombers outfitted with comfortable seats, soft lighting, soundproofed interiors, and air-conditioned comfort.[3] Airlines conveyed their brand sensibilities through design-defining elements including brand marks and the outfits worn by pilots and flight attendants. Over time, different airlines introduced innovations as part of their brand appeal: Pan American spurred the development of jet planes, which were able to travel distances in half the time of propeller planes. In the 1970s, American Airlines debuted discounted "Super Saver" fares and, in the '80s, a frequent-flyer plan that gave travelers incentives for brand loyalty.

Nowadays, travelers make their decisions based on price point and brand experience. Low-cost carriers offer no-frills service at sometimes extraordinary discounts from fares on other more traditional airlines. The barebones experience is part of the charm for some travelers, or the discomfort, for others. With offerings like unlimited snacks, more comfortable seats, in-flight WiFi, and on-demand television services, newer brands like JetBlue and Virgin America have sought to establish themselves as much more

nimble, hip, and accommodating than their stodgy predecessors—more amply capable of giving travelers an entertaining, comfortable, and enjoyable experience. These new airline brands have changed the rules and expectations of air travel. Other airlines offer elaborate comfort at a much higher price point.

Another essential brand touchpoint of the new millennium has less to do with individual enjoyment and more to do with collective responsibility. Oil depletion and environmental destruction have become major issues, and this has changed the way we define ourselves as human beings, not to mention as travelers. The branding messages of transportation are changing as a result. Certain airlines and travel websites offer carbon offsets while booking your flight. In the car category, a whole new era of branding began in earnest with the introduction of the Toyota Prius and has continued with subbrands like Nissan Leaf, Chevy Volt, and Ford Focus. Certain

A propeller plane for passenger air travel

high-profile celebrities are going electric, and everyday drivers are looking for a car that is both economical and environmentally responsible. It seems increasingly likely that social cachet will come from adhering to a more sustainable manner of traveling, creating opportunities for new brand touchpoints.

What emerging or unheard-of brands will capture the public imagination in the future? As we head into the later years of the two thousand teens, transportation brands are continually evolving in parallel with shifts in economic realities and cultural predilections. Pan Am has come and gone, as has Saturn, once heralded as an innovator and now a historical footnote. United is now United Continental. Once upon a time, there was only one brand of passenger train travel in the United States, which then proliferated to many and subsequently reduced to one. We are now on the cusp of a new era of emerging transportation brands that are seeking to capture the public imagination. The

electric motorcycle manufacturers Mission Motors, Zero Motorcycles, and Brammo are striving to gain converts and brand enthusiasts. And there are other, new frontiers of transportation: The Virgin Galactic brand may seem like a storybook, farcical lark in 2012, but it might one day be a commonplace brand among a constellation of others. What amenities and brand experiences would Final Frontier Air or JetBlue use to entice intergalactic travelers? Those iconic blue chips might need to be redesigned for zero-gravity edibility.

Extra hands assure extra luxuries
on DELTA *Royal Service Flights*

Not two, but three alert stewardesses assure you of every attention in the brief span of a Delta Royal Service Flight. So linger over your luncheon or dinner with its complimentary champagne and choice of entrée (*tenderloin steak to order, Rock Cornish hen, or seafood on appropriate days*). There's also music by Muzak, fast baggage handling and beverage service for the discerning passengers who specify these luxurious flights.

These flights serve:
NEW YORK · WASHINGTON · ATLANTA · HOUSTON · CHICAGO
MIAMI · NEW ORLEANS · DALLAS · PHILADELPHIA
BALTIMORE · MEMPHIS · DETROIT

Delta's DC-8 Jetliners are on their way!

Key Exports

Who would you say is leading the Export race ? Textiles ? Motors ?
Heavy Industry? Light? B.O.A.C. has at least shown plenty of pace
n the early stages. Our exports are the men who bring back export
ders; and never before have orders so large come back from so
so fast! Among the 8,900 we have carried, the record is held by
Miles Thomas, Vice-Chairman of the Nuffield Group. 14,000
in ten days, and back with £1,200,000 of business. But all did
sly. Faced with the job of wiping off six years' arrears of
calls, they proved to have everything it takes—except a

B·O·A·C

SPEEDBIRD ROUTES
ACROSS THE

Between :
CANADA · U.S.A. · MIDDLE
SOUTH, EAST AND WEST AFR
INDIA · FAR EAST

13

CHOOSE ME

THE EVOLUTION OF BRANDING RETAIL ENVIRONMENTS

ROCHELLE FAINSTEIN

Beginning with the Industrial Revolution, a new consumer value surfaced: self-indulgence. Retail brands and marketers raced to encourage this new value in consumers, responding with more styles of clothing, more variety at the local grocers, as well as nonessential items like children's toys and entertainment products for adults, too. Consumers were now inundated with choice and with it, the recognition of the power of their spending dollars. With the boom of new products and competing brands, came many more "rules" to follow. Increasingly, retail shopping developed into a game—some might say "a war"—of competitive pricing.

In-Store Experience

One of the earliest examples of fixed pricing in the United States came with the 1846 opening of A.T. Stewart, the country's first department store. Located in lower Manhattan, the store offered European retail merchandise and the first set prices on many dry goods—in the past, consumers

could haggle with shop proprietors about prices. But while setting the standard for all future retail stores with its fixed prices, A. T. Stewart also offered an experience of shopping unlike any other.

The store embodied sheer immensity, as shoppers made their way from the clothing department to shoes to housewares within the largest retail space in the city. It was an experience of luxury, a treat, to be in the store's sublime setting of expensive marble, Italian architecture, and light streaming light from French plate glass windows. Women were especially drawn to the in-store fashion shows, and soon enough, a number of imitation stores sprang up on the same strip of Broadway, all of them becoming popular among the city's fashionable elite.

Choose Me: The Evolution of Branding Retail Environments

Globally, the department store category proliferated with store likes Le Bon Marché in France and Bainbridge in England, providing inspiration for retail monoliths that had serious staying power, like the now world-famous Macy's, which has roots going back to 1858.

The true revolution in retail shopping, however, did not arrive until 1916, when Clarence Saunders introduced the marvelously new concept of self-service shopping in his grocery store, Piggly Wiggly. Before Piggly Wiggly arrived on the scene, shoppers would generally present their orders to store clerks, who would gather the goods. Yet, Piggly Wiggly allowed shoppers to save time by serving themselves, and in turn, the store made more sales. This new method introduced the concept of convenience to grocery store shopping, an attribute that would dominate the retail landscape ever after.

Catalog Sales

In 1859, The Great American Tea Company, the first mail-order tea house, sprang up, advertising primarily in religious dailies and delivering items to tea enthusiasts by horse-drawn cart. By 1869, with the expansion of the railroads westward, the company was renamed the Great Atlantic & Pacific Tea Company and can be seen as the earliest ancestor of our modern-day catalog companies. The option to order by catalog was one among many evolutions of convenience that included door-to-door sales, in-home demonstrations, Tupperware parties, infomercials, and direct-response TV ads—not to mention web shopping—allowing consumers to shop on their own and from their homes.

OPPOSITE:
The modern shopping mall experience is marked by airy architecture complemented by spectacular backdrops and set pieces.

LEFT:
Sears catalog, 1962

The Great Atlantic & Pacific Tea Company pioneered several important innovations that allowed it—known as A&P—to trail-blaze the retail landscape and provide a lasting legacy. After extending operations to the West Coast, the company gave birth to the first national supermarket chain and, in 1880, the brand introduced the first private label product, baking powder. Many more store-branded goods would follow. A&P also ushered in the first customer loyalty program with store savings coupons. The debut contributed to the most exciting and simultaneously, the most detrimental, innovation of the retail market: the sale.

Listen to Your Customers

While initially an exciting concept, sales have long since lost their luster. In recent years, many brick-and-mortar retail stores have felt the pinch of their own extreme discounting and put themselves out of business. Yet some store brands that compete on price, like the behemoth Walmart, continue to have legs, while others have faded from existence. The success of retail brands of the twenty-first

Choose Me: The Evolution of Branding Retail Environments

century relies heavily on their integration into the digital landscape, namely through an online presence, and their ability to stay relevant.

The reason why certain retail chain stores such as Walmart may survive where others fail is their willingness to listen and evolve with the consumer. Walmart, which was founded in 1962 as the premier discounter in the United States, with a promise of "Always Low Prices," experienced rapid growth over four decades. In 2010, Walmart invested in a complete rebranding campaign, creating consistency across its in-store and web, advertisements, and collateral marketing materials. The branding agency Lippincott also developed a new slogan for the business to extend its appeal to a wider audience without alienating existing customers.

The new tagline of "Save Money. Live Better," enabled Walmart to speak to a new group that did not associate themselves with discount shopping, but still enjoyed saving money. Walmart also smartly invested in its digital presence by creating a website that was much simpler and more elegant in terms of design at a time when retail shopping on Internet-enabled devices had begun to surge. By understanding how to position itself to appeal to a wider customer base and also utilizing the latest channels for brand communication, Walmart remains at the helm of modern retail.

The Online Retail Experience

Many recent brands have found themselves a new retail space online, the technology for which emerged in the early '80s. In 1981, Michael Aldrich developed the first business-to-business online

purchasing system for the travel brand Thomson Holidays. Online shopping services made shopping far more efficient, cutting out the need for a retailer—or travel time.

One of the largest ventures into online retailing was Amazon.com. Founded in 1995, Amazon offered an extensive collection of books and made them much easier to purchase. After its launch, the company nearly went out of business and did not show a profit until 2003, reflecting the slow

The reason why certain retail chain stores such as Walmart may survive where others fail is their willingness to listen and evolve with the consumer.

adoption of online shopping. From its base of books, Amazon has expanded into music, video, electronics, and more, and improved its user experience so much that it has become one of the most successful ecommerce sites to date. When regular customers log on to the site, intuitive technology "recommends" products based on previous purchases. Easy navigation, speedy shipping, partnerships with select vendors, and a welcoming feedback forum all combine to provide a seamless retail experience that is much richer than those we might have in-store. Even more significantly, Amazon is one of the original retail brands to exclusively live online.

The Walmart shopping experience throughout the world is defined by low prices and large stores.

The successful launch of Amazon opened doors for other etailers, such as the auction site, eBay, as well as the opportunity for brick-and-mortar retailers to move into the Internet retail space.

Social Media Influences Buyer Behavior

Today the Internet retail space continues to be shaped by new technologies and trends, most noticeably through social media and mobile Web access. Social media has fostered a conversation between consumer and retailer over the interface of the Web. Where previously shoppers struggled to determine which online stores were safe to buy from and where to click for customer service, now they can get tips from friends and online reviewers and feel more comfortable shopping online. Additionally, consumers can ask questions, provide feedback, and send each other recommendations over a number of social media forums.

Some of the most vibrant subsets of social media are user reviews and product category blogs, where consumers search for information before they make their purchases—both online and off. Brands that participate in these conversations, by viewing and responding, or by building their own feedback forums, are able to engage consumers, and in some cases, gain long-term loyalty.

Online shopping seems to have become a permanent fixture in the way we purchase products and has naturally extended to Internet-enabled mobile devices. During 2010 and 2011, mobile-centric technology, marketing, and websites

have experienced a boom and brands are scrambling to catch up. Half of smart phone users make purchases with their phones, and brands like Virgin America, Converse, and Lexus are investing heavily into their digital marketing and presence. Here, we even see Walmart resurface with the company's new division @WalmartLabs, which will support mobile and social strategy. But as screens get smaller, how will logos and other visual representations of the brand be affected? On the consumer side, other questions remain unanswered, such as issues concerning privacy. Will brands find mutually agreeable ways to engage consumers on their iPhones and Androids?

In the midst of all these technological and seemingly impersonal methods of shopping, there continue to emerge a number of organic and experiential retail channels and brands.

Pop-up stores began springing up in 2004 as a low-cost alternative for new and established brands to generate excitement about their products. Brands would find a storefront or a streetscape to occupy for a limited time—from a day to longer periods—and create buzz around the limited opportunity to purchase limited-edition goods. This type of store model was a very effective and low-cost method to get consumers offline, out of their homes, and in personal contact with brands. In an apparent contradiction, these same pop-ups are now helping brands drive traffic to their websites, but they are still a great way to raise brand awareness, even for national chains that want to push a trend. Target is a prime example of an established company that has used the strategy; the retailer has set up pop-up stores to promote the Rodarte clothing line. Other brands like Nike and J. C. Penney have also popped up in

The retail environment of modern shopping malls features multi-level atriums that provide exposure for stores while allowing consumers to people-watch.

major cities. By providing goods that are unattainable elsewhere, pop-ups have brought the thrill back to shopping.

As a struggling economy has shifted consumer spending habits, there has been a shift in how stores pitch to consumers. Clearly, many households don't have the discretionary income that they once did. Similarly, the social experience of going out and shopping is evolving. Perhaps this can explain the sudden upsurge of farmers' markets and flea markets, which encourage attendees to buy local goods and spend a day surrounded by a de facto community, often in open-air environs with snacks and entertainment. Are markets back to stay, or are they simply the flipside to our plugged-in options? If we look to New York as a cultural epicenter that reflects significant trends, the flea market success story at the hip Brooklyn Flea seems to suggest the trend has inertia. This revival of market-style retail is closing the loop on a long cycle of retail innovation by returning us to our roots; these counterpoints to "convenience" are reignited our sense of adventure.

14

USE ME

THE EVOLUTION OF BRANDING APPLIANCES

TIMOTHY A. HARMS

The novelty and allure of domestic appliances in the booming postwar years can be seen in the August 1948 issue of *House & Garden* magazine, whose cover rather prosaically featured little more than the interior drying rack of a Hotpoint dishwasher. The accompanying feature story, "The Vanishing American," outlined the decline of what had been an essential fixture of every upper to upper-middle class home for centuries: the domestic servant. Replaced by a seemingly endless parade of chromed and enameled appliances for cooking, cleaning, and comfort, the maid

Sergej Razvodovskij/Shutterstock.com

Reddogs/Shutterstock.com

House & Garden

SERVANTLESS LIVIN
HOUSES AND PLAN
U.S.A. TRAVE

Of the hundreds of thousands of owners

NOT ONE HAS PAID A CENT FOR SERVICE

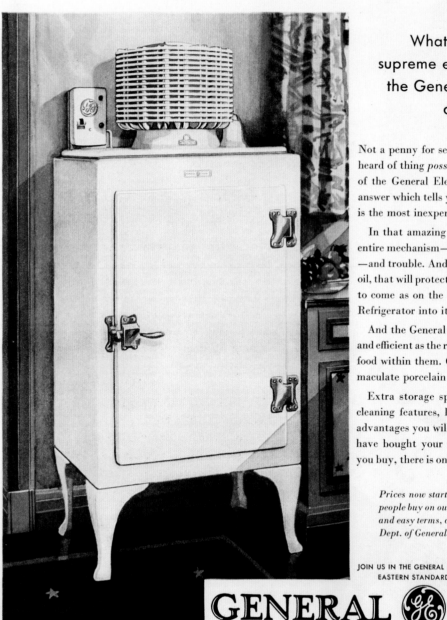

What greater proof of the supreme efficiency and economy of the General Electric Refrigerator could be asked?

Not a penny for service! What is it that makes such an unheard of thing *possible?* Look at that small round unit on top of the General Electric cabinet. Your answer is there—the answer which tells you why the General Electric Refrigerator is the most inexpensive refrigerator you can own.

In that amazing unit on top is housed your refrigerator's entire mechanism—sealed forever against dirt, rust, moisture—and trouble. And sealed up with it is a *permanent* supply of oil, that will protect the mechanism as thoroughly in the years to come as on the day you first plug your General Electric Refrigerator into its socket.

And the General Electric cabinets you will find as durable and efficient as the remarkable mechanism that preserves your food within them. Glistening white inside and out, with immaculate porcelain lining, they are *all-steel*—every inch.

Extra storage space, accessible freezing regulator, easy-cleaning features, low running cost, quiet operation—these advantages you will often think of and appreciate, *after* you have bought your refrigerator. If you think of them *before* you buy, there is only one refrigerator you will even consider!

Prices now start as low as $205 at the factory—and most people buy on our easy time payment plan. For our catalog and easy terms, address section J-4, Electric Refrigeration Dept. of General Electric Co., Hanna Bldg., Cleveland, O.

JOIN US IN THE GENERAL ELECTRIC HOUR, BROADCAST EVERY SATURDAY AT 9 P. M., EASTERN STANDARD TIME, OVER A NATION-WIDE N. B. C. NETWORK

GENERAL ⓖⓔ ELECTRIC
ALL-STEEL REFRIGERATOR

had become a relic of a bygone era, and by the latter half of the twentieth century, she had disappeared from all but the wealthiest of households.

This transformation in American domesticity shifted the center of the home away from parlors and dining rooms. Throughout the Victorian era, kitchens had been seen as primarily off limits; a strictly functional space relegated to the basement or back of the house, to keep all practical and labor-related activity away from guests and visitors.

But with the introduction of electricity and cooking gas—and all the gadgets that utilize them—people started seeing the kitchen as the mechanical heart of the home rather than the origin of noise, grease, and soot. The "electronic servants" that replaced human labor were totems that symbolized the rising affluence of the boomer generation. The appliances transformed the kitchen into a consumer showpiece for the new American lifestyle. Walls that separated the kitchen were removed, breakfast nooks added, and gleaming Formica countertops installed to provide more space for all the time-saving appliances eagerly purchased by new homeowners. The kitchen began to look less like a place of toil and drudgery and more like a modern laboratory.

The Iceman's Demise

Few appliances have had as much an impact on the quality, variety, and preservation of our food than the modern refrigerator. Prior to mechanical refrigeration, horse-drawn wagons delivered ice to customers and the visits of the iceman were as common as those of the postman. Zinc-lined iceboxes held ice blocks in a top cabinet, allowing

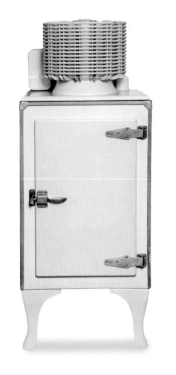

the cold air to circulate down to the lower food cabinet—a process that was only effective with the frequent replacement of ice. Temperature consistency was impossible. Drip trays needed emptying often. With the invention of the refrigerator, however, the ice industry withered and our relationship to fresh food was forever changed by the availability of unlimited cold air.

A home refrigerator had been available from General Electric as early as 1911, but it remained little more than a modern marvel for many years after. By the 1920s, brands like Kelvinator and Frigidaire were beginning to mass-produce refrigerators, but their high price tag kept them out of most American kitchens. The least expensive model cost an exorbitant $300 at a time when a Model T could be had for the same money. In 1927, General Electric decided to lease its Monitor Top refrigerator through utility companies for an extra monthly fee; with that increased accessibility, the refrigerator started to become as affordable as it was indispensable.

Resembling the ironclad gun turret atop the Civil War–era USS *Monitor* warship, the GE Monitor Top housed its namesake cooling mechanism in a cylinder at the top of the contraption. Since heat rises, it made the most sense to keep the mechanical equipment "On top—where it belongs," as one print ad touted. Another ad in the May 1932 issue of *The Saturday Evening Post* featured the Monitor Top prominently as it told readers to "Look to the Mechanism."

Part of the success of the Monitor Top can be attributed to the unorthodox marketing techniques used to promote it. These included such novelties as a neon billboard that could be read from more than 3 miles (4.8 km) away, a touring railroad exhibition, and a series of animated window displays. One display featured an animated play inside the refrigerator cabinet, while another consisted of a "wearied housewife in an old-fashioned kitchen without electrical conveniences." GE's marketing strategies proved so successful that by 1931 more than 1 million Monitor Tops had been produced.

The Greatest Discovery Since Fire

Like many modern inventions, the microwave oven has its origins rooted in wartime research and manufacturing. Magnetrons, the high-powered vacuum tubes that emit enough electromagnetic radiation to warm a cup of coffee in thirty seconds, are also one of the key components in radar technology—which was used extensively in World War II submarines.

In 1945, Percy Spencer, an engineer at the military subcontractor Raytheon, noticed that the chocolate bar in his pocket melted when he stood near a magnetron. Intrigued, he decided to run more experiments with different food items. An egg exploded, popcorn kernels popped; a fabulously fast way of cooking was born.

Raytheon's main expertise was in developing high-powered tools for the military, a fact that was evident with their first iteration of a production microwave oven in 1947. Weighing almost 700 pounds (318 kg), it stood at 5 feet (12.7 cm) tall and sold for more than $2,000. It also needed an electrician to install a dedicated 220-volt line; a plumber was required to install a water line to cool the vacuum tube. Even when marketed to restaurants and ocean liners, the microwave oven clearly wasn't ready for show time.

The concept for a more consumer-friendly version was revived under the name Radarange in 1953, but still failed to catch on for at least a decade longer. In the mid-1960s, just as Raytheon was attempting to acquire refrigerator manufacturer, Amana, the company hired an industrial design

Original Dreft packaging

You can do much more with an
Amana® Touchmatic™
Radarange®
MICROWAVE OVEN

Model RR-9

Because it does much more for you

**The first microwave with a memory . . .
It's like having a computer in your kitchen!**
The Amana Touchmatic Radarange gets food from the freezer to the table as simple as 1-2-3. Because its computer "remembers" and performs your cooking program in sequence.
1. It "remembers" how long to defrost.
2. It "remembers" exactly how long to cook—with split-second accuracy.
3. It "remembers" to shut off and to call you for dinner with a "beep".
At the same instant, it even "remembers" and displays the time of day—in lights.

Amana Cookmatic Power Shift™ . . . Puts You In Full Control Of Everything You Cook.

COOKMATIC WARM SIM LOW MED ROAST HIGH

With Amana Cookmatic Power Shift . . . you can instantly change fast boiling to a simmer . . . change a simmer to a roast. Just slide the shift lever to a lower or higher speed. Adjust while you're cooking to achieve special effects desired in slow-cooked recipes, or to pamper delicate items like cheeses, milk and eggs so they turn out perfect. Keeps foods warm without overcooking.

Amana Features . . . Quality And Convenience
675 Watts of Power cooks almost everything in one-fourth the usual time. **Stainless Steel Interior** won't rust or corrode. Reflects more cooking power for faster, more efficient cooking. **Chrome-plated Zinc Diecast Pull-down Door** permits easy entry from either side. **See-through Window** and **interior light** lets you see what's cooking. **Removable Glass Oven Tray**—catches spills. Dishwasher proof. Operates on ordinary, 115-volt household current. **Saves Energy**—uses 50% to 75% less energy than a conventional electric range. See a demonstration of the remarkable Amana Touchmatic Radarange at your Amana Retailer or write Ann MacGregor, Dept. 649, Amana, Iowa 52204.

If it doesn't say *Amana®* -it's not a *Radarange®*
MICROWAVE OVEN

BACKED BY A CENTURY-OLD TRADITION OF FINE CRAFTSMANSHIP.
Amana Refrigeration, Inc., Amana, Iowa 52204

A Raytheon Company

Print ad for an Amana Radarange microwave oven, 1977

Like many modern inventions, the microwave oven has its origins rooted in wartime research and manufacturing.

firm to make the device more appealing to housewives, using more elegant materials and designing knobs to fit a woman's hand. New technology from Japanese manufacturers also made components cheaper and smaller.

To effectively market the new device, an all-women sales team was assembled under the direction of Air Force veteran JoAnne Anderson. She instructed her team on how to demystify the technology for skeptical audiences, explaining how microwaves agitate water molecules to create friction and heat. Cakes were to be avoided, but baked potatoes were a must in any demonstration. Women's groups and church organizations were invited to see the demonstrations and marvel at the "space-age wonder." Print ads touted the Amana Radarange as "The Greatest Discovery Since Fire."

15

PRETTY ON THE OUTSIDE

THE EVOLUTION OF BRANDING BEAUTY

KATHRYN SPITZBERG

The idea that beauty is subjective is not new. Yet, we all yearn to be beautiful, so we seem continually subject to the latest appeal for that ideal—makeup, hair coloring, perfume, skin conditioner, eyeliner—that will allow us to attain perfection. Each of these products is part of an aesthetic DNA that, when assembled in the right combination, will achieve the desired effect: gorgeous.

Throughout the history of innovation in beauty, brands have sought to give women the power to make themselves beautiful. These beauty pioneers understood that beauty is timeless and yet it can change. By carefully navigating this contradiction, they have both succeeded in building brands and continually redefined what is beautiful.

Max Factor Makes Up Makeup
(Late 1800s–Early 1900s)

Cosmetics use is nothing new to our society, considering the widespread use of cosmetics as early as in ancient Egypt. However, it was the advent of photography and the birth of film in the late 1800s that had a tremendous impact on the mass market of cosmetics. With the birth of photography and film, beauty was no longer just a moment captured in a passing gaze, but an image captured in a more permanent medium for many eyes to see. In 1914, Max Factor, a Russian immigrant and wig maker, began building his cosmetics empire when he invented a "flexible greasepaint" to be used for film, and which gave film stars a more natural look on-screen and wouldn't crack under the hot studio lights.[1]

Factor is credited with inventing the term *makeup* and starlets of the time relied on Factor to help them achieve signature looks. He worked on some of the most iconic faces of the time, shaping the features of beauties such as Judy Garland, Joan Crawford, Bette Davis, and Jean Harlow. Factor not only made these women appear flawless, he also built lasting relationships with each so that as his cosmetics trickled down from the screen into mass retail, his beautiful starlets voluntarily appeared in full-color magazine ads to promote his products. Factor understood the power of aspiration, making flawless beauty on the big screen attainable for every woman. Through his cosmetics and the use of celebrity endorsements, Max Factor strategically molded and shaped the face of beauty for American woman.

Max Factor with Hollywood starlets, 1937

BELOW:
Vintage packaging for
Max Factor

OPPOSITE:
A 1930s advertise-
ment for Max Factor
cosmetics

Chanel's Serendipitous Suntan
(1920s)

Not every symbol of beauty is as calculated to perfection as Max Factor's cosmetics line. Some icons and influences just happen naturally. With the birth of Hollywood and a new awareness of celebrity, all eyes were focused on the who's who. During the roaring twenties, attitudes began to shift, freeing women from the confines of clothing, especially at the beach. Having spent a little too much time in the sun, French designer Coco Chanel was photographed with a golden tan after a Mediterranean cruise to Cannes aboard the Duke of Westminster's yacht. Knowing her iconic status, she embraced her bronzed body, commenting, "The 1929 girl must be tanned and a golden tan is the index of chic!"[2] Though her tan may have very well been a mistake, her confidence and ownership of her new glow began America's love affair with a sun-kissed look. It wasn't long before Hollywood starlets and fashion models showed off their golden tans and the masses followed suit, trying to capture some of the glamour of their favorite stars.

The Allure of Lashes and a Vulnerable Public
(1930s)

At the time a suntan was seen as having true health benefits, however, not every beauty product introduced to the public had the public's best interests at heart. In 1933, Paramount released a newsreel about the proposed changes to the 1906 Food and Drug Act that included footage describing how several women had suffered corneal damage and blindness from using an "eyelash beautifier."[3]

Though the actual product was called Lash-Lure, the newsreel failed to mention this product name, causing market-wide consumer skepticism and the sale of all eyelash products plummeted. Especially concerned was industry leader Maybelline, which used the phrase "eyelash beautifier" liberally in its advertising. In a letter to *Time* magazine, Tom Lyle Williams, the founder of Maybelline, wrote, "we have suffered untold damage to our old established business by the ambiguous publicity given out" during the newsreel and "how utterly damaging this was to us, inasmuch as the phrase 'eyelash beautifier' is practically synonymous with our trade name Maybelline, due to our product being the most extensively advertised mascara on the market for the past 16 years."[4] From a

Coco Chanel in Paris, 1935

branding standpoint, the Lash-Lure scandal was a wake-up call to Maybelline to differentiate its products from its competitors' products, and in 1934, Williams replaced "eyelash beautifier" with "mascara" in all Maybelline advertising. In 1938, Congress passed the Federal Food Drug and Cosmetic Act to better regulate the growth of the cosmetics industry and protect the general public from letting their desire for beauty override their general well being.

Revlon Paints on Patriotism
(1940s)

The idea of government as the protector of public interest was especially believable at the time the Federal Food Drug and Cosmetic Act was established because America had just entered World War II. Consumers were focused on doing what they could to support the war effort, and savvy brands jumped on the flag-waving bandwagon. Revlon, a well-known producer of nail enamel, replaced company expansion with "patriotic activities, producing first-aid kits, dye markers for the navy, and hand grenades for the army."[5] Though Revlon's war efforts were admirable, the company still capitalized on American patriotism, focusing its efforts on a new product that had become a symbol of alliance: red lipstick. Wearing red lipstick became a way for women to do their part, maintaining beauty and morale in the face of adversity, and lipstick became "an essential nonessential."[6] Female recruits were told their lipstick and nail polish should match the scarlet hat cord of their uniform.[7] Since Revlon already had a firm hold on nail enamel, lipstick was the next logical step. In a brilliant campaign that leveraged the idea of patriotism through detailed beauty, in 1940

Revlon began introducing seasonal, coordinated colors of lipstick and nail polish with enticing names like Fatal Apple and Kissing Pink. These alluring names, combined with full-color ads and an advertising campaign showing "matching lips and fingertips," enabled Revlon to double sales from 1930 to 1940.[8] By the end of the war, Revlon was the number two cosmetics producer in the United States.[9] Staying in tune with wartime enabled Revlon to simultaneously empower its consumers and boost the brand and business.

Color at Home with Clairol
(1950s)

Although Marilyn Monroe was born with reddish hair, she is most known for the bleached blonde curls that have made her an icon. A starstruck public sought to keep up with the hairstyles of their favorite celebrities; however, there was still some stigma around coloring hair, which was viewed as low-class, immodest, and daring.[10] One brand, Clairol, helped break this stigma by bringing Hollywood color into every woman's home. By developing the first home hair-coloring kits and creating a variety of colors to choose from, Clairol enabled women to color their hair privately at more affordable prices than going to a salon. They also didn't have to face the public stigma of sitting in a salon and potentially being seen by nosy neighbors. Along with a new line of home coloring products, Clairol launched ad campaigns that were designed to make hair coloring more socially acceptable and mainstream. Featuring mothers and daughters with similarly colored hair, Clairol demonstrated that respectable, married women colored their hair. From 1956 to 1962,

Sheer Genius
...the beautiful difference!

RED ON RED LIPSTICK BY MAX FACTOR

© 1961, MAX FACTOR & CO

Women everywhere are looking lovelier with
Sheer Genius®—wondrous new make-up in a tube!

MOST DRAMATIC CHANGE IN MAKE-UP in 24 years! Soft liquid drops in a tube! Sheer Genius is the first *complete* make-up, combining the lustre of liquid and the softness of powder for a flattering, delicate finish. Never shiny, never powdery—won't streak or fade. Sheer Genius keeps you always looking fresh...and lovely!

IT FEELS SO GOOD TO BE BEAUTIFUL with Sheer Genius. Your skin feels fresh, young, floating on air. Ever so lightly, Sheer Genius pampers your skin, keeps it always feeling fresh and natural. Discover for yourself the beautiful difference of Sheer Genius. In 10 complexion-balanced shades. $1.50 the tube.

MAX FACTOR

Does she...or doesn't she?

Hair color so natural only her hairdresser knows for sure!™

She's as full of fun as a kid — and just as fresh looking. And this is a lovely thing in a mother! But staying young is not only thinking young, it's *looking* young too. And the fresh, young, even color you get *every time* with Miss Clairol, makes the beautiful difference. It's like knowing how to turn back time. It certainly is the best way to keep gray hair from ever showing.

Keeps hair in wonderful condition — soft, silky. Because Miss Clairol carries color deep into the hair strand, it shines outward with a clear, all-over even tone the way natural color does. That's why hairdressers recommend it and more women use it than any other haircoloring. So quick and easy. Try it yourself. Today.

MISS CLAIROL®
HAIR COLOR BATH is a trademark of Clairol Inc. © Clairol Inc. 1964

MISS CLAIROL HAIR COLOR BATH® THE NATURAL LOOKING HAIRCOLORING

Even close up, her hair looks natural. Miss Clairol keeps it shiny, bouncy. Completely covers gray with the younger, brighter, lasting color no other kind of haircoloring can promise — and live up to!

Good Housekeeping

the number of American women who colored their hair increased from 7 percent to a whopping 50 percent.[11] Through strategic use of advertising and by making a unique cultural commentary, Clairol helped to shift societal perspective for the benefit of its consumers and the brand.

Clinique Makes the Masses Individual
(1960s and 1970s)

After the rigidity and repression dictated by conformity in the 1950s, women looked to let their hair down and embrace a more individual beauty regime. Established in 1968 as a subsidiary of Estée Lauder, Clinique was the first line of skincare products to target the individual beauty needs of every woman with the belief that beautiful skin could be created. Clinique revolutionized the idea that a woman was "stuck" with the skin she was born with and created a branded, scientifically driven three-step system to help women achieve the skin they had always dreamed of. Instead of selling fragrance-laden promises, Clinique offered a simple, allergy-free system that enabled women to take charge of their beauty regime. Clinique embraced the idea of clinical skin care through all touchpoints of the brand, keeping the product line simple with minimal typography, a muted color palette, and soft, rounded corners. The Clinique counter is staffed with skin "consultants" in pristine white lab coats, ready to prescribe the correct formula to solve any skin care problem. With this process, Clinique became the first beauty brand to bring individualized consulting services to a mass market.[12] Clinique leveraged the science

behind beauty, owning an innovative, customized take on skin care that differentiated the company from its competition.

Bare Escentuals
(1980s to Present)

As the pendulum of beauty swings back and forth, new brands and products are constantly being developed to keep pace with the changing times. One of the most influential brands that has once again changed the masses' view of beauty is Bare Escentuals, created by Leslie Blodgett. The Bare Escentuals brand was developed by Blodgett with the belief that makeup can change the way people feel, which can empower them to create larger changes in the world. Using the concept that makeup should be considered skin care, Blodgett created a range of products that were "good for you" based on the "mineral" makeup that was sold in boutiques. Getting her innovative products to the masses was a challenge in an oversaturated beauty market. Inspired by a bought of insomnia, Blodgett realized her brand would be best established with QVC as a distribution channel in 1994. In her second appearance on QVC, Blodgett sold $180,000 of foundation in ten minutes, and before long, she was selling $1.4 million an hour.[13]

What really drove the brand's success was the community of consumers who purchased the brand and volunteered positive testimonials on the QVC message boards. Though this was before the advent of social media, Blodgett saw the importance of staying in touch with her brand's community and would stay up for hours after a show, writing personal messages to purchasers. Blodgett's hard work to build a strong brand paid off in 2010 during one of the largest takeovers in cosmetics history, when the brand was acquired for $1.7 billion by Shiseido.[14] By staying in touch with individual consumers and enabling the community to participate in the brand, Bare Escentuals transcended its line of pure products to become a connected and vibrant community.

Clinique revolutionized the idea that a woman was "stuck" with the skin she was born with.

Though icons like Max Factor and Coco Chanel have long passed, their spirit of innovation continues to live on in their product lines and the strong brands they created. By shifting societal perspectives on beauty, by making iconic beauty accessible for everyone, and by empowering consumers to create strong communities, successful beauty brands will continue to resonate with us on a deeper, more emotional level.

The most exciting thing you'll ever wear

Fashion is important, but well-dressed eyes are vital to beauty. That's why, the world over, lovely women always choose Maybelline ...use ULTRA+BROW to transform brows to feathery-soft perfection...blend veil-soft flattery onto lids with ULTRA+SHADOW ...define, shape and enlarge the eyes with FLUID LINER... and know the luxury of lashes brushed long, longer, longest with ULTRA+LASH mascara. Remember, beautiful eyes—exciting woman!

Maybelline

16

THIRST

THE EVOLUTION OF BRANDING BEVERAGES

SASCHA DONN, BRIAN GAFFNEY,
and **ZACHARY LYND**

In 1975, a very important taste test was conducted by the perennial soda underdog Pepsi. It was appropriately coined "the Pepsi Challenge," and in true battle fashion it seemed the goliath Coca-Cola Company had finally been slain. Blind taste testers gave a clear edge to Pepsi and with it, claim to superiority. Subsequent tests, however, confused the matter. Now presented with proper identification, taste testers declared Coke the overwhelmingly leader. Was the discrepancy in the label?

In fact, it was. MRI scans revealed that taste testers' brain activity changed when subjected to a brand image. Social psychology researchers refer to it as the Pygmalion effect, whereby expectations tend to rule outcomes. It is a powerful agent for psychology and, perhaps unsurprisingly, for buying as well.

The test revealed the power brands hold, not only in defining purchasing habits but also in their ability to override the sense of taste. The strength of brands and their multiple expressions via labels, bottles, and other devices has played a key role in deciding the successes and failures of every variety of beverage brands.

Carbonated Beverages

It's difficult to imagine a product that has been able to sustain popularity for over 200 years, overcoming a multitude of practically identical competition and evolving customer needs. Yet this has been the extraordinary history of many carbonated beverages, a history much indebted to brand. It is the strength of brands like Perrier, Coca-Cola, and Dr. Pepper that has made them immediately recognizable to customers and has trained loyalists to demand these brands throughout generations.

The idea of carbonated beverages extends back to the 1700s when people traveled to carbonated mineral springs that were believed to have curative power, but it was not until the mid-1800s that carbonated beverages started becoming what they are today.

Pepsi design through the years

The potential for carbonated beverages to become the mass-produced goods we now enjoy began with Dr. Joseph Priestley's creation of the first drinkable manmade glass of carbonated water in 1767, but it wasn't truly feasible until 1832 when John Mathews refined a device to mass-produce carbonated water.[1] During this era, carbonated water or "soda water," as it was termed in 1798, was marketed as a health tonic by companies like Perrier, which began to realize the potential of bottling and selling the water health seekers traditionally traveled to their spas to enjoy. As more and

more soda water brands came to fruition, companies began to introduce bottle and label designs to create distinction from competitors. Visual executions provided a platform to instill brands' beliefs and create strong connections between customer and brand. One infamous design is that of Perrier's bottle, which was inspired by Indian exercise clubs, a reference to its positioning as a health tonic, and is still an identifying shape for Perrier today.[2]

The late 1800s and early 1900s introduced many new flavors to the carbonated beverage world, including ginger ale, root beer, and cola. The brands introducing these flavors—Canada Dry, Hires, Coca-Cola, and so on—initially took on the curative powers of soda water perceived since the previous decade by positioning themselves as health tonics. The popularity of flavored carbonated beverages, termed "pop" in 1861, grew steadily during Prohibition as both an alcohol alternative and a mixer for home-brewed alcoholic concoctions.[3,4] Pop brands continued to use label and bottle design as a means of distinction and brand building, and so with the launch of its unique contour bottle in 1916, Coca-Cola introduced one of the most recognizable icons in the world.[5] Possibly beginning as a reflection of the beverages' apothecary foundation, the contour bottle has become a manifestation of Coca-Cola's mission to refresh the world and inspire moments of optimism and happiness.

As increasing varieties of flavored pop were introduced, brands began to explore new ways to differentiate. One pop brand in particular, Dr. Pepper, discovered that one of its ingredients, sugar, provided energy to the drinker, and that the average person experiences periods of sleepiness during a typical day at 10:30 a.m., 2:30 p.m., and

ABOVE:
Coca-Cola branding, in bottle and can form

OPPOSITE:
Limited-edition Diet Coke bottles by fashion designer Karl Lagerfeld

4:30 p.m. Dr. Pepper exploited this discovery with its famous advertising slogan, "Drink a bite to eat at 10, 2, and 4," a campaign that would continue to appear in advertising and on bottles and bottle caps for decades to come.[6] The 10, 2, and 4 campaign and philosophy set Dr. Pepper apart and paved the way for a transformation of the entire carbonated beverage category. The transition away from health tonic and toward energy drink took full charge in the 1950s and 1960s and set the foundation for an influx of energy drinks like Red Bull and Jolt Energy, which started in the 1980s.[7, 8]

Throughout history, beverage brands have been changing to meet society's needs. Their ability to establish recognizable and distinct identities has formed loyal customers who stand across generations and demand their brands in crowded marketplaces. From health tonic, to alcohol mixer, to energy drinks, carbonated beverages have been able to shift with the times and maintain an important place in our lives. As lifestyles become more hectic and we see people trying to accomplish more in less time, the number of energy drinks available has grown tremendously, even to the point of introducing alcoholic energy drinks like Sparks and Four Loco. As the pace of life continues to speed up, what need will we look to carbonated beverages to fulfill next?

Coffee Isn't Just Coffee Any Longer

A great cup of coffee is evidence of the existence of modern-day alchemy. Freshly roasted beans, appropriately ground and combined with clean water, heated to, and held at, the proper temperature for the optimal brewing time, will yield a

As the pace of life continues to speed up, what need will we look to carbonated beverages to fulfill next?

beverage whose preparation its most loyal and dedicated imbibers will liken more to chemistry than cooking; more to ritual than routine. Coffee is a community and a culture, and America is fully committed to coffee's culture and economy.

As a nation, the country ranks eighth in global coffee consumption, importing more than $4 billion worth of coffee per year, for which Americans pay, on average, $1.38 per cup, for the three cups of coffee consumed each day. The United States' contribution to the global $80 billion coffee market: 23 percent.[9] Given that coffee is a widely recognized commodity on the world market and a mature product on the shelves of America's stores, one might wonder whether or not there is anything left to learn about communicating coffee's story to its existing and potential buying public. There is.

The basic components of branding coffee are captured in this brief comment by Howard Schultz, CEO of Starbucks, who acknowledges advertising as the opportunity to emphasize his company's "passion, care, and integrity [for] the coffee"[10] that it buys, roasts, brews, and sells. The translation of Schultz's philosophy, into a branding context, can be best seen in work of the coffee roasters that make up the Third Wave, coffee companies whose buyers form direct relationships with growers, all over the world, helping them to produce the best-quality bean, for which the coffee company pays top dollar. Mark Pendergrast, author of *Uncommon Grounds,* describes the first two waves as 1) makers of bad coffee, and 2) pioneers of specialty coffee, respectively. Examples of Third Wave Coffee companies include Intelligentsia (Chicago), Counter Culture (Durham, NC), and Stumptown (Portland, OR).

Evidence of the Third Wave's commitment to coffee culture can be seen on the face of their brands, on the packaging itself:

1) The Intelligentsia logo and bag, designed by Planet Propaganda in Madison, Wisconsin, was designed to "signify the intent to elevate coffee to a new level, hence the cup held by wings." In addition to the logo, the coffee bag holds a stickered label, which identifies the region and name of the farmer/farm from which the coffee was sourced, which speaks to authenticity, the date of roasting, which speaks to freshness, and tasting notes, for consumer education.

2) At the heart of the Counter Culture Coffee brand is authenticity. The goal of Carrboro, North Carolina–based the Splinter Group's design and marketing work for Counter Culture is a "reflection of the roaster's mission to transport coffee drinkers to a specific place of origin." Its packaging gives coffee a wine-like treatment.

3) When Stumptown decided that it needed its packaging refreshed, it engaged fellow Portlandians, the Official Manufacturing Company. Stumptown already had a simple brown bag with a slit in the front, and "wanted a way to display a ton of information about growers, farms, flavors, and more." The Official Manufacturing Company made color-coded cards for each region, with latitude/longitude locations, elevations, descriptions, and certifications.

American coffee consumption is shifting to coffee companies who use their brands as platforms to introduce consumers to the highest-quality beans and improve the quality of life for the growers from whom they buy.

ABOVE:
The first Starbucks logo

OPPOSITE:
Intelligentsia coffee packaging, designed with the intent to elevate coffee to a new level

★

INTELLIGENTSIA

FRESH ROASTED COFFEE

DIRECT TRADE

HOUSE BLEND

BOURBON, TYPICA, CATURRA, CATUAI GROWN AT 1400 - 1900 M

This medium-bodied blend offers subtle fruit notes with milk chocolate and caramel
close behind. The balanced acidity finishes with notes of baked apples.

HONDURAS, EL SALVADOR, GUATEMALA
REGION

NET WT. 12 oz (340 g)   ROASTED ON 08.18.11   300039

INTELLIGENTSIACOFFEE.COM

Why do consumers buy bottles when water is nearly free from the tap?

Branding Bottled Water

Advertising and marketing veteran Barry Silverstein was spot on when he observed that, "[the bottled water category] is one in which the product itself is an internationally recognized commodity that is colorless, tasteless, and (hopefully) odorless."[12] Yet, with hundreds of brands of bottled water stocked and sold by retail stores, the space is literally overflowing with competition. In 2009, 8.5 billion gallons of spring, purified, mineral, and artesian water were sold for $10.6 billion in the United States, where the typical price for a $1/2$-liter bottle was 99 cents.[13] We are a thirsty nation!

Why do consumers buy bottles when water is nearly free from the tap? The answer to this question can be traced back to two primary sources: 1) the misinterpretation of a 1945 guideline recommendation from the Nutrition Board of the National Research Council (NRC), which led to the misconception that we must drink eight to ten glasses of water a day to remain properly hydrated; and 2) a common misperception that municipal water is not as safe as it should be or could be, making bottled water a "healthier" alternative, by default.

How can consumers determine the benefits of one bottle of water over the next? Effective branding helps consumers choose. In light of the few assets at the command of bottled water brands, ownable equities are few in number; the most salient being package and source. The Danone Group, owner of the French mineral water Evian, and Voss, owner of Norwegian artesian water VOSS, are two companies that have successfully capitalized on the concept of the bottle as brand canvas.

Elias Fayad, Evian's zone director for the Middle East, explains how Evian's use of package design as a brand differentiator led to the production of limited-edition bottles annually, in collaboration with global fashion icons. "Every year, we cultivate creativity and complicity with a new designer. What they are really doing is looking into the spirit of the brand and adding a little bit of each of their souls. Our water is untouched by man and perfected by nature, so we attempt to give the bottle an artistic expression." [14] To date, Evian has collaborated with Christian Lacroix (2008), Jean Paul Gaultier (2009), Paul Smith (2010), and Issey Miyake (2011).

Neil Kraft, a former creative director for Calvin Klein, designed the VOSS water bottle. His team "was inspired by both the purity of the untouched source and by fragrance industry experts who define brands by developing brand personality through a unique bottle and overall packaging." [14] Kraft describes the VOSS brand as "a new way to think about water. Beyond refreshing … to beautiful." [15] The VOSS bottle, available for sale today, is the result of endless hours of research and development, hundreds of sketches, months of brainstorming, and nearly a year of entertaining possible glass and cap manufacturers.

Creating Taste on a Wine Label

Wine exemplifies the rule, not the exception. In terms of perceived expectations and motivating purchase, the label has proved as important to wine as it has to all beverages. It is a complex product with roots dating back to the Stone Age, a mythology from the Greeks, the Old World, and now a new one. Today it enjoys wide international distribution and consumption in nearly every country in the world. The United States alone bottles over 6,500 brands that collectively impact the national economy to a yearly tune of hundreds of billion of dollars. Increased domestic support, along with the growth and success of wine, are welcomed problems for American vintners. Look to the label, not the vine, for those who will lead the market.

A 2001 study by French researcher Federic Brochet illustrates the point. Brochet invited subjects to experiment in a wine tasting where he served two wines of average and similar quality in differentiated bottles: Vin de Table and Grand Cru, respectively. The experiment produced results congruent to the Pygmalion, an effect uncovered in the original Pepsi Challenge. Brochet pushed his study further, infusing a white wine with a tasteless red food colorant. Remarkably (to some) the visual queue of the color was enough to affect tasters' perception of taste and smell, thereby significantly affecting their judgment.

In truth, it is difficult to imagine that a disparity of that proportion is directly attributable to a visual queue. After all, the wine experience is predicated on taste and smell. The job of a branding specialist is to hear the ring of opportunity inside alarming facts. If visual queues hold great power, then our challenge is to wield the proper symbols in order to stage the forthcoming experience with earnest appeal and communication. Should doing so in a category that spans thousands of competitors not appear challenging enough, consider that it also requires meeting existing mechanical processes and supplier guidelines, and must be legally defensible against other wineries of indistinguishable ingredients, regions, price points, and principles. It is a complex process whose final product can achieve the power and pleasure of a short story in merely a few square inches.

Of the successful wineries, two such examples happen to also run the spectrum on quality. Yellow Tail has exploded to international fame and achieved the holy grail of branding; becoming a household name. The wine epitomizes New World techniques for strategy and market positioning. Yellow Tail built its brand around ownable and immediately recognizable traits such as the bracketed lowercase logo, a bright color palette, and its symbolic kangaroo all set against the dark black label. A luxurious winery achieving a more critical acclaim has also invested heavily into the power of branding and package design. Ridge Winery uses large, beautiful type that compels further investigation. The particular lot is weighted equally against its parent, Ridge, speaking to its important and unique origin. Crowned with a branded cork ever so slightly revealed by its shortened seal, Ridge is truly set apart from its foe. Like Yellow Tail, Ridge has created brand equity through distinct packaging and clear communication.

White Rock

Psyche at Nature's Mirror
The Trademark of
America's Finest Mixers

Those who appreciate the finest choose **White Rock** *sparkling water*

17

UNPLUGGED

THE EVOLUTION OF BRANDING ELECTRONICS

JAMES GADDY

In 1883, Thomas Edison filed the first U.S. patent for an electronic device, fourteen years before the "electron" was even discovered and three years after he had observed an effect known as thermionic emission: visible, visual evidence of invisible parts of matter. The discovery would become a crucial insight in the subsequent development of electronic devices that have similarly magical properties—devices that can eliminate distance, bring the future and past together, and make both the word and image visible. This magic, the ability to see, hear, and record experiences from across great distances and time, has profoundly influenced how telephones, computers, televisions, music players, and video games have been branded since: Early RCA advertisements promoting the television referred to it as a "magic lamp," while Apple introduced its iPad as a "magical device."

But legendary figures like Edison and Alexander Graham Bell weren't just great American inventors; they understood, before it was even a word, that branding was essential to the overall mythology—and profitability—of their new products and services. Bell was directly involved in the creation of the American Telephone & Telegraph Company, incorporated in 1885, as well as the collective patchwork of regional telephone exchanges known as the Bell System. Edison, for his part, established mass-production electric utilities and displayed a preternatural understanding of how to turn an idea into a practical, useful object. He even got a magician's slogan when a newspaper columnist dubbed him the "Wizard of Menlo Park."

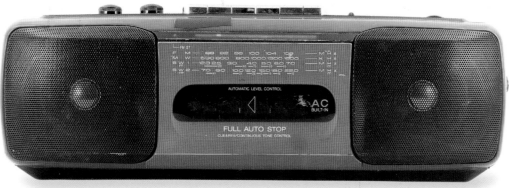

By the 1950s, the basic technology for just about every electronic device we use today had already been developed.

By the 1950s, the basic technology for just about every electronic device we use today had already been developed—1946 was especially momentous: RCA, then primarily known for its radios, produced the first consumer-ready television; AT&T engineered the first mobile telephone call; and ENIAC, the first general-purpose electric computer, the original version 1.0, was announced. (The IBM 610, the first keyboard-operated computer, would come out two years later.) And the transistor, the key component in nearly every modern electronic device, would be produced by 1954. If the first half of the twentieth century was primarily devoted to harnessing this new technology, the second half was devoted to perfecting the branding and promotional syntax of these new devices using three basic themes: size, control, and contact.

From the beginning of electronics branding, most companies have sought to tap into the yearning for quality design married with iteratively smaller technology. As early as 1959, when AT&T introduced the Princess Phone by boasting "It's little!" electronics companies have realized that size is key. With a design based on extensive market research, the Princess Phone was created to be a telephone for the bedroom, small enough to fit

LEFT:
Memorabilia from the first half of the twentieth century

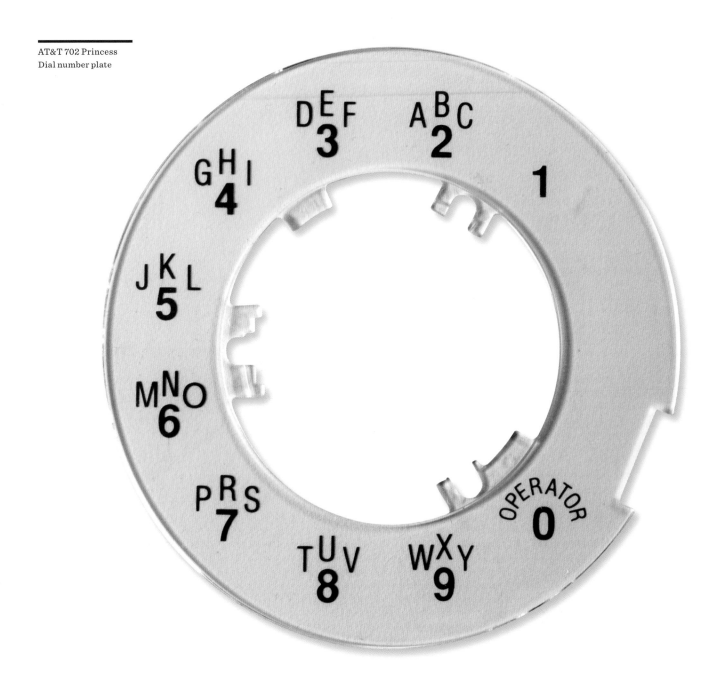

on a nightstand, with a light added to the rotary dial that served as both a nightlight and a visual aid for late-night phone calls. Nearly fifty years later, the iPod, with its sublime operating system and so-easy-a-baby-can-manage-it navigation, made its pitch by promising 10,000 songs in your pocket—all on that exquisitely designed, slim piece of electronics. And the iPad continues that trend: The technology—on a device so thin (and getting thinner with each new version) that it's practically invisible—is a sorcerer's tablet, allowing its premium-paying users to access experiences that have, until now, been unavailable.

Introducing Portable Sound

But when it comes to "branded by size," nothing changed the game quite like the Sony Walkman, the first portable stereo cassette player. Introduced in 1979 (and discontinued in 2010), the Walkman became such a massive hit that cassettes outsold vinyl records by 1983. Sony founder Akio Morita gave one of the first copies to Steve Jobs, then in his first go-round leading Apple, setting the stage for the iPod revolution more than twenty years down the road. That first Walkman was chunky by today's standards: Weighing in at 14 ounces (397 g), it contained three basic functions: play, stop, and fast forward (rewinding required the user to flip the tape over and fast forward). Morita had long established the Sony brand as the company at the forefront of the electronics revolution and its miniaturizations: One year after the invention of the transistor, Sony introduced the transistor radio, the first pocket-sized radio of its kind; later in its history, it debuted an 8-inch (20.3 cm) television. And the Walkman was the product of the simple

When it comes to "branded by size," nothing changed the game quite like the Sony Walkman.

observation that young people enjoyed playing music all day long; the idea that they would carry their music around with them—if given the opportunity—proved extraordinarily prescient.

One thing that Apple did better, besides the ingenious move to brand its music player with the now ubiquitous white headphones—and thus the culture that went along with them—was to explicitly tap into the desire for control, the yang of size's yin. The act of bestowing the consumer with power has often been electronics brands' underlying promise. Video game companies, for instance, were going bankrupt in droves during the early '80s until Nintendo filled the void with a memorable tagline that alluded to its gaming experience: "Now you're playing with power." Even more important, the new video game system turned the industry away from joystick controllers to pad-centric versions: a collection of small, smooth buttons that would define one's progress through the game. It revolutionized video games, but it, like the iPod, had an antecedent: the remote control.

Giving the User Control

It's no surprise that the invention of the television precipitated the invention of a product to control it—the "clicker," which successfully permeated the market in the mid-1950s with names like "Flashmatic," "Lazy Bones," and the "Zenith Space Commander," a model introduced in 1956. The remote offered more of the convenience that American families of the postwar era were longing for—a convenience marked by all the comforts of suburban life: the autonomy of one's own home and car, nearby shopping, and, even in that early era, the effortlessness of channel-surfing to avoid commercials. Zenith's ads for the device promised freedom from advertising while others playfully hinted at husband-and-wife power struggles.

But that early positioning hints at tapping into a desire that is more fundamental than the impetus to control. Brands have continually appealed to that human yearning—some might describe it as a basic need—to contact, whether in a tactile way, as in physically touching a screen or pressing buttons, or in a more abstract way, to "keep in touch" with a community of like-minded people. When RCA introduced its 630-TS television, it promoted the device as a way for families to be together, whether it was a father and son watching baseball or a husband and wife bonding over a shared love of mystery movies.

And more recently, the element of contact has become more literal, where *touch* has become the operative word. From the first touchtone telephone, in 1941, to the iPod Touch, brands have promoted their electronic experiences as something, if not equal to "living breathing, physical presence," then at least the next best substitute for it. As our lives have become more indoors and virtual, games like Nintendo's *Guitar Hero* and Xbox's *Dance Central* allow us to interact and get active without even leaving the house, an interesting turnabout from the remote control that allowed viewers to lift only one finger to change channels.

This distinct human-ness of our electronic devices continues to mark the branded experience: Four years before *The Social Network,* Cisco was claiming to be "the human network," and IBM promises to "build a smarter planet." This ability to "reach out and touch someone" from afar, as AT&T once pitched, remains forever an opportunity to connect. But with the advent of touch screens, the branded experience, though still mediated by the screen, is no longer a boundary as much as it is an accomplice, allowing us to push and pull and expand these points of contact as if on command. The other tools needed to direct our experience— whether a remote control, channel knobs, cassette tapes, or even pressing phone buttons—are less and less necessary. The screen is contact, community, and control, rolled into a device that can fit in your pocket. It's a product that's as magical as ever: Touch it, and the entire world appears.

A BRAND CALLED YOU

THE EVOLUTION OF MULTIMEDIA BRANDS AND BEYOND

JEREMY DIPAOLO
and **KATHRYN SPITZBERG**

Playboy, **Oprah, and Disney** would seem to have little in common. All three are media icons, to be sure, but they have vastly different takes on what is meaningful content. Yet, there is commonality: Each began the vision of a single person and sought to create brand experiences that tapped into cultural mythologies. The brands comprise empires that transcend mere media conglomerates; they used rich storytelling and compelling narratives to reach audiences; and they branched out into numerous media, giving consumers different ways to experience and participate in the brand narrative.

The Playboy Bunny Comes Alive

Playboy magazine started as a countercultural publication. Having observed the cultural trends and publishing milieu of the early 1950s, Hugh Hefner recognized there was need (and space) for a men's magazine that addressed the sensibility of the postwar generation. Taking a swipe at the buttoned-up, Puritan ideals that prevailed in American culture, Hefner sought to give men a glimpse into an alternative lifestyle rooted in freedom of choice rather than cultural mandate. Politics, humor, women; these topics became *Playboy's* focus. Hefner produced the first issue of *Playboy* magazine—featuring a now famous photo of Marilyn Monroe on the cover—on a kitchen table in his Chicago apartment.[1] When that first issue sold more than 50,000 copies, it was clear that Hefner had tapped into a mythology that was deeply captivating. The sophisticated mix of photography, journalism, interviews, and essays from the nation's top writers at the time began to solidify *Playboy* as no less than an outlet of freedom.

Within the decade, the magazine would see a rise in sales to over 1 million copies per month and the debut of the first Playboy Jazz Festival in Chicago. Hefner and the beloved bunny symbol became the icons of "the good life," as Hefner began to further embody his version of the lifestyle depicted in *Playboy's* pages, and as the brand's enterprises evolved into an empire. Hefner, Playboy's smoking-jacket-clad prime minister, oversaw a massive expansion of the brand into numerous clubs, resorts, and casinos in the 1970s. He bought and sold mansions that became epicenters for the brand lifestyle. Understanding the importance—and market potential—of extending the brand

Hefner and the beloved bunny symbol became the icons of "the good life."

into as many platforms as possible, Hefner was among the pioneers of paid television with the 1982 launch of Playboy TV. The company produced films, records, events, television shows, licensed goods, and much more.[2]

Though the transitions may not have always been smooth (the brand has weathered financial crises, consolidations, and broad technological shifts during its almost sixty years of existence), the brand's core mythology remained, allowing for its expansion into numerous media. Weaving through all the brand's extensions, touchpoints, and platforms, however disparate the elements may seem, has been an invitation to partake in the good life. Whether rubbing elbows with Playmates past at the Playboy Club in Las Vegas, enjoying a night under the stars at the Hollywood Bowl for the Playboy Jazz Festival, or simply browsing the collection of every issue ever published on the iPlayboy iPad app (for the articles, of course), Hefner's belief in freedom and his vision of the Playboy lifestyle are omnipresent.

Oprah and Harpo

The year 1973 was important for daytime television. *The Phil Donahue Show,* based in Dayton, Ohio, was in its second year of national syndication and on its way to becoming one of the highest-rated talk shows of the next decade. In Nashville, Tennessee, the local WTVF-TV took a chance on a youthful African-American woman to anchor the news, ushering in a number of firsts for the station. The nineteen-year-old Oprah Winfrey would become not only Donahue's biggest rival, but the nation's most influential talk-show host.

In 1984, Oprah took the helm on the program AM Chicago. Within two years, the show had taken on her moniker and had gone national.[3]

During its twenty-five-year tenure, *The Oprah Winfrey Show* was the highest-rated talk show for a consecutive twenty-four seasons, reaching more than 40 million viewers in 145 countries.[4] By simultaneously embodying both personal struggle and success, Oprah became an icon of the mythology that she and her brand represent: the limitless power of the human spirit. From the earliest days of *The Oprah Winfrey Show,* Oprah formed a very human and meaningfully authentic bond with her audience—she seeks to inspire, to educate, to inform. She encouraged both guests and audiences to realize their possibilities, to confront their inner demons, to explore art, to contend with important social issues.

The early success of her original television program, along with her Academy Award–nominated acting debut in Steven Spielberg's *The Color Purple,* quickly established her as a celebrated media icon. She shrewdly began capitalizing on her celebrity to expand her influence into many media channels. Her reverse-namesake

Harpo Studios produces television and film projects, *O, The Oprah Magazine,* features its mascot on almost every cover (she has shared it once with First Lady Michelle Obama), and the recently launched OWN: Oprah Winfrey Network, as a home for Oprah's brand-aligned programming. In each medium, her perspective and worldview are undeniably clear and present: Her products and interactions serve as a positive-feedback loop where her influence reinforces brand messages through every touchpoint; the brand messages in turn fortify her cultural authority.

She also sells books—a lot of them. In 1996, she launched Oprah's Book Club, placing her seal of approval (literally) on various titles that resonate with her messaging, from *Anna Karenina* to *A Million Little Pieces.* Since the program's launch, more than 22 million copies of the books have been sold, a number of them instant best-sellers.[5] Her "Oprah's Favorite Things" program segment was almost guaranteed to sell out any of the products she featured, whether it was gourmet popcorn or Thanksgiving turkeys. By casting her influential light on projects and products that align with her brand, but extend outside the arena of what she actually produces herself, Oprah continually establishes affinities that perpetuate her popularity as not merely a talk show host cum media magnate, but as cultural arbiter nonpareil.

She has even obtained political clout through her successful brand management, as 1993's "Oprah Bill," creating a national database of registered sex offenders, was signed into law.[6] While it may seem callous to examine her impact on policy as part of a branded message, it is indeed an extension of a carefully managed strategy that allows Oprah to put her own experience at the forefront of the mythology. The Oprah brand has become a forum for storytelling where personal experience is the ultimate truth, addressing through its various platforms the holistic well-being and yearnings of viewers—intellectual, emotional, existential, psychological, creative. She is a one-stop shop for self-exploration and realization of the human spirit.

Creating the Disney Experience

Unlike *Playboy,* whose complex freedom myth is embodied by the brand's creator, and Oprah, whose golden aura of influence conjures images of the saints, "Disney Magic" is a self-created, self-contained mythology. Certainly, since Walt Disney first put pencil to paper to create the world's most famous mouse, the brand has channeled archetypal myths in the stories selected for its features and programming. But whether refurbishing beloved fables like the Arthurian legend or spinning a yarn about ragtag pirates from the company's own theme-park ride, the stories, products, and experiences in the Disney brand have a common genome. They all filtered through—and build upon—the narrative that becomes the fabric of the Disney macrocosm: an ever-expanding patchwork of magic realms and dreams, carefully shaped to feed people's thirst for fantasy.

At the outset of every Disney experience, audiences are invited to leave their troubles at the door and enter a world of imagination. A recent cinematic variation of this overture begins with the shot of a distant horizon where a pirate ship lolls on the water. The camera begins its flight over the Disney landscape to the tune of "When

urmoments / Shutterstock.com

Unlike *Playboy,* whose complex freedom myth is embodied by the brand's creator, and Oprah, whose golden aura of influence conjures images of the saints, "Disney Magic" is a self-created, self-contained mythology.

You Wish Upon a Star," the music building to a crescendo as Cinderella's castle sweeps into the frame and with a wave of Tinkerbell's wand, the sparkling signature "Walt Disney Pictures" materializes. This sensory cue reinforces the brand's mythology—that magic *is* attainable. The icon evokes a canon of storytelling and imagination that includes films like *Pinocchio, Cinderella,* and *Mary Poppins* as well as more recent movies like *The Little Mermaid, Toy Story,* and *Up.* Thanks to Disney's master conjurers (and a healthy dose of CGI) the worlds of the imagination and of fantasy are palpably within grasp. By referencing a brand experience now familiar to several generations, the opener conveys the idea that regardless of age, we can all rely on Disney to satisfy our collective yearning for magic and entertainment.

The worlds and experiences evoked by the Disney brand show how a powerful mythology can attract consumers to a brand and, ideally, provide them opportunities to experience and participate in the myth across a wide range of media, over a lifetime. The brand becomes irresistibly compelling when its shepherds build and maintain a meticulous culture that can be distilled into every interaction, regardless of time or place—behavior that is only further enabled by the progression of mobile technology that allows consumers to connect with the Disney magic anywhere.

As the Walt Disney Company has matured, however, its leadership has come to realize that not all stories can take place in a realm of fairy tales, animation, and charm; the company has acquired or launched media properties—ESPN, ABC, and Hollywood Records, among them—that don't necessarily fit into the patchwork of magical realms that the brand's fictional productions cater to, per se, but still fit into the Disney mythology. Where Disney mastery is evident in this arena is in the blurring of reality and fantasy, producing such films as *Cars,* which features NASCAR-style automobiles as main characters; a fitting and generations-friendly analogue to ESPN's coverage of the actual racing league. This is but a recent example of a concept the brand has excelled at for decades in producing its theme-park adventures, cruise ships, live events, and retail stores: taking the myth from the realm of the imagination and injecting it into tangible, real-world experiences for children of all ages to enjoy.

The reliance on a core mythology is essential, whether for Disney, *Playboy,* Oprah, or any other multimedia brand. The magic, and power, of myth allows us to believe that our dreams can come true.

PART THREE /
DESIGNING BRANDS

HOW TO BRAND

19
HOW TO BRAND
A BOOK

JADALIA BRITTO

Rodrigo Corral

Rodrigo Corral Design

Creative Director, Farrar, Straus & Giroux

Creating culture, one book at a time

What do you think Rodrigo Corral is best known for? Just book design—or more than that?

I'm known for book design, but I would certainly like to do more. I'm capable of more than just that.

Do you consider yourself to be a brand?

No. The approach I take with my work doesn't really lend itself to building a brand because each project has its own character and issues that can't have a brand ID placed on them. Finding a style and saying, "This is the look or palette I want to carry out on the next dozen projects," would not work in the projects and clients my studio works with.

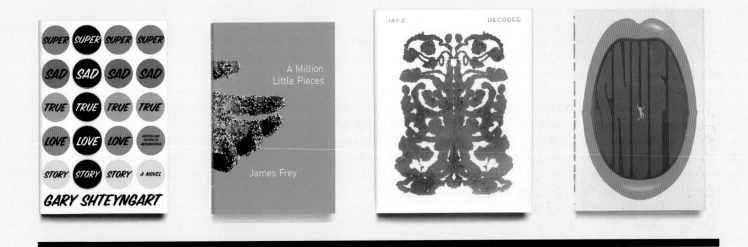

How does branding play a part in book design?

It plays a part in every cover. Once it has been handed to the marketing department, they take the imagery you craft and borrow elements for use in advertisements and promotion. Whether it's in a three-by-three-inch ad space in *The New Yorker* or a full-page ad in the Sunday *Book Review,* that's the measure of the importance of branding in book design: being able to take the cover you designed and chop it up into smaller pieces to use as a selling tool.

What's the relationship between the book and the design? What makes a cover successful?

The writing and the reviews. The book itself has to be well-written and the design has to translate that for the reader, making sure it is genuine and clear in its message. The more attention a book can garner for its literary merits, the more you will see the cover, and that's when a cover becomes important. If a book has gone on to sell very well, designers automatically start to look at the cover as successful. I think it's just

a lucky coincidence. When I think about *A Million Little Pieces,* which I designed, I am so excited that that cover was for a best-selling book, but I would not say that cover played any part in it becoming a best seller.

What are the biggest misconceptions in the world of book design?

From the perspective of an author, publisher, and agent, I think they feel that the designer isn't really thinking about the life of the book—about what will happen to the book once it's published. I think designers are more invested in the process of coming up with a great solution for these concerns than the publishers give them credit for.

From the perspective of the designer, I think there's a feeling that publishers don't understand the process well. There's a feeling that publishers and designers speak different languages. It's definitely arranged so that when you go into a meeting with the publisher and the editors to talk about the cover,

THIS PAGE AND FOLLOWING PAGES: A selection of book covers by Rodrigo Corral Design

you don't really have a dialogue. It's a group of people saying they like it or they don't like it. This is a challenge that will continue, but it's something I relish nonetheless—I like creating something irresistible and working through the challenges.

What are some of the brands you think are particularly iconic?

Apple is visually iconic. BP is brilliant—it is one of the most notorious companies, but its look says, "We are all about the environment." There is something very twisted but successful about that. I love Dunhill, and I'm a big fan of American Express—I want to work with them. It's the messages—the messages conveyed in an instant by all these companies that interest me.

When prospective clients approach you, which projects do they usually reference as their reason for wanting to work with you?

For years, it was *A Million Little Pieces* or all the Chuck Palahniuk books. More recently, it's been *The Brief Wondrous Life of Oscar Wao*, by Junot Díaz, or *Super Sad True Love Story*, by Gary Shteyngart.

Can you talk about designing the covers for those two books?

Super Sad was such a challenge. Gary captured how an individual can feel alone in a city of millions—that was the toughest thing to get across. As for Oscar Wao, it was completely the opposite challenge, in that emotion was easily found on each and every page and violence as well. Violence is a strong thread throughout the book, and I wanted to find a way to convey this without being offensive.

How did you approach the design for Jay-Z's book, Decoded?

That was really exciting and scary at that the same time because I've been a fan of Jay's work since he started. But he is an incredible person to work with and incredibly disarming, so I was able to follow my instincts, knowing how much I've listened to his music and his lyrics. I knew his story very well, and knowing how comfortable he was as a person made the process a success.

If you could redesign any of your most high-profile book projects, which would it be?

I want to redo *The Brief Wondrous Life of Oscar Wao* as a graphic novel, but not as we know graphic novels to be. I want to redefine the genre. That's the book I would love to put another face on. I don't get those feelings often. Usually, when it's done, it's done.

How has the rise of electronic devices reshaped the book business?

There's fear in the air, and fear usually causes people to be slightly paralyzed or take really cautious steps as they move forward. Overall, there are clearly less books being published and fewer chances taken on manuscripts from first-time authors. Publishers are definitely taking less chance on design, and when they do take a chance, the process becomes a lengthy one. Everything feels like it's slow going. Everyone is afraid to make a mistake or to even make a move.

Mary-Kate and Ashley
Olsen's *Influence*,
designed by Rodrigo
Corral

MARY
TOMER

Mrs. O

THE FACE
OF FASHION
DEMOCRACY

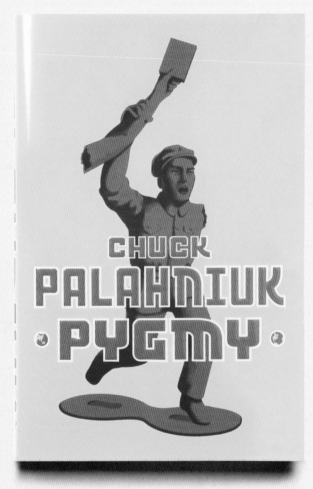

20
HOW TO BRAND A RESTAURANT

ZACHARY TYLER LYND

Matteo Bologna

Mucca Design

Creating design as delectable as the cuisine it represents

Mucca Design's work was featured in a Cooper Union exhibition titled "Appetite," which examined the history of design and food, and how design can stimulate the appetite. Is that something you hope to achieve in your work?

My first thought is, "No." As an Italian, I believe that the food should always be the "protagonist"—the sole reason why we eat at a particular restaurant. For Italians, generally, this is true. But because we're in America, where food is primarily the protagonist in an obesity epidemic, restaurants need design. Restaurants need design not to create appetite, but to add to the culinary experience.

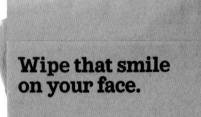

Wipe that smile on your face.

BrooklynFare.com

In Italy, restaurant design is loathed—a case study on the Mucca website refers to it as "an anathema."

Absolutely. Design is something that comes between you and the experience of tasting the food. It's not necessary. When you go to Italy, some of the best restaurants are ugly, but the food is amazing. Here, we live in a different context. Traditionally, food here is bad. People eat mostly packaged food provided by corporations. But in the last twenty years in the United States, there has been a movement led by people like Alice Waters, who have helped food to reclaim the importance it should have had from the very beginning. There are two groups related to this. There is a group of chefs who are trying to improve the quality of food, and who have actually succeeded quite well. And there are other chefs who are trying to improve or add to the experience.

What role does design play in this experience?

As designers, we're setting the stage. We have to help the customer enjoy every moment in the restaurant. Everything we do is about giving personality to a venue so that the event remains very memorable for the customer. The design and materials we create for the restaurant help to elevate the food in a very particular way, without interfering in the relationship between the customer and the food.

Does that make your design more intuitive or more intellectual?

For a restaurant, the design should be transparent and functional. A menu should be easy to read, so the customer can find things easily: You don't want to spend too much time reading a long page of text. Usually, we design in such a way so that the menu

is easy to scan—this way, the customer can give a quick look at it and know what to get. For the restaurateur, our design is functional in the sense that it needs to promote certain items to help facilitate a certain experience during the evening. Or get rid of old fish [laughs]. Either way, our job is to highlight certain items that are more profitable or more significant for the restaurant's identity.

Does that present challenges that other kinds of design do not? Does it make the menu a very unique canvas?

The menu is definitely a unique canvas. When you design a menu, you need a lot of experience to achieve certain goals that your client has. Menus have a lot of rules that are very subtle—but every specialty in design has specific rules. Book jackets have their own rules. Signage has its own rules.

BELOW AND PREVIOUS PAGE: Branding for Brooklyn Fare, a grocery store, using a custom typeface

Carry the day... and the groceries.

You've been able to convince many clients to use customized typefaces. Why, and what do you think restaurateurs would benefit from knowing about design?

We live in a world where competition is fierce. Most restaurants don't hire good graphic designers, so most of them use standard typefaces. For instance, you see Copperplate everywhere. But if you're in a competitive environment, you want to stand out. And the typeface is the voice of the restaurant.

Imagine if we needed to dub a movie starring Brad Pitt, Robert De Niro, and Robert Redford—but my voice was used to dub all three. The actors may look different and may be saying different things, but the voices would still be identical. If you really wanted to do a good job, you would use different people to dub them. Having a custom typeface is the same as giving Brad Pitt a unique voice. Nobody else can ever have that voice.

You created four different variations of one typeface for the restaurant Pastis—why?

We built three or four variations of the logo. We wanted to give Pastis a history, as though it was established by the owner in 1906 and then passed to his son in 1920. The son reprints the materials at another printer who doesn't have the exact logo, but tries to create something slightly similar because they don't have the original anymore. Then someone else takes over the restaurant and changes the logo. Every time the restaurant changed hands or was passed along, it was slightly changed. It's still the same place, but we played with the design in this way to include layers of history.

You've said that there's no such thing as inspiration. So where does this idea for Pastis come from?

That's not inspiration. That's research. You look at history and you try to replicate it in a way that looks authentic. Yet it's totally fake, so you have to put in a lot of love. Otherwise, it looks like Disney.

From a personal viewpoint, what do you stand for? What gives you satisfaction?

I stand for honesty. I stand for good storytelling and easy access to good communication. I want you to leave the restaurant feeling satisfied intellectually and emotionally. The menu should give you information, but it should also have something that makes it unusual—something that makes you want to stop and look at the details. As Mies van der Rohe said, "God is in the details." I think God is in the kerning—in between letters. Zoom into the space between two letters, and that's where you find honesty and integrity and the love of making something.

BELOW:
To-go cups for
Brooklyn Fare

RIGHT:
Menus (above) and
wine list (below) for
Morandi, an Italian
restaurant started by
restaurateur Keith
McNally in New York
City, featuring custom
typefaces Morandi
Serif and Grotesque

Morandi Serif

MORANDI SERIF LIGHT
abcdefghijklmnopqrstuvwxyz
ABCDEFGHIJKLMNOPQRSTUVWXYZ
12345678910

MORANDI SERIF REGULAR
abcdefghijklmnopqrstuvwxyz
ABCDEFGHIJKLMNOPQRSTUVWXYZ
12345678910

MORANDI SERIF HEAVY
abcdefghijklmnopqrstuvwxyz
ABCDEFGHIJKLMNOPQRSTUVWXYZ
12345678910

MORANDI SERIF BLACK
abcdefghijklmnopqrstuvwxyz
ABCDEFGHIJKLMNOPQRSTUVWXYZ
12345678910

Morandi Grotesque

MORANDI GROTESQUE LIGHT
abcdefghijklmnopqrstuvwxyz
ABCDEFGHIJKLMNOPQRSTUVWXYZ
12345678910

MORANDI GROTESQUE REGULAR
abcdefghijklmnopqrstuvwxyz
ABCDEFGHIJKLMNOPQRSTUVWXYZ
12345678910

MORANDI GROTESQUE HEAVY
abcdefghijklmnopqrstuvwxyz
ABCDEFGHIJKLMNOPQRSTUVWXYZ
12345678910

MORANDI GROTESQUE BLACK
abcdefghijklmnopqrstuvwxyz
ABCDEFGHIJKLMNOPQRSTUVWXYZ
12345678910

God is in the kerning—in between letters. Zoom into the space between two letters, and that's where you find honesty and integrity and the love of making something.

Logo and collateral for
French bistro, Pastis

21
HOW TO BRAND
A PAPER PRODUCT

JESSIE MCGUIRE

Christine Mau

Kimberly-Clark

Giving Kleenex new relevance to young and old consumers alike

What does branding mean to you?

It's all about "the brand promise." Every brand communicates to the public what it promises to deliver on. This is done through marketing, communications, and design, and all of that adds up to how the brand presents itself and its products. The public then evaluates that brand on whether or not it's keeping that promise. Does the brand messaging ring true? Is it resonating? Is the company acting the way it told you it will? People develop an affinity for a brand because they believe in the promise the company makes. If the brand keeps, and even over-delivers on that, then the affinity continues to grow. And that's how someone begins to feel passionate about that brand.

What do you find compelling about the Kleenex brand?

I came to Kimberly-Clark because of my affinity for the brand. To me, the Kleenex boxes were these little pieces of art that could go into everybody's home. This is a really powerful idea. We're not talking about one piece of art that goes into one home— we're talking about something that becomes part of the everyday landscape, because it's in millions of homes and other settings. At Kleenex, I got to work on the branding and graphic design, and I also got to focus on the print, pattern, and style I was passionate about. I liked the opportunity to leverage both of these, to define the interplay of the print and pattern with the brand's positioning.

What is Kimberly-Clark's approach to brand positioning?

In 2009, Massimo Vignelli said that if you can design one thing, then you can design everything. At that time, Kimberly-Clark realized that a successful strategy for the company needed to be a brand-centric one, so our leadership dedicated the top-level talent to one particular brand. In this approach, each person evaluates and creates a design strategy for that brand, no matter what the channel or medium is. I'm the Brand Design Director of Family Care Brands. My scope of design encompasses everything from product development all the way through to overseeing television production.

How has Kleenex evolved since you became involved with the business?

Early on, the Kleenex brand had a strong propensity to use design to create an affinity with its consumers. In 1967, Kleenex came out with the upright cube box—what consumers call "the cube." That box featured the hippest, trendiest, grooviest graphics. Then the business went back to the plain pattern—what we call "the tortoise shell, flame stitch pattern"—something that was more expected and traditional. Looking at the entire tissue category after a few years, Kleenex realized that it was flat and stagnant. I kept asking, "What's wrong?" It turns out that Generation Y was not purchasing facial tissues as previous generations had.

So I started interviewing every twenty-year-old I could find—at the airport, at family reunions, wherever I was. I would ask them about Kleenex, and they would tell me these stories about the fact that when they were kids, it was a big deal to choose which Kleenex box to buy. People would light up as they were reminiscing about this.

ABOVE:
Two packages for Kleenex Boutique Tissues, 1970s

BELOW:
Contemporary Kleenex packaging

I would say, "Great—do you still buy facial tissue today?" Inevitably, the answer would be, "No, there's nothing for me on the shelves." The Kleenex brand had not capitalized on the aesthetic that it had started years ago. The brand was sticking to what I call the "vanilla wafer solution." It was creating designs that were generally acceptable and that were liked by the masses—that were "good." But it hadn't really taken advantage of the "personal style statement aesthetic"—the way that personal style becomes an aesthetic statement.

How was the actual packaging a response to this?

I argued that if we're going to get Generation Y to buy Kleenex, the brand is going to have to do what it did in 1967 when the boomers fell in love with "the cube." We started thinking about that, and that's when we came up with the oval design for the box. Essentially, we gave this new generation its own icon. Then we began looking more closely at the graphics, thinking about how we could create designs that would resonate better. And we began creating graphics that were a little more cutting edge—that were higher up on the trend curve.

How do you determine when a design has been successful?

It's driven a great deal by the changes we see in the trend curve. When I started on the brand, the trend curve was about a six-year projection showing the "incoming" and "outgoing" trends. At that time, the graphics would stay on a product for about that long—six years. In the early 2000s, we saw a shorter trend cycle that was more of a three-year span from incoming to outgoing. We take these trend criteria and look at each and every design to see what role it plays in the portfolio, and then we apply the design strategy accordingly.

How long is the trend curve currently?

That's a question I'm wrestling with myself. I think it's in flux—it's becoming specific to different products. Some product forms still have a curve that's longer, which might have to do with their manufacturing process. Those that can be more nimble are taking advantage of that agility and doing things rather quickly.

Of the tissue box designs that you've worked on, which one is your favorite?

Can I pick two? The first one that I ever did, probably in 1998, was a graphic interpretation of reindeer in snow. It was a big milestone to see something I had worked on going out to the all the retailers in the United States. I would joke about it with some of my friends who were fine artists—I'd say, "You might have work at MoMA, but I'm on display every day at the Piggly Wiggly." My second favorite design was out this year, 2011—it's called "Spellbound."

HELLO:
May I offer
you a Kleenex?

You might have work at MoMA, but I'm on display every day at the Piggly Wiggly.

Summer Kleenex
packaging for Target,
2009

How to Brand a Paper Product

22
HOW TO BRAND
USABILITY

KATHRYN SPITZBERG

Dan Formosa

**Cofounder/
Smart Design**

Creating objects that are irresistible to touch and exquisite to use

How did the OXO line come about?

When we started Smart Design in 1980, we began with the premise of "designing for people," which the general design consultancies at the time were not practicing. We had a conviction that we needed to understand not only how a product works but also how the body works, and how a person interacts both physically and psychologically with a product. We had been in business as consultants for ten years, and we had previously done a lot of work with Corning, so we knew housewares pretty well.

Sam Farber, OXO's founder, called Davin Stowell—apparently in the middle of the night—with this idea of designing a line of housewares that would be functional and usable by everyone, including people who may have some physical challenges, like arthritis. I had a master's degree in biomechanics, so I had a good understanding of the body and the hand, and I recognized that this was a great opportunity. Sam had an idea and a clear vision.

A lot of products on the market haven't evolved for decades—like the carrot peeler, for example. What stunts the design of such basic tools?

People get used to seeing things in a certain way and, as a result, there's no new life pumped into certain categories. Like the carrot peeler, they are what they are, and they've been that way for a long time. There are still opportunities in numerous categories where we've gotten so used to seeing things in a certain way for such a long time that we stop thinking about rethinking them.

OXO describes its products as embodying a "universal design" philosophy. Is that a philosophy you strive for at Smart Design?

At Smart, we never use the term "universal design"—we actually try to avoid it. "Universal design" gets interpreted as meaning one design that should work for everybody. Our philosophy is that design should be for everybody, but everybody doesn't necessarily need just one design. For us, design is about eliminating segregation. We shouldn't artificially divide people by design. People will always have individual preferences on what they like or dislike. But we believe people shouldn't be forced to use products and services that are being designed for the people in the middle of the population. Those may not suit the needs of the people at the edges of the population.

At Smart, we are coming at this work from a different angle: We think design in general should be for everybody and that design doesn't have to be reserved for expensive stuff. Design shouldn't be an elite enjoyment. We should be able to find good design in high-end stores, but we should also be able to find good design in supermarkets or in the local department stores.

What were the biggest challenges you had when developing the OXO product line?

In a way, the problems we were solving were easy because kitchen tools at the time were so bad. We applied basic principles of ergonomics and biomechanics to make the tools easier to use. Design-wise, we had a field day, and we ended up creating some really touchable things. The first handles had fins on them that were rather playful.

Was there anything in particular that inspired the "touchable" aspect of the OXO designs?

For inspiration, I went to some bike shops in New York City and looked at handlebars and grips on kids' bikes—the ones with streamers and other decorative elements coming off of them. We noticed that the little fins on the handlebar grips added friction, which is what we were looking for. We also noticed that the grips were really touchable. Whenever we had a bunch of things on the table during meetings, someone would always pick up the grip and fiddle with it. It was like a touch "magnet"—people couldn't stop themselves from touching it. On the original product packaging, we included an image of a thumb squeezing the rubber fins to show how touchable it was.

What makes OXO unique?

OXO was based on a vision that we totally supported from the start. The company never did any marketing studies. What's happening with companies now is that they're trying to use market research and design research to find a vision, and they end up

spinning their wheels. The best thing a company can do is assemble a cohesive team that is open minded and willing to explore, but that can still make decisions that help define the direction of the product or the company. Looking to a group of consumers to define a vision or define a direction is usually not a path to success.

What do you anticipate for the future of product design?

There's still tremendous opportunity to improve quality of life. The fact that people are now talking to each other and sharing their experiences is keeping a lot of companies on their toes. This type of communication is really helping to develop a culture in which we celebrate good design in products and services. Since not as many companies can compete on technology, it isn't giving businesses a competitive edge like it used to. The real chance to innovate may not be centered on technology, alone, but on the design of the experience. The design field is growing more and more important for innovation.

How do you define innovation?

As a blanket statement, I'd say innovation is improving quality of life.

If you couldn't do what you're doing today, what would you do?

I'd be a rock star. Definitely. Though I'm not sure how anyone grew up playing music, since music notation is so poorly designed. It's god awful.

ABOVE:
An early version of a potato peeler

OPPOSITE:
In-store display and branding for the full line of OXO Good Grips products, encouraging customers to follow through on their impulses and touch the items (top).

A selection of OXO Good Grips Kitchen Tools (bottom)

Companies are trying to use market research and design to find a vision, and they end up spinning their wheels. The best thing a company can do is assemble a cohesive team that is open minded and willing to explore, but that can still make decisions that help define the direction of the product or the company. Looking to a group of consumers to define a vision or define a direction is usually not a path to success.

How to Brand Usability

23
HOW TO BRAND
A HOTEL

ABBY MCINERNEY

Scott Williams

Founder and President/ Scott Williams & Co.

Developing cachet through innovation— and discovering the obvious

Your background is in theater and television— how did that lead into branding?

Great branding involves great storytelling, and that's what theater is all about. At its core, branding, too, is about getting on stage and telling an amazing, indelible story. Up until recently, we didn't talk about theatricality and stagecraft in the world of brands. But in my experience, stagecraft can become a palpable form of witchcraft when it comes to branding because there's an alchemy that happens—there's a certain magic or pixie dust that people use in order to create these moments that become forever locked in your memory and tied up with your emotions.

At Starwood, you were responsible for the visual and verbal communications for all Starwood creative projects. How did you decide what to prioritize and where to implement new strategies?

The first issue when I started was the Starwood brand. The only thing defining the brand was the customer loyalty program, Starwood Preferred Guest. The program had a unique point of view and offered benefits such as no black-out dates, and we had to make sure the focus was on highlighting these killer brand equities because we were being outspent four to one by our competition in the hospitality arena. We constantly had to prioritize those benefits so we didn't represent ourselves as a commodity. It's so easy to become a points program where your identity seems to be about giving away free stuff. Giveaways don't necessarily generate brand loyalty. In fact, most of the time, this approach has the opposite effect. If you look at the great premium brands, one of the strongest loyalty factors—which is key to building a cult around the brand—is that people are willing to pay a little bit more because they have a love and an almost irrational attraction for the brand.

The second priority was to contend with the fact that many of our divisions had their own agencies, and as a result, there were some inconsistencies in the brand platforms. For instance, Westin had a campaign running in Japan and Korea when I arrived that hadn't run in North America for a couple of years. We walked a very fine line of making sure that the general managers could control their own businesses but when business travelers went from North America to Japan, the messaging was inconsistent, and we wanted a global look and feel. But we didn't

TOP:
Promotional material
for the Sheraton Hotel

BELOW:
Website redesign for
Morgans Hotel Group

always have the money to do that on a worldwide basis. My task was to try to create as much consistency as I possibly could.

What did you determine were the core values of Starwood?

Ultimately, Starwood represented innovation, leadership, and agility. When we identified these values, they were all aspirational, but it certainly was who we wanted to be. We innovated around the *W* brand as a chain. Our CEO, Barry Sternlicht, scaled up the *W* brand, and then with Westin and the "Heavenly Bed" and all the products that followed, we dramatically changed the face of hotel bedding. Ian Schrager had done the white bed before, but he never scaled it with the reach that Westin had. Schrager said that Sternlicht legitimized the boutique hotel industry as a business to investors.

What advice do you have on how to be a good client and how to work productively with outside agencies?

Be decisive and stick to the brief. The better the brief, the better the work. And, when you have input for the agency, be specific and make sure the feedback is valuable, and not driven by ego. There's nothing worse than having someone say they don't like the color blue or similar such subjective comments. The critique must always be in response to the objectives of the brief.

After Starwood, you moved over to Morgans, which made an appeal to customers during the recession with campaigns like "Fuck the Recession." Was that successful?

"Fuck the Recession" was an attention-getter to say, "Hey, we feel the same way." We wanted people to notice us in a really awful market, and we wanted to say, "The world's not going to end, yet—it definitely sucks, but come in to our properties, and we will deliver you a very different experience." We had two main goals with the campaign: The first was to remind the core Morgans audience that now—more than ever—they deserved to "recess" with Morgans. The second goal was to deliver a bold brand statement that Morgans is always daring, even in the face of adversity. The campaign was polarizing, which is good, because you want to know who your customers are and who they aren't—and the whole point was to get people talking about the brand.

You're a big believer in "observational design research." Can you share some interesting discoveries that you've found?

Observational research is one of the best tools for bringing obvious flaws to the surface and fighting indifference at the same time. When people come to accept the status quo and stop innovating, they've become indifferent. If you want to fight that, you find the obvious by looking for it. You observe. Great innovation can come from observing the obvious, from paying attention to the things that are taken for granted. It's not hard to figure out once you see it—you get it immediately. And you wonder why no one had recognized it before then. For instance, the fact that no one ever considered "remaking" the bed is remarkable. Why did every other hotel company miss this? How obvious! The "Heavenly Bed" worked for us, but that doesn't mean we always get it right.

Collateral for the "Fuck the Recession" campaign for Morgans Hotel Group

MORGANS HOTEL GROUP

Dearest Recession,

As even you are aware, it is in our nature, as well as our trade,
to be accommodating. Still, and please forgive our uncharacteristically
inhospitable tone, we find that we are completely unable to accommodate you.
Morgans is the very model of living life with the stops off.

And considering the dastardly manner with which you rob people of their joy,
not just their assets, you sir have become Public Enemy #1. This is your notice
that our doors will never swing wide for you. Not ever.

Towards this end, we are putting our considerable resources and talents into
thwarting you the best way we know how -- we're throwing a party, dare we
say it, a bacchanal. And we warn you, style, feasting and reveling will rule the
day and no doubt continue on past dawn. By the way, don't think that you can
sneak under our velvet rope once the party has cleared. We intend to defy you
every chance we get.

Hear that sound, Mr. Recession? That's right. It's laughter.
Now, with all due respect, ~~go away~~ *fuck off.*

None of our love,

MHG

MHG

FUCK THE RECESSION.

ATTITUDE IS EVERYTHING. RECESSISON.COM

Great innovation can come from observing the obvious, from paying attention to the things that are taken for granted.

LESS TRADING FLOOR. MORE DANCE FLOOR.

HEY, DOWNTURN... UP YOURS.

DECLARE RECESS ON THE RECESSION.

24

HOW TO BRAND PACKAGED FOOD

MO SAAD

Rob Wallace

Managing Partner and Strategic Director/ Wallace Church: Iconic Redesign

Inheriting and reinventing legacies

What makes a great brand?

Cheryl Swanson says that a great brand is something for which there's no substitute. For me, there's no substitute for my iPhone, my kayak, or my '65 Ford Mustang. Some brands can offer that experience and others do not.

If a great brand is about creating an experience, where does the designer's role come in?

Every designer wants to work on brand design for the next Apple or Grey Goose. The design challenges are relatively easy to manage on a prestige brand with an already established emotional experience. It's much harder to work on a brand that doesn't already have a relevant experience. In that case, designers need

to create this experience. Do we decorate a package? Yes. Do we make it more ergonomically easy to use and dispense? Absolutely. That's all part of the process. However, telling a relevant brand story is what makes a designer's job exciting.

You redesigned Lean Cuisine and created a new visual architecture for the brand. What was the genesis of the project?

Nestlé created this particular brand category of prepared food in 1981. Since that time, the brand has grown from eleven products to ninety-eight across three price points, and numerous competitors have entered the market. We needed to help differentiate the brand from all of the newer competitors that had similar strategies centered [on] dieting. Instead of positioning Lean Cuisine as a kind of diet food, we determined that the brand should stand for wellness—a wellness that was attainable and approachable. So, we created a brand story around being healthy. We wanted consumers to feel there was an aspect of their lives where they could have

some control, and we wanted them to recognize that they could be fit without necessarily being an athlete. There was a level of empowerment that we expressed through this positioning: Lean Cuisine could help consumers feel better about what they ate.

If you consider this in the context of Maslow's hierarchy of needs, we moved the brand from the arena of the basic needs to that of the emotional, and then from the emotional to the arena of self-actualization. Laddering the brand from diet food into a tool for self-actualization was a real monster challenge, particularly for a $900 million category leader that first created this category.

How did you create the new visual language for Lean Cuisine?

We started by "deconstructing" the original experience and then creating a visual story that we introduced to a small group of consumers. Our audience could remember certain elements of the brand, but these elements didn't necessarily make them feel

Redesigned Lean Cuisine packaging, 2005

good. We soon realized that the Stouffer's logo on the package—the products had long been known as "Stouffer's Lean Cuisine"—was creating a negative association for the brand. In the consumer's mind, Stouffer's meant giant pans of lasagna and large portions of comfort food. These were things that were diminishing the story of wellness that we were trying to convey. Nestlé, which owns the brand, then made a decision to remove the Stouffer's logo from the package.

Once that was done, we determined that "wellness white" could be an "ownable" color in the category. We also used colors inspired by nature to define the different categories of the food. And we used the product as the hero on the front of the packaging. To keep the visual focus on the beautiful food and to drive appetite appeal, we put the brand name on the bottom of the package, something that has been done very rarely. We stripped out all the ancillary information on the pack and placed the photograph of the food on a clean white background. We worked with multiple photographers to create a consistent look for is all ninety-eight products.

You also worked on the rebranding of Quaker Oats. What was your approach to working with such an icon?

Quaker represents our heritage. It's believable and authentic. That stuff—all the cultural associations that come with the brand—is not baggage! When we ask consumers if they'd like to see a legacy brand's packaging change, they say, "No—I've used this brand since I was five years old. Why would I want it to change?" Previously, Larry—the name for the Quaker man—sat atop the Quaker word mark. We created a

visual design "unit" by placing Larry in the center of the Q. We then applied this identity to a series of new products. When we showed consumers how change would be portrayed, they agreed that the brand should have been this way since they were five years old.

Is it more appropriate to approach a brand redesign as a more evolutionary undertaking or as a revolutionary one?

It depends entirely on the brand. Lean Cuisine was a revolution—Quaker Oats is an *evolution*. The goal is for every brand to own an experience and to keep that experience relevant. We're not going to reinvent wellness in the context of oatmeal. There's also nothing else that can be communicated about oatmeal that would encourage you to eat oatmeal if you're already doing so. But you can certainly evolve the oatmeal experience, whether you do that by creating a bite-sized energy bar or by adding an ingredient to the product.

Maintaining the heritage of legacy brands to fit the twenty-first-century mindset is one of the great challenges of branding. How can Scotch tape grow its market share from 70 percent when its only competition is from private label tape brands? We'll have to wait and see, but I would predict that the experience will certainly change. How does Kleenex sell a box of tissues that costs $7 when the content inside is identical to what you can get from the same company for $3? Design has changed these expectations and experiences. Design has made brands more relevant.

FOLLOWING PAGES: A selection of Lean Cuisine packages

SIMPLE FAVORITES
LEANCUISINE®
Fettucini
Alfredo:
tender pasta with a
creamy cheese sauce
discover the
goodness
FAT
5g
CALORIES
250
FIBER
4g
NO PRESERVATIVES
NET WT 10 OZ (283g)
SERVING SUGGESTION • KEEP FROZEN
COOK THOROUGHLY

Maintaining the heritage of legacy brands to fit the twenty-first-century mindset is one of the great challenges of branding.

THIS PAGE:
Quaker, then (top)
and now (bottom)

25
HOW TO BRAND
A BEVERAGE

NOAH ARMSTRONG

Mike Bainbridge

Executive Vice President, Sterling Brands

Finding the essential in packaging for Tropicana

You're in charge of the Design Intelligence division of Sterling Brands. What's the focus of your work?

We provide the insights and inspiration so that we and our clients can understand everything that a brand is in its current state and everything that it can become through design. We seek to understand the role that design plays in the relationship that a consumer has with a brand today and in the future.

Design Intelligence helps set the course for design, but our process is not purely analytical. It's equally influenced by consumer insights and our own power to imagine. Our process would be entirely ineffectual if it involved a bunch of strategists sitting in a room coming up with ideas and then hoping a designer could interpret them. When those two sides work to weave together imagination and design from the outset, we get something truly special.

Tropicana came to Sterling for help with its orange juice packaging. What was the genesis of the project?

At one time, Tropicana was the orange juice industry leader. They had essentially created the not-from-concentrate category, and they owned that space as the premium brand for many years. Over time, several other brands became competitive, and Tropicana was no longer the only not-from-concentrate option on the shelf. We were asked to help the brand reclaim the superiority of its flagship product: Pure Premium orange juice. Tropicana needed to reassert itself as the industry leader.

How did you begin work on this project?

The project of "reclaiming superiority" presents the problem in very theoretical terms. That charge, alone, is not inspirational enough or directional enough to be solved through design. The first task of Design Intelligence was to distill that somewhat vague notion into something that could be addressed through design.

We spent the first few weeks identifying problems and suggesting themes that could be used for potential solutions. We then developed some concepts that focused on the feel of the brand. One theme was centered [on] the idea that drinking orange juice in the morning is a very grounding and peaceful moment—but the outcome is very energizing. Another concept was structured as a celebration of the product's "goodness."

This project allowed us to do some early research to find out from consumers where Tropicana's brand equity lies today, and where it could be taken in the future. Quantitative research findings told the Tropicana leadership that the brand's name recognition was extremely solid. We also learned that though consumers' affinity for the product was strong, it showed signs of erosion. It's important to remember that if brands aren't communicating their message, they're positioned in the market either by what other people say or by what the brands don't say. Even though Tropicana's leadership believed wholeheartedly that their product was better than any other, it became apparent that they hadn't devoted the time and resources to remind consumers of that.

We conducted qualitative research—which has its pitfalls—to find out what aspects of the brand resonated most strongly with consumers. Through a first phase of research, we found that the brand's straw-in-orange icon had a strong resonance in consumer's minds, even if they didn't identify it with Tropicana. But when consumers were asked to connect symbols with specific brands, we found that the straw-in-orange icon was very much associated with Tropicana. In fact, that symbol was the essence of Tropicana: a premium product that tasted exactly like what juicy oranges should taste like. It was very apparent that this was the quintessential visual representation of the Tropicana brand.

What else did you gather from your research?

We learned that Tropicana had two major problems. First, it was impossible for the brand to claim superiority when it looked like everyone else. And second, it had become increasingly difficult to distinguish its product in stores.

ABOVE:
Tropic-Ana, an early
Tropicana character

Tropicana's straw-in-orange trademark

Tropicana is a case study of how to evolve a brand responsibly. In these types of projects, our fundamental challenge is to keep the integrity of the brand intact, but also spur its progress in a way that's respectful to the relationship with the brand's consumer.

Essentially, the orange juice packaging formula had become the following: Make the logo green, put a slice of orange on it, and you're pretty much done—because that's what Tropicana does, and it's the market leader. Different designers had tinkered with the package many times over the years, but the process usually resulted in the addition of more elements. We needed to find out which elements held equity and which did not. And most of all, we needed to reassert the superiority of Tropicana.

Through research, we concluded that the superiority of the brand is expressed through the mark. The straw-in-orange is heroic, iconic, and what consumers identify as the complete mark. It was also the only element over which the company could truly claim ownership. That mark needed to be front and center, not tucked away, as it had been. We also determined that we should keep the contributing elements—like typography, specific colors, and language that worked in the brand's favor, but weren't necessarily unique to the brand. And we learned that there was something special about the typography of the Tropicana name, but that it wasn't sacred. It could be evolved. The nonessential banners, bars, and names could all be removed from the package. In order to reinforce the premium aspects of the brand and reassert their superiority, we needed to simplify the design.

What was your biggest challenge in working on this project?

Tropicana is a case study of how to evolve a brand responsibly. In these types of projects, our fundamental challenge is to keep the integrity of the brand intact, but also spur its progress in a way that's respectful to the relationship with the brand's consumer.

When do you know if you've created a good design?

Simon Lince, Sterling's chief creative officer, says that good design should look absolutely effortless. It's my job to make sure that our designers are given the tools they need to make that happen.

Tropicana's packaging before the straw-in-orange was brought front and center.

Tropicana packaging
from recent years,
after the trademark
had been brought front
and center.

How to Brand a Beverage

26
HOW TO BRAND
A DEPARTMENT STORE

JEREMY DIPAOLO

Michael Bierut

Pentagram

Design narratives from a master storyteller

You tapped into Saks Fifth Avenue's design heritage when you developed the new brand language for the store. Why look to the past when developing something for the future?

In the case of Saks, there are three reasons: First, the brand shepherds were simultaneously trying to capitalize on the authority of Saks' heritage and express a progressive, forward-looking fashion attitude. The store on Fifth Avenue really feels like it's been around for a long time, and the Saks leadership likes that. That's a good thing. Because of that, they can commission interior spaces that are progressive and lively, but that are within the context of a brand that has real history.

But we were told not to be restrained by that history. We were invited to come up with anything we wanted. We started by setting "Saks Fifth Avenue" in a million different typefaces. In Gotham, Helvetica, Bodoni. What happened—and this is the second reason we ended up going in the direction we did— was that these different versions all felt "sad" somehow. It was like taking a name that had real power and resetting it so that it was representing a store that could have opened yesterday. It was dismaying to look at these options. The brand felt denuded— castrated, almost.

Third, it's difficult to find a legitimate new position that you can own typographically. You take the words *Saks Fifth Avenue,* you set it in Helvetica like JCPenney, you set it in Bodoni like Giorgio Armani, you set it in any number of options—you name it, and no matter what neighborhood you're trying to move into, there's always somebody living there already.

Considering those kinds of constraints, what did Saks want you to accomplish?

What Saks really wanted was something easily identifiable from across the street—like Tiffany's blue or the Burberry plaid. Those visual iconographies are well established, and the only reason they mean anything is because they've been around for a while. When we started the project, it didn't seem that Saks had anything like that.

Did you have some kind of a "eureka" moment when you realized what the new design would be?

I remember one meeting where we gathered together some inspirational imagery. One set featured examples of mid-century New York School Abstract Expressionism, which included paintings by Barnett Newman and Franz Kline that had huge, overscale, very organic gestures on them. The clients really liked those and said, "This looks modern, but it has warmth to it." At that point, we were still experimenting with the logo by setting it in Helvetica and other variations. We'd revisited the script logo and someone had magnified it very large on their screen. I said, "Wait a second; that could be something."

So then we did a quick cleanup of the existing Saks script logo, divided it up into smaller squares, and started shuffling those around. We discovered that some of these images had an abstract power—yet they weren't patterns that came from nowhere. They were all derived from a way of writing the Saks name that has a sixty-year history. And the designs we created

looked new, and startlingly so. We'd found the ideal combination of both modernity and tradition, and it was really thrilling to see that because once you had these sixty-four squares, you could mix them up any way you wanted, and the result would always be compelling. When you do the math, it turns out that there are more combinations possible than there are particles in the known universe.

Why go for a system with almost infinite expressions? Many brand identity systems stick to a kind of formalistic rigidity.

For Saks, we were considering its collection of fifty-plus packages. There are two different ways to contend with a project like that: In one, you make all the packages part of a monolithic system. Tiffany's is monolithic, and Massimo's plan for Saks was monolithic. Massimo had a men's and a women's package, two different colors, and the same hang tag

Shopping bags for
Saks Fifth Avenue

A good identity is one where there are a lot of narratives you can project onto it—some fanciful, and some more plausible than others.

on both. That's one way you can go with it, and there's a certain power in that. We were trying to develop something with slightly idiosyncratic variations.

In essence, a department store like Saks is a frame around all the brands that you can buy there. So the store itself has to represent some larger idea. Part of that idea is that Saks defines the mark of quality, and it deems that these other brands are worthy of being sold as part of the Saks family. But the company is also trying to represent the kind of frenetic energy that is present when these choices are put together, and what happens when you're doing that on a very busy block in midtown Manhattan.

And unlike any other store you'd rank at the same level, Saks alone has its address in its basic name. It's not just "Saks," it's "Saks Fifth Avenue." In our design, the grid you get when you juxtapose the abstracted squares suggests the predictability of the New York City street grid—but the variation within each block is about the lack of uniformity and the diversity of life in any big city. It's the same variation you get from area to area, floor to floor, moment to moment in a store like Saks, which is constantly striving to surprise you.

I also like that the visual treatment makes a claim about the connoisseurship of the people who work at Saks and who buy and curate what you find at the store: They all attend to all those small details, those minute differences. And the same applies to the people who shop there.

A good identity is one where there are a lot of narratives you can project onto it—some fanciful, and some more plausible than others. In this case, people were able to articulate a lot of stories about what this identity meant, which was satisfying.

27

HOW TO BRAND
A CITY

NATASHA SAIPRADIST

Joyce Rutter Kaye

NYC & Company

The metropolis
as muse

**You transitioned from being editor in chief of
Print magazine to your role as senior editorial
director of NYC & Company, New York City's
official tourism organization. How did your
perspective change?**

As an editor, your primary responsibility is to know
your audience. Regardless of the medium you're
working in—print, Web, or video—you have to deeply
understand who you're writing for and be able to
craft a message to reach them in a meaningful way.
Once you've gained experience immersing yourself
in a particular audience's needs and delivering the
appropriate content to them, it becomes natural to
gravitate toward the challenge of connecting with
new and different audiences.

I've also been very fortunate to be engaged with brands that I can feel passionate about. *Print's* been around since 1940, and was long respected as a leading voice in design and visual culture. My job as editor was to maintain its integrity and to keep it relevant as a source of information, criticism, and design inspiration. I was able to do this with an extremely focused, talented group of editors, writers, and designers who were equally as passionate as I was about design and about continually expanding the boundaries of design journalism.

When the opportunity came up to work at NYC & Company, I jumped at it—who knew you could be the editor of New York City? As a longtime New Yorker, it was thrilling to realize that I could support the city I love, get people excited about visiting and living here, and continue to work with great writers and editors. There were, and are, many challenges in transitioning from a primarily print-based discipline to a more interactive environment, especially during a time when social media is evolving so rapidly and becoming so influential in the way we deliver information and editorial content. One of the great benefits of working in this environment is knowing almost instantly how readers are responding to what you're publishing. It's not always predictable, which makes it fun. Our readers love "Must-See NYC" itineraries, as you might expect, but they also love the arcane insider trivia we throw their way, such as the fact that there's a vaulted whispering wall in Grand Central Terminal near the Oyster Bar or a boat graveyard in Staten Island.

The NYC logo, created by Wolff Olins, has a multitude of applications.

What are your primary goals and objectives in your role?

Our goal as an organization is to fulfill Mayor Michael R. Bloomberg's goal of bringing 50 million visitors to New York City in 2012. We're well on our way, having hit 48.7 million in 2010. As senior editorial director, I need to ensure the consistency of our voice and editorial quality is maintained in everything we produce, which is vast and ranges from publications to the nycgo website, and from numerous e-newsletters to speeches and social media channels. Through all of the content we produce, we are trying to make the experience of visiting and living in the city as enjoyable, manageable, and accessible as possible.

NYC is definitely a brand. But being such a diverse city, how does NYC position itself?

Because NYC is such a diverse city and means so many things to so many people, we don't need to position it in one certain way, and as one kind of experience. Instead, we can emphasize the vibrancy and the energy of New York City and remind people why they want to come here now. Our recent "Get More NYC" campaign, with the tagline, "Be More. See More." plays against the message conveyed by a campaign like, "What happens in Vegas stays in Vegas." The underlying message of our outreach is, "What happens in NYC transforms you, and stays with you forever." All of our content, whether we're talking about a marketing campaign or an nycgo feature, speaks authentically to the true experience that New York City offers.

How effective has social media been in the branding and marketing of NYC?

Social media has been a great way to engage our audience with the content on nycgo—Twitter and Facebook have become substantial platforms for us to drive traffic to the site. We also use social media to promote NYC & Company marketing programs like Restaurant Week, and have been successful in using it for giveaways, such as tickets to performances. The features that get a lot of retweeting on Twitter are usually about free deals, timely events, and topics that New Yorkers tend to have strong opinions about, such as where to find the best pizza in the city.

Who decides what part of the city gets to be promoted and be featured on the nycgo website?

The editorial is shaped by a variety of things, including our own editorial vision and our ongoing mandate to promote all five boroughs of the city. The organization as a whole is responsible for shaping the strategy and creative for numerous City Hall programs all year round, and those all get a presence on the site. Some of those initiatives involve promoting biking in the city, encouraging people to visit Harlem, Coney Island, and Lower Manhattan, supporting the Mayor's Cup athletic competitions, and encouraging volunteerism. We get a lot of input on a formal level from inside and outside the organization, but there's nothing like going outside and talking to visitors themselves. Most New Yorkers love to share what they know about the city, so it's fun to be able to do this every day and actually get paid for it.

Collateral for NYC & Co, including guide books, website, and outdoor banners

28
HOW TO BRAND
A CULTURAL INSTITUTION

MYLES GAYTHWAITE

Rob Giampietro
Project Projects

Rob Giampietro, designer, educator, critic, and principal in the design firm Project Projects, discusses crafting the identity for SALT, a cultural institution in Istanbul, Turkey.

Thoughtful evocations of identities influx

When Vasif Kortun, SALT's director, first approached you, what did he want to accomplish?

The idea was that three institutions would be joining together under one umbrella: the Garanti Gallery, which focuses on contemporary art; Platform Garanti, which focuses on architectural and cultural projects; and the Ottoman Bank Archive and Research Center, which is part of the Ottoman Bank Museum. Those three entities coming together under one roof presented a very different kind of cultural institution.

In what way?

One of the things that stood out was that Vasif and his colleagues talked about SALT being an exhibiting and researching institution, rather than a collecting institution. The emphasis was not on having materials hidden away in an archive collecting dust. Instead, the focus was on creating exhibitions and nurturing public discourse. As a result, the institution would always be changing, always experimenting. So the question for us was, "How can we approach that kind of problem?"

And what was your initial approach?

We went to Istanbul and talked about different ways of thinking about this problem, and we discussed how identity projects had been approached in the past. After we were awarded the project, we outlined some specific design directions, each of which played off the idea of fludity and change. One touchstone was MTV's identity from the 1980s, which constantly adapted for different on-air situations and contexts. We were interested in this idea of something that is consistent but also mutable. And yet even as it's constantly changing, it's also perpetually becoming more itself—no one ever mistook MTV for something else.

Why this idea of "perpetually becoming"?

We felt that because SALT was so active, it was an institution that was defined by its present and its future, rather than its past. It seemed appropriate that the identity was always going to be in a state of flux—it was always going to be developing layers upon layers, rather than being fixed at a certain point.

Another reference for us was Matthew Carter's Walker typeface, which was designed for the Walker Art Center in the 1990s. Carter took the institutional typeface model—where an organization would have this one proprietary typeface—and made it more dynamic. Even though Walker was a proprietary typeface, that typeface didn't have a singular look. So we thought, "Well, what would a contemporary approach to this kind of typographic solution be?"

We started experimenting with an alphabet, and we decided to alter the letters *S, A, L,* and *T,* almost like DNA code. Those four letters are different from the others, while the rest of the letters have a typographic consistency. But the letters for *SALT* would

ABOVE:
Kraliçe, a custom geometric sans serif typeface, designed to work within the new identity for SALT, a new institution in Istanbul.

BELOW:
Speculative future versions of Kraliçc by other invited designers.

always stand out. Early on, SALT referred to itself informally as an "institute of difference." So we like that the identity of the institution would always itself be changing—even if it's embedded in this more specific context of the organization itself.

What other typographic influences did you consider?

When we went to Istanbul, we noticed the typeface DIN a lot, and we became interested in how to use DIN without using DIN—we thought we would tweak it a little. We were also really interested in the typefaces that were used for playing cards because cards are a mutable, shiftable set of items with gamelike, mutiplayer qualities. It turned out that a typographer friend—Timo Gaessner in Berlin—was working on 123Queen, a typeface that was based on playing card numerals and letters with echoes of DIN. We took the name "Queen" and translated it into Turkish, which is "Kraliçe," and that typeface forms the basis of the alphabet. The letters *S, A, L,* and *T* will be redesigned by different designers over time as the institution goes forward. So, in a way, the design becomes a curatorial program, an institutional typeface, and a solution to the identity problem.

Different designers will be changing the SALT letterforms over time—how is that going to work?

SALT is interested in finding ways to bring new creative people to Istanbul and generating new conversations as a result of that interaction. We thought that it was an interesting idea to invite contemporary typographers, designers, and artists to Istanbul to give a talk about their work at SALT and then—as a way of paying it forward—they would then be invited to change the Kraliçe typeface.

How future designers will approach the typeface is up to them. It's up to us as curators to ask designers to give the face a different perspective, but we're still figuring out who we'll approach. As these different versions of the typeface are used, they'll start to layer on top of one another, in a sense.

What are the different considerations you have for designing a cultural identity as opposed to a more commercial enterprise?

With a cultural institution, the public is a third term. It's important that the public is considered during the design process, and that there's some way of engaging them—or even representing their contribution to that institution—within the identity itself. With SALT, we were very conscious of the public—there's Garanti, there's SALT, and there's the public. The shifting relationships between these three groups allowed us to frame this particular design intervention.

Place and time had an influence on this project.

Yes. I think the best ideas are always strongly contextual, even site specific. Some identities emerge from interesting conversations with interesting clients. It's an iterative process: We have an idea, that idea gets refined, and so we change it. Then, it gets changed some more. Out of that back and forth comes something that neither we nor the client would have conceived initially. When that happens, the identity represents a melding of our two viewpoints.

ABOVE AND RIGHT: The typeface applied to the overall brand identity, including posters, the website, signage, bags, and T-shirts

SALT GÖRSEL VE MADDİ KÜLTÜRDE KRİTİK KONULARI DEĞERLENDİRİR;
YENİLİKÇİ PROGRAMLARI, DENEYSEL DÜŞÜNCEYİ VE ARAŞTIRMAYI DESTEKLER.

MERHABA

saltonline.org

HELLO

How to Brand a Cultural Institution

SALT

◄ ► C + ⌂ http://www.saltonline.org

📖 Apple Yahoo! Google Maps YouTube

🏠 ⭐ 🏷 TR

DISTRIBUTED WORK:
KAREN VERSCHOOREN,
EMEL KURMA,
HASAN YALÇINKAYA

ONLY
5 DAYS
LEFT

NEW VIDEO
Lastwinterspringneve
rcame

salt channel | video

New
Summer
Hours!

Galleries: 11am–6pm
Shop: 11am–6pm
Coffee Bar: 11am–3pm

announcements | beyoglu
summer

Get Inv

get involved

exhibitions | on view | beyoglu

29

HOW TO BRAND
PRINT

PORTIA HUBERT

Gail Anderson
SpotCo

Reflections on typography, entertainment, and design as performance

You've worked primarily in print design when at *Rolling Stone* and when creating branding campaigns for Broadway productions. What are your feelings about the power of print?

There are emotions and memories associated with print that I don't think you can experience without actually holding and touching something. Consider an old copy of one of the magazines from your youth—that rolled-up issue of *Tiger Beat* that had your groovy preteen handwriting on the love quiz on page 12. Or your battered copy of *Catcher in the Rye*. I don't think there's a digital equivalent for these things. That said, I could end up caring more about saving space, and being able to access information immediately, than keeping all these mementos. But I haven't yet reached that point when my reading material has become a burden that outweighs my sentimental leanings.

SpotCo has done such important work in advertising and branding for arts and entertainment. When you are designing or art directing for specific projects, are you thinking of the audience?

In my ten years at SpotCo, I learned to very attentively consider the audience. It's not that I didn't do that in the past when I was working in magazines. But it felt like the stakes were a little higher when designing artwork to generate an emotional response from potential ticket buyers—that would usually be the first thing that they see.

In theater, there were often many folks involved in the decision-making process, which was new for me. And for the most part, we presented anywhere from six to a dozen ideas for larger shows. That was a complete surprise after refining only singular ideas at *Rolling Stone.* Perhaps that's also a function of the era when I was at *Rolling Stone,* where we only had a single "client."

When you were awarded the medal of AIGA in recognition for your contribution to design, critic Steven Heller wrote that your work at *Rolling Stone* showcased your "theatrical typography." Do you feel that description fits?

Steve Heller has suggested that since my typography was "theatrical," the move to SpotCo in 2002 was a natural one. I myself remember thinking, "Well, the magazine spreads were like posters, so I can make theater posters—right?" The transition was actually much more difficult for me than I'd ever imagined—and the design part was the least of it! My world was turned upside down, because I was used to working in a two-week cycle, and I was now sitting with projects that sometimes lingered for months. I had to learn a

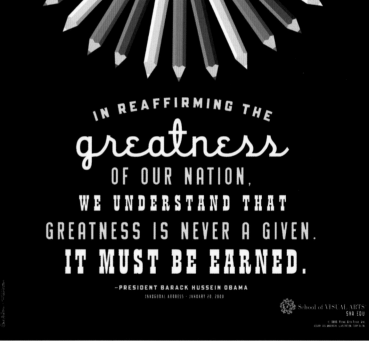

IN REAFFIRMING THE *greatness* OF OUR NATION, WE UNDERSTAND THAT GREATNESS IS NEVER A GIVEN. IT MUST BE EARNED.

—PRESIDENT BARACK HUSSEIN OBAMA
INAUGURAL ADDRESS · JANUARY 20, 2009

School of VISUAL ARTS
SVA.EDU

One of a series
of posters for the
School of Visual Arts

whole new vocabulary relating to theater—for who did what on a show, not to mention the theatrical pecking orders that often weren't entirely clear. In terms of design itself, the work had to become a bit louder and less fussy. There are definitely pieces that are a little too heavily Photoshopped for my personal taste, but that's outweighed by the projects featuring "theatrical type" that still hold up. In the end, I built up a body of work that I'm proud of. My time at SpotCo was a tremendous learning experience.

How do you translate the sensibility of a theatrical production into design? How do you use typography to express emotion?

I can't imagine not being able to use typography to express emotion. It's essential to what I do—I belong more to the "ornamental" school of design than to the "clean and simple" one. That said, I really admire designers who can generate the same experience using juxtapositions of unusual photography and straightforward type solutions. I'd like to do some of that kind of work now, to see if I'm capable of it.

Now that you've started your own firm, are you considering working in new media?

I had little interest in designing for the Web when people were first shifting into that medium. It felt like the visual executions were way too limited by the technology—in particular, as this applies to text fonts. But thinking about ways that people receive information is pretty intriguing, as are all of the navigational subtleties. And even though I'm not quite sold on reading magazines on the iPad, the device itself just makes me giddy. I hope that there'll be a way for me to incorporate apps into my work, but I get the feeling that I would need to go back to school to do that, which makes my head hurt.

What skills does a designer need today to survive the dynamic world of visual communication?

I was part of the generation of designers who moved from drafting table to desktop computer, and who were hands-on by necessity. While I'm not as comfortable in the Adobe Creative Suite as a designer a few years younger, I can get through most projects with a limited amount of hand-holding. But a student entering the current marketplace needs to have many more skills under his or her belt than I had to have in 1984. The expectation is that you've got to know something about motion or the Web—or, now, the iPad—since you grew up with a mouse in your chocolate-stained hands.

An important skill that is way too low on the list, though, is basic written communication skills. I can't believe how many designers are incapable of composing a clear, coherent email. While you don't have to be Hemingway, knowledge of basic English grammar should be a given and not a bonus. And come on—the computer pretty much shakes you by the shoulders with all of those green underscores when you screw up.

TOP:
Poster for a production of Peer Gynt

BOTTOM:
Book cover for *New Vintage Type*

RIGHT:
Spread for *Rolling Stone* magazine

The Next Queen of Soul

ALICIA KEYS IS IMPOSSIBLY YOUNG (20) AND EXTRAORDINARILY GIFTED ("SONGS IN A MINOR") – A NEW YORK GIRL WHO'S POISED TO TAKE OVER THE WORLD

30
HOW TO BRAND
A NONPROFIT

BRIAN GAFFNEY

Jennifer Kinon & Bobby C. Martin, Jr.

Original Champions of Design

Updating a classic for modern times

You recently redesigned the Girl Scouts logo. What were the organization's goals for the identity refresh?

JENNIFER: The Girl Scouts had made a lot of internal changes and they were ready to communicate them. They wanted to convey that the Girl Scouts is as appropriate to today's girls as it was to their moms.

BOBBY: They wanted to figure out ways to keep girls involved and excited about being a part of Girl Scouts even as they get older, when Girl Scouts is no longer seen as the cool thing to do.

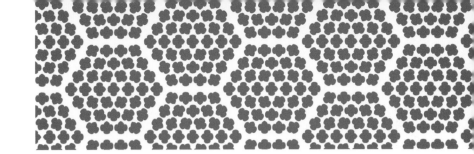

How did the goals translate into design objectives for OCD?

JENNIFER: The Girl Scouts have 108 councils, recently consolidated from over 300. All these individual councils are contractually allowed to do whatever they want to do with their identity. The usual approach for the organization was to take the Saul Bass stamp—a beautiful, iconic mark—and stamp everything with it. They were hanging their whole brand on a single mark, but the brand is more expansive than that. The brand needed to be able to sit on the desk of Michelle Obama or on a banner out on a soccer field. The brand needed to be fashionable.

We were determined to give them some flexibility and "ownability" so that the brand could extend through all possible touchpoints. Our goal was to take the Saul Bass mark and base an entire system on it. We wanted to empower the Girl Scouts with a broad enough spectrum of graphic language so that they could make any flier they wanted and still be "on brand."

BOBBY: We used a handful of elements to challenge the way that girls and women are typically thought of—we moved away from pinks and childish graphic devices, and worked to engage girls and inspire them in a new way.

Girl Scouts also had a massive brand book, filled with guidelines dating all the way back to 1978 when Saul Bass created the mark. Every time a company had come in to do minor modifications, new guidelines were added. We created a short brand guide—a cheat sheet of sorts—that anybody could pin up or keep in a drawer. This short guide provided simplicity and flexibility.

What did the research process for this project involve?

JENNIFER: The first step was to learn as much as possible about the visual history of the Girl Scouts. We went through the archives, looked through each and every bag and tag on every outfit and every pin and badge. Then we interviewed key internal players. We also talked with the girls, and we made art collages with them. We hung out with them and listened to them talk about the brand.

BOBBY: We were also given prior research material, and we surrounded ourselves with all of the quantitative research that had been done. We looked at things that were currently happening in the world of girls' pop culture. We wanted to be archaeologists of design and find the things in the brand that were there in the beginning.

How had the trefoil mark evolved over time?

JENNIFER: Before Saul Bass, the trefoil had a point on the i. Bass took the point away when he made his beautiful mark. Our goal was to create a system where

The iconic trefoil mark, designed by Saul Bass, updated for the Girl Scouts and grouped into patterns

the point and the Saul Bass mark live together. That iconic trefoil mark signified the Girl Scouts. When Girl Scouts started, there was an eagle in it—then the eagle went away. Later, they put a *GS* in it. At another time, they made it into an outline. Our challenge was to consolidate these iconic marks into one icon.

How do you handle the challenge of refreshing an iconic brand that was designed by such a legend?

BOBBY: From people like Paul Rand, Saul Bass, and Massimo Vignelli, we learned the things that got us excited about being designers. We wanted to keep the integrity of the design as much as possible, while, at the same time, making subtle tweaks that helped it to stand out as a design and organization that is alive and well. Once we actually understood where the Girl Scouts wanted to be and discovered why they refreshed the brand in 1978, we knew what tweaks had to be made.

The result was to take the trefoil back to its more distinct shape; one that was less symmetrical, to a more distinct trefoil shape, with a bit more of a point at the bottom. Going back to the true trefoil shape required some additional, subtle changes. As we made those changes, we asked ourselves, "WWSBD?"—What Would Saul Bass Do? We did that with every decision we made.

Decisions about the bangs, noses, and lips were made based upon our observations of the Girl Scouts and our conversations with them. When we started to look at the silhouettes, we noticed that there was a very specific kind of girl that was in the illustration. We started to make some tweaks to see if we could make her a little less specific, while still keeping a lot of the same elements.

JENNIFER: We wanted to age the girls down and we wanted to make them iconic. We wanted to make them "everygirl" through simplification and the use of shape. Simplifying and stretching out the mark made it a symbol of a strong, young woman, in all of her many colors, shapes, and sizes.

BOBBY: Beyond the benefit of returning the trefoil to its distinct shape, the process then gave us the opportunity to build a visual system. The trefoil shape can now be used for patterns, for punctuation, for other visual elements—it can be used in many exciting and creative ways.

ABOVE:
The trefoil, used here on business cards and letterhead, can be used for patterns, for punctuation, and for other visual elements.
RIGHT:
The Girl Scouts brand guide "cheat sheet"

We wanted to be archaeologists of design and find the things in the brand that were there in the beginning.

31
HOW TO BRAND
A CORPORATION

MANAL NASSAR

Steff Geissbuhler

C&G Partners

Vocabularies of design, symbolism, and what makes a memorable brand

How would you describe your approach to branding?

I like problem solving. That is at the core of what I do and what I'm interested in visually. Branding and corporate identity projects consolidate all the attributes you associate with a company's products or services into a visual form. Distilling those traits into a mark is a challenge, because the design can only express so many things. My approach is to find the simplest means to express the big idea and depict the company not necessarily as it is at that moment, but in terms of what it aspires to be.

Can you give me an example? For instance, how did you approach the redesign of NBC's corporate identity when you did that in the early '80s?

NBC originally used a peacock made out of colorful paintbrushes as a device to indicate that a program was going to be in "living color," back in the era when color TV was a new and exciting phenomenon. The peacock image was not originally the network's corporate identity.

Before we were called in, NBC had gone through all sorts of logos. The "snake" consisted of the network's letters linked together in one connected line. Another was the letter *N* rendered in a patriotic blue and red that was very abstracted and looked "hard." That design didn't seem the right tone for NBC, which is far more entertaining than that mark would suggest. The letter *N* didn't mean anything, and there was no reason to abbreviate a three-letter abbreviation like CBS and ABC, even though people no longer know what the letters stand for. We felt that the peacock, which the network had used in the past, was actually a very appropriate symbol. It's a proud bird showing off its feathers, and it's associated with color. People could relate to that. We redesigned the peacock, simplified it, and then assigned the colors based on the color bars the technicians use to calibrate the broadcast equipment.

The identity you created for Merck is both a brand mark and a word mark. What are the challenges in this type of project?

There are many. Merck is one of the oldest pharmaceutical and chemical companies in the world. We created a symbol for the company that was made out of simple, geometric forms that are obviously related

to tablets, pills, capsule shapes, petri dishes, and other objects associated with medicine. In the white space, you can even see a mortar and pestle shape, an ancient symbol related to drugs and medicine. With the symbol we created, the simplest geometric forms communicate what is necessary. At the same time, the aqua color associated with hospital scrubs made sense. Previously, every division of Merck had its own individual symbols and logos. We created a graphic nomenclature system to allow Merck to be consistently communicated as the overarching brand and parent company while still allowing the company's many divisions to be represented within that system. Even in Europe, where the company name is *MSD,* the symbol and type tie it back to the parent corporation's brand. We wanted to consolidate it and make it all one aesthetic.

What trends do you see in branding today?

There's an unbelievably competitive situation at the moment. Not just between design firms, but between brands. Everybody wants to have a very memorable brand that people recall instantly and associate with the right attributes and storyline. And it gets more and more difficult to find that—especially for companies that don't have tangible products that you

can relate to. For instance, with financial companies, you can no longer show a dollar bill or a coin, because the financial world is not about cash anymore. It's about transactions, futures, stocks and bonds, investing, portfolio management, mortgages. These are abstract ideas and concepts that you can't easily grab onto visually. So you need to get philosophical and metaphorical to represent the attributes and culture of a company, and that makes the design more difficult. Since there are more established brands and designers coming up with smart ideas, it gets tougher to compete.

You've worked on projects for clients like Alhurra TV, Radio Free Europe, and Voice of America where the identities are used in different regions of the world. In the era of globalization, how does branding change?

Your symbolism cannot be based on your own national vocabulary—it has to be understood everywhere in the world. So you find symbols that have a much more common denominator so that everybody is clear about what they're looking at. Radio Free Europe had originally used a Liberty Bell as their symbol, and of course that only means something in the United States. In the countries where it was broadcasting, not only was that meaningless, but it was wrong. In an Islamic country, the bell is associ-

ated with church. In Russia, it means "party time" and that's obviously wrong, too. That was clearly an oversight and based on not doing the necessary research. You cannot communicate in different countries around the world assuming that everybody understands your language.

Anything you wish you could have changed?

I did an identity for NPR years ago. It was a very flexible corporate identity, and it was redesigned by someone else on the basis that my logo wouldn't work on the Web. The new designers took the same idea of three squares that I had created and set the letters lowercase, which made it much less memorable and less fun to play with than the "sound tiles" that I had designed. I regret that the client didn't come back to me to tell me that something had changed. I wish that they would have asked me to update the identity and move it forward, rather than going to somebody else to redesign it. These identities are like my children, and I would like to see them grow up, mature, and be successful.

ABOVE:
A previous NPR logo, designed by Geissbuhler, before the public radio station's most recent redesign

LEFT:
Logos for Time Warner Cable, pharmaceutical company Merck & Co, the Nonprofit Finance Fund, and The Signature Theatre Company

RIGHT:
Exhibition graphics for the Museum of Jewish Heritage

32
HOW TO BRAND
TELEVISION
PROGRAMMING

SASCHA DONN

Kenna Kay

MTV Networks

TV Land

Creating an identity that moves along at sixty frames per second

As the person in charge of branding TV Land, what does branding mean to you?

In our case, a good brand tells you what you're going to get. For example, when you go to Starbucks, you know the experience you're going to have: You know the quality of the coffee you're going to get, you know the kind of music you're going to be listening to, and you know that all of that is going to be the same every

The most recent brand
for TV Land

time. Successful brands create loyal customers who come back again and again because they feel the brand is an extension of their personalities.

That idea relates to the MTV brand in the sense that MTV packages a group of entertainment products in a way that all of the programming is going to appeal to the customer. Viewers know what they're going to get if they watch one of our shows. And our goal is to make sure that if they like one thing that we feature, they're going to enjoy the other things we offer them, too.

In television, there's a real push and pull with the overarching consumer brand as it relates to the individual properties. Some people can't even tell you what channel their favorite shows are on. Yet some media properties develop a very distinct personality, and they want customers to feel a deep sense of connection. They want customers to be consistently loyal to that channel and have a sense that when they turn it on at 9 p.m. on Wednesday, let's say, they'll always find something they like.

But there's a debate within the television industry about this approach, as you see with certain networks that let the shows stand for themselves. For example, HBO features a collection of wonderful individual shows. How do all the shows add up in the context of the network's overall identity? Maybe the identity is expressed in the quality of HBO's programming, but network branding has certainly taken a backseat to the promotion of the individual programs.

What do you think is a television brand that has done a good job branding itself?

I love PBS. One thing that's been said about the network is that "it's like going to a good friend's house for dinner—you don't know what they're going to cook but you know it's going to be good." And that's the way I feel about PBS. I'm not really that interested in volcanoes, but I know if I sit down and watch a PBS program about volcanoes, I'm going to be engrossed in it. There are very few programs on PBS that I don't like to watch. That level of engagement and brand integrity is what I strive for with TV Land.

You're beginning a brand "refresh" project. Can you talk about that and give some background on how the project evolved?

This project came about because most consumers have an outdated perception of TV Land. Most consumers think of the network as "the home of classic television"—that actually used to be a tagline for us. But over the past five years, we've been creating original programming. And original programming is really the future for us and for all of MTV Networks. For us, that includes original programming like *Hot in Cleveland* and *Retired at 35*. So we've been making our forays into this arena and trying to redefine ourselves. It's been very difficult because we don't have gigantic advertising budgets that would allow us to go out there and say, "TV Land has changed." The way we reach our consumers, of course, is on the channel itself. TV Land has 90 million viewers, so we put our advertising and promotion on air. But how do you reach the rest of your potential viewing audience without spending huge amounts of money on ads?

To emphasize that we've changed, we've been tweaking TV Land's identity and refreshed our look last spring when we launched two new sitcoms in June 2011. And we didn't call it a "rebranding," per se, because there are things we like about where we are as a brand. For example, we don't want to redesign the logo—but we feel we need a new spring outfit, so to speak.

TV Land has gone through a lot of changes in the past few years as it's moved away from being "the home of classic television." The brand went through a refresh only a few years ago. How does this refresh differ from the last one?

We "refreshed" about a year and a half ago, close to the beginning of 2010, and in terms of mechanics, it's been a difficult package to work with. We transitioned into high definition last June [2011], so we needed to be a little cleaner in terms of rendering and graphics so we could deliver our branding and design work in a timely manner. With the need to simplify the design for HD, we saw an opportunity to assess where TV Land stands as a brand. I also think that in our transition away from "the home of classic television," we lost a little bit of our brand personality.

Our sweet-spot audience is women, but we want to appeal to the entire twenty-five- to fifty-four-year-old age range. As an entertainment channel, we want to be fun, upbeat, and escapist. We're not trying to be the moral at the end of the story—it's more about letting viewers "have their own time," the hour when they can put their feet up and watch TV. We've been trying to reflect this idea in the graphics, but it's difficult. And another factor we have to consider is that the amount of time for promotions on the channel has been reduced over the years. There's less time for messaging. So we're figuring out how to do more with less. Everything has to count: The color palette, the typeface—all of it has to convey some kind of meaning, some kind of messaging, some kind of feeling about the brand.

33

HOW TO BRAND
A BRANDING AGENCY

CHANGZHI LEE

Michael Ian Kaye

Mother

The necessity of self-reflexive branding and not trying too hard

The Mother brand has a very distinct identity— the agency has a working kitchen, living room spaces, and lots of ephemera. How do you create a brand experience like this that seems so easy and natural?

The genesis of Mother, both as a brand and as an idea, comes from the notion of a bunch of people who sit around a table—a table like the one that your mother might set. The idea is also that the environment generates a sense of warmth and fun, as well as a sense of mystery or conflict—it evokes the complex vocabulary of emotions and experiences we can have with our family members. But it also reminds us that we all come from a common space and have a common purpose. A family's common purpose is to sustain and nourish the new generations that can propel it into the future.

Our sole intention in creating the space that is Mother was to materialize a place where you felt comfortable, where you were surprised, and where you feel intrigued but not taken off guard.

In that sense, the experience is not really theater but about authenticity?

There's a fine line between trying and tying too hard. This is all about creating an experience that doesn't look like we're trying to create an experience. I think that the premise was never about theater but about the effort to create a culture.

Having the kitchen at the heart of the agency is crucial because that's where people go to get their coffee, and that's where the most interesting conversations happen. That's also where people congregate during a party, so making the kitchen the "hero" of the agency is a key dimension of our personality.

Beyond the studio being a comfortable environment to walk into, we foster a certain sensibility by working at a common table. There are no offices, there are no walls, and we move around. We change seats every four months so that we can meet different members of the family. One week, I can be sitting next to a "co-partner"—as we refer to the partners here—and the next month, I can be sitting next to an intern. Through these interactions, we build a culture that is not based on stature or status but on what makes us uniquely us.

Has your approach to branding been successful with the clients you've worked with?

Every brand is different. Our brand is defined by the collection of diverse creatives who've gathered together, and that's what we've tried to embrace when designing this building and this experience. We knew there would be people coming in from diverse backgrounds with many unique aesthetic sensibilities. Our objective was to use that influence to create a place of warmth and creativity.

The process of how we define our Mother brand experience is very similar to how we define a client's brand experience. We ask ourselves, "Who is the audience? What's the objective? How do we want to make the guest feel?" And then we figure out the best way to communicate that.

The process is always going to be the same, in the sense that we always work according to our particular design algorithm, but the outcome should never be the same, because brands are like people. They have their own voices and their own personalities. Our agency is devoted to responding to that unique essence and making it our focus.

Is the crux of the branding process defined by a relationship between the consumer and the brand?

What a brand needs is a certain pull, a pull that works on its core audience and beyond that core to its "aspirational" audience. There are some brands, as there are some people, who command attention loudly. There are some brands that are the "strong, silent type" who draw people to them through their elusiveness and evasiveness, by generating a sense of mystery.

The key to this process is trying to define what that brand is, because once we do that, we can determine a voice that communicates outward and draws inward.

Take a brand like Target, for example. With their bull's-eyes and smiley faces, Target has a visually loud design language. Part of that sensibility is about being a mass brand, and part of that is being about fast, fun, and friendly. That's the tone of voice that Target needs to speak outwardly, either to influencers or to its core audience.

Conversely, New Balance is a brand that's a bit more intellectual—we're now working for them on a fashion-based project. New Balance's consumer doesn't want to be told that New Balance is the best; they want to discover the brand. So how can we build an experience that allows the consumer to discover and feel part of the brand instead of feeling like they're being spoken to? In each brand's case, we're looking for a way to engage the brand's target consumer— and we do this in the same way that a person would engage somebody who they wanted to hang out with.

Our process is focused on discovering a brand's point of view and defining that—instead of letting the outside world define the brand.

We have a limited amount of time throughout the day. How much time do you think should be spent on technology and how much time spent on observing reality?

As many doors as the computer has opened for us, it's clear that everything is not always online. I think there's a perception among younger people that all the answers to life can be found on the Web. But there are so many things that can't be experienced, seen, or read there, and that don't exist online. My fascination is not so much about observing reality but in observing how people interact with spaces, with film, or even with theater. All of those things are so important in developing brand communications.

Wall of portraits and assorted ephemera at Mother's New York City studio

SOURCES

REFERENCES AND FOOTNOTES

Chapter 1

1. Gregory Curtis, *The Cave Painters, Probing the Mysteries of the World's First Artists*, (New York, Anchor Books, 2006), 92-95.

2. Gregory Curtis, 97-105.

3. Gregory Curtis, 93.

4. David Lewis-Williams, *The Mind in the Cave, Consciousness and the Origins of Art*, (London, Thames & Hudson Ltd., 2002), 237.

5. *Gregory Curtis, 96.*

6. Joseph Nechvatal, "Immersive Excess in the Apse of Lascaux," Technoetic Arts 3:3, 2005, 181–192, doi: 10.1386/tear.3.3.181/1.

7. Richard Gray, "Prehistoric cave paintings took up to 20,000 years to complete," *The Telegraph*, October 5, 2008, http://www.telegraph.co.uk/earth/3352850/Prehistoric-cave-paintings-took-up-to-20000-years-to-complete.html.

8. Gregory Curtis, 230-238.

9. David Lewis-Williams, 228-229.

10. David Lewis-Williams, 75.

11. Tracy Staedter, "Ancient Shell Beads Could Be First Sign of Modern Culture", *Scientific American*, June 23, 2006, http://www.scientificamerican.com/article.cfm?id=ancient-shell-beads-could

12. David Lewis-Williams, 78.

13. David Lewis-Williams, 237

14. Gregory Curtis, 96.

15. Nicholas J. Conard, "A female figurine from the basal Aurignacian of Hohle Fels Cave in southwestern Germany," Nature, Volume 459, 14 May 2009, 248—252, doi:10.1038/nature07995

16. Denis Vialou, 29-31.

17. David Lewis-Williams, 95-96.

Chapter 3

1. Grant McCraken. *Culture & Consumption* (Bloomington, IN: Indiana University Press, 1988).

2. Forbes.com, 2005, www.forbes.com/2005/07/05/wedgewood-pottery-businessman-cx_0705wedgewood_print.html

3. Gaye Blake Roberts and Robin Reilly. "Wedgwood." Grove Art Online. Oxford Art Online, March 16, 2011.

4. Ibid.

5. *Time.* "Prince of Pottery," www.time.com/time/printout/0,8816,712258,00.html

6. Oxford Art Online.

7. Neil McKendrick, John Brewer, and J. H. Plumb. *The Birth of a Consumer Society: The Commercialization of 18th-Century England* (Bloomington, IN: Indiana University Press, 1982), p. 1.

8. McKendrick, et al., p. 103.

9. McKendrick, et al., p. 110.

10. McKendrick, et al., p. 133.

11. Robin Hildyard. *English Pottery* (London: V&A Publications, 2005), p. 198.

12. McKendrick, et al., p. 138.

13. McKendrick, et al., p. 141.

14. Hildyard, p. 198.

15. McKendrick, et al., p. 135.

16. McKendrick, et al., p. 121.

Chapter 5

William Cahn. *Out of the Cracker Barrel: The Nabisco Story, From Animal Crackers to Zuzus* (New York: Simon & Schuster, 1969).

Alec Davis. *Package and Print: The Development of the Label and Container* (London: Faber, 1967).

Hal Morgan. *Symbols of America* (New York: Viking Penguin, 1986).

Susan Strasser. *Satisfaction Guaranteed: The Making of the American Mass Market* (New York: Pantheon Books, 1989).

A&S, January 1913, "Principles and Practice of Advertising," Gerald B Wadsworth.

Chapter 8

1. *Century of American Icons*, Edited by Mary Cross, Chp 7, p. 131.

2. Pepsi FAQs website. "Ads and History–Highlights," www.pepsiusa.com/faqs.php?section=highlights

3. http://designhistory.org/advertising_fall_08.html

4. Mary Cross (Ed.). *A Century of American Icons* (Westport, CT: Greenwood Press, p. 148).

5. Alfredo Marcantonio. *Is The Bug Dead?* (New York: Stewart, Tabori & Chang, p. 6).

6. Walter Henry Nelson. *Small Wonder: The Amazing Story of the Boklswagen Beetle* (Cambridge, MA: Bentley Publishers, p. 219).

7. Phil Patton. *Bug: The Strange Mutations of the World's Most Famous Automobile* (New York: Simon & Schuster, pp. 95, 98).

8. Bob Garfield. "Top 100 Advertising Campaigns." *Advertising Age.*

9. *Graphic Design History,* Steven Heller, Georgette Balance, p. 305.

10. *A Century of American Icons*, p. 123.

11. *Cool Rules: Anatomy of an Attitude*, Dick Pountain and David Robins, p 19.

12. www.45cat.com/artist/the-majorettes

13. www.youtube.com/watch?v=BTvKh64sl_w

14. *Levi Strauss & Co.* by Lynn Downey.

15. *Levi Strauss & Co.* by Lynn Downey.

16. Email with Lynn Downey.

17. *1000 Covers–A History of the Most Influential Magazine in Pop Culture*, Introduction by Jann Wenner, pg. 5-6.

18. *Encyclopedia of American Journalism*, Stephen L. Vaughn, p. 456.

19. *Rebels Wit Attitude: Subversive Rock Humorists*, Iain Ellis, p. 92.

20. CNN, "A life made famous by 'Almost Famous'", September 25, 2000.

21. PIB People was ranked number one in ad revenue since 1991 by the Audit Bureau of Circulations.

22. Interview with Dick Stolley, Founding Managing Editor, *People* magazine.

23. Bill Hooper, Archivist, Time Inc., Time Inc. Archives.

24. Interview with Dick Stolley, Founding Managing Editor, *People* magazine—backup on figures.

25. "Historical Dictionary of the 1960s" by James Stuart Olson; p. 248, found on Google books.

26. http://americanhistory.si.edu/collections/object.cfm?key=35&objkey=33

27. "Pan Am" Lynn Homan, p. 106, found on Google books.

28. http://www.bls.gov/opub/cwc/cm20030124ar05p1.htm

29. "Pan Am" Lynn Homan, p. 106, found on Google books.

30. "Pan Am's Steep Dive," *New Yorker*, June 22, 1981.

31. "When flying was caviar," Corey Kilgannon, *New York Times*, 2003.

32. Pan Am ad examples: link + link.

33. "Flight of the Imagination," *Eye Magazine* #73: http://www.eyemagazine.com/feature.php?id=168&fid=773

34. "Flight of the Imagination," *Eye Magazine* #73: http://www.eyemagazine.com/feature.php?id=168&fid=773

Chapter 9

1. Birth of an MTV Nation, *Vanity Fair*, November 2000.

2. *Rebels and Chicks: A History of the Hollywood Teen Movie*, Stephen Tropiano, p. 197 Random House Digital, Inc. 2006.

3. Inside MTV By R. Serge Denisoff, p. 81 Transaction Publishers, 1988.

4. No Logo, Naomi Klein, p. 44, Picador 2002.

5. Design Literacy (continued): "Understanding Graphic Design," Steven Heller, p. 202 Allworth Communications, Inc., 1999.

6. http://kclibrary.lonestar.edu/decade80.html

7. www.bankrate.com/finance/credit-cards/credit-cards-for-the-rich-american-express-platinum.aspx

8. www.mhhe.com/business/management/thompson/11e/case/starbucks.html

9. www.achievement.org/autodoc/printmember/cas1int-1

10. www.time.com/time/magazine/article/0,9171,985751,00.htm

Chapter 11

1. www.icmrindia.org/casestudies/catalogue/Business%20Strategy/BSTR194.htm

2. www.bizcult.com/content/?p=432

3. www.reuters.com/article/2011/01/19/us-nokia-idUSTRE70I25P20110119

4. http://articles.economictimes.indiatimes.com/2011-01-19/news/28429397_1_brand-trust-sachin-tendulkar-survey

5. Edwin Colyer, India, a Hot Brand Climate? May 31, 2006, www.businessweek.com/innovate/content/may2006/id20060531_711820.htm (March 2011).

6. Brand Culture Failures: Kellogg's in India. November 15, 2006, http://brandfailures.blogspot.com/2006/11/brand-culture-failures-kelloggs-in.html (March 2011).

7. D'Altorio, Tony. The Number One Reason Why Google Failed in China...And It's a Big One. January 28, 2010, www.investmentu.com/2010/January/google-fails-in-china.html (March 2011).

8. Fisher, Linda. China: Economic Powerhouse—and Land of Branding Opportunities. August 7, 2006, www.aiga.org/content.cfm/china-economic-powerhouse-and-land-of-branding-opportunities (March 2011).

9. www.slashgear.com/htc-quietly-brilliant-campaign-goes-global-video-2661709/

10. http://en-za.havaianas.com/en-ZA/about-havaianas/history/

11. (Thai source) Red Bull. September 26, 2009, http://chor-chang.exteen.com/20090926/red-bull (March 2011).

12. Purnell, Newley. Thailand's 6 Coolest Self-Made Millionaires. February 28, 2011, www.cnngo.com/bangkok/play/thailands-6-coolest-self-made-millionaires-010934 (March 2011).

13. www.overcaffeinated.org/database/energy-drinks/red-bull.php

14. www.fastcompany.com/articles/2001/10/redbull.html

15. www.redbullflugtagusa.com/

16. www.consumergoodsclub.com/cgc-official-blog/78-marketing/575-red-bull-it-gives-you-still-wings

Chapter 12

1. http://online.wsj.com/mdc/public/page/2_3022-autosales.htm

2. www.boeing.com/history/narrative/n036boe.html

3. www.creativepro.com/article/heavy-metal-madness-come-fly-with-me [Also images].

Chapter 15

1. *The American Beauty Industry Encyclopedia*, by Julie Willett, p 115.

2. Randle, Henry. 1997. "Suntanning: Differences in Perceptions throughout History."

3. http://cosmeticsandskin.com/bcb/lash-lure.php

4. http://cosmeticsandskin.com/bcb/lash-lure.php

5. www.enotes.com/company-histories/revlon-inc/nail-polish-company-founded-1932

6. *Encyclopedia of the Exquisite: An Anecdotal History of Elegant Delights*, by Jessica Kerwin Jenkins.

7. *Encyclopedia of the Exquisite: An Anecdotal History of Elegant Delights*, by Jessica Kerwin Jenkins.

8. www.enotes.com/company-histories/revlon-inc/nail-polish-company-founded-1932

9. *Encyclopedia of American Business History*, Volume 2, by Charles R. Geisst.

10. *Encyclopedia of Hair: aCultural History*, by Victoria Sherrow, p 157.

11. *Encyclopedia of Hair: a Cultural History*, by Victoria Sherrow, p. 157.

12. www.en.clinique.com.hk/clinique/zhen/24/_www_clinique_com_hk/customerservice/brand_story.tmpl

13. www.nytimes.com/2011/06/12/fashion/leslie-blodgett-of-bare-escentuals-the-queen-of-beauty.html?pagewanted=3&_r=1

14. www.nytimes.com/2011/06/12/fashion/leslie-blodgett-of-bare-escentuals-the-queen-of-beauty.html?pagewanted=3&_r=1

Chapter 16

1. Bethanne Patrick and John Thompson. *An Uncommon History of Common Things* (Washington, D.C.: National Geographic, 2009), p. 27.

2. www.perrier.com/EN/entrezbulle/rubrique4.asp

3. www.canadadry.ca/history.html

4. Andrew Smith. *Encyclopedia of Junk Food and Fast Food*, p. 134 (Westport, CT: Greenwood Press, 2006).

5. www.thecoca-colacompany.com/ourcompany/historybottling.html

6. www.drpeppermuseum.com/About-Us/History-Of-Dr--Pepper.aspx

7. www.redbull.com/cs/Satellite/en_INT/How-it-all-started/001242939605518?pcs_c=PCS_Article&pcs_cid=1242937556879

8. www.joltenergy.com/about.html

9. Coffee Statistics: www.coffeemarvel.com/blog/post/2010/05/11/Facts-and-Statistics-about-Coffee-Consumption-in-the-United-States.aspx

10. Howard Schultz quote: www.businessweek.com/magazine/content/01_32/b3744014.htm

11. Intelligentsia Logo: http://popsop.com/2193

12. Brandchannel.com–March 5, 2007. Voss- high water. Barry Silverstein.

13. 2009 Water Sales - www.bottledwater.org/files/2009BWstats.pdf

14. Evian Package Design: www.labbrand.com/brand-source/evian-strives-brand-differentiation-build-brand-equity

15. VOSS Bottle Design: www.vosswater.com/

Chapter 18

1. s.com/home/content.cfm?content=t_template&view=admin&packet=00061D22-C172-1C7A-9B578304E50A011A

2. www.hmhfoundation.org/default/index.cfm/about-the-foundation/hmh-biography/

3. www.oprah.com/pressroom/Oprah-Winfreys-Official-Biography/2

4. Nielsen Cassandra Ranking Report - Nov'86 to May '99 and Wrap Sweeps, Nov '99 to May '10, major sweeps only. Wtd Avg DMA HH Rtg, Primary Telecasts Only.

5. www.mediabistro.com/galleycat/top-10-bestselling-books-in-oprahs-book-club_b30637

6. www.oprah.com/pressroom/Oprah-Winfreys-Official-Biography/2

DIRECTORY OF CONTRIBUTORS

Editorial Director
Jeremy Lehrer
www.unifyingtheorymedia.com

Producer
Taryn Espinosa
www.tarynespinosa.com

Designer
Rodrigo Corral Design
www.rodrigocorral.com

**School of Visual Arts Masters in Branding
Student Writers and Contributors**

Richard Shear
www.shearpartnership.com
http://richardshear.wordpress.com/

Noah Armstrong
www.cmncmplx.com

Jadalia Britto
www.jadaliabritto.com

Lee Changzhi
www.leechangzhi.com

Jeremy DiPaolo
jeremy.dipaolo@gmail.com

Sascha Donn
www.sascharocks.com

Rebecca Etter
rebecca.etter@gmail.com

Brian A. Gaffney
bgaffnbk@gmail.com

Myles Gaythwaite
myles@gaythwaite.com

Margaux Genin
mgenin@gmail.com

Maxine Gurevich
http://magnifyingculture.tumblr.com/

Timothy Harms
timothyaharms@gmail.com

Portia D Hubert
www.portiahubert.com

Chi Wai Lima
www.vitamincdesign.com

Daniel Lin
www.minus31.com

Zachary Lynd
zacharylynd@gmail.com

Jessie McGuire
www.Colorfulbrands.com

Abby McInerney
abby.mcinerney@gmail.com

Manal Nassar
manal.nassar@gmail.com

Mo Saad
www.mosaad.com

Natasha Saipradist
www.saipradist.com

Kathryn Spitzberg
http://about.me/kathrynspitzberg

Curtis Wingate
www.curtiswingate.com

Additional Writers

Rochelle Fainstein

James Gaddy
http://jamesgaddy.com

Featured Firms and Practitioners

Rodrigo Corral Design
www.rodrigocorral.com

Matteo Bologna
www.mucca.com

Christine Mau
www.kimberly-clark.com

Dan Formosa
www.danformosa.com
www.smartdesignworldwide.com

Scott Williams
www.scottwilliamsandco.com

Rob Wallace
www.wallacechurch.com

Mike Bainbridge
www.sterlingbrands.com

Michael Bierut
www.pentagram.com

Joyce Rutter Kaye
www.nycgo.com

Rob Giampietro
http://projectprojects.com/

Gail Anderson
http://gailycurl.com/

Jennifer Kinon & Bobby C. Martin, Jr.
http://originalchampionsofdesign.com/

Steff Geissbuhler
www.cgpartnersllc.com

Kenna Kay
www.tvland.com

Michael Ian Kaye
www.mothernewyork.com

ABOUT THE EDITOR

Debbie Millman has worked in the design field for over twenty-five years. She is president of the design division at Sterling Brands where, after nearly two decades, she has contributed to the redesign of over 300 global brands.

Debbie is President Emeritus of the AIGA, the world's largest professional association for design, a contributing editor at *Print* magazine, a design writer at FastCompany.com and co-founder and chair of the first Masters in Branding Program at the School of Visual Arts in New York City. In 2005, Millman began hosting the first weekly radio talk show about design on the Internet: *Design Matters with Debbie Millman*, and now 150 episodes are featured on DesignObserver.com and iTunes.

In addition to this title, Debbie is the author of *Brand Thinking and other Noble Pursuits* (Allworth Press, 2011), *Look Both Ways: Illustrated Essays on the Intersection of Life and Design* (HOW Books, 2009), *How to Think like a Great Graphic Designer* (Allworth Press, 2007), and *The Essential Principles of Graphic Design* (Rotovision, 2008).

ACKNOWLEDGMENTS

Very special thanks to Jeremy Lehrer for his editorial genius.

Very special thanks to Taryn Espinosa for her tremendous organization and production skills.

Special thanks to Rodrigo Corral, Noah Armstrong, and Steven Attardo for their beautiful design.

Special thanks to Richard Shear for helping to create the framework for this book.

Thank you to Emily Potts for allowing us to make this book and for her infinite patience.

Thank you to the kind people at Rockport: Betsy Gammons, Cora Hawks, and David Martinell.

Thank you to Rochelle Fainstein, James Gaddy, Caitlin Dover, and Marli Higa for their editorial contributions.

Thank you to Brent Taylor for all of his wonderful photography.

Thank you to Shutterstock.com for the breadth and depth of their catalog.

Thank you to Sibylle Wolf for allowing us to use her historical photographs.

Thank you to the faculty and staff of the School of Visual Arts Masters in Branding program: Rob Giampietro, Dr. Tom Guarriello, Scott Lerman, David Weisman, Pamela DeCesare, Richard Shear, Dr. Daniel Formosa, Sem Devillart, J'aime Cohen, and Rainy Orteca. Also, thank you to Lisa Grant, Jennifer Simon, and Gonzalo Muiño.

Thank you to the incredible inaugural students of the School of Visual Arts Masters in Branding program, who, without their contribution, this book would not be possible: Maxine Gurevich, Zachary Tyler Lynd, Abby McInerney, Manal Nassar, Kathyrn Spitzberg, Taryn Espinosa, Jadalia Britto, Jeremy DiPaolo, Margaux Genin, Daniel Lin, Mo Saad, Chi Wai Lima, Noah Armstrong, Natasha Saipradist, Lee Changzhi, Myles Gaythwaite, Portia Hubert, Rebecca Etter, Curtis Wingate, Sascha Donn, Timothy Harms, Jessie McGuire, and Brian Gaffney.

Thank you to the Proctor & Gamble Corporation, especially Phil Duncan, Elizabeth Olson, Olga DelaRoza, Amy Brusselback, Carolina Rogoll, Jeanbaptiste Salvado, Sidney Fritts, Martha Depenbrock, and Kathy Welker for all of their assistance with the MPS Branding Program and with this book.

Thank you to the Johnson & Johnson Corporation, especially Rusty Clifton.

Extraordinary thanks to the many, many people we interviewed for this book and who allowed us to feature their work.

Thank you to David Rhodes and Steven Heller for everything.

INDEX